EYEWITNESS TRAVEL

PARIS

EY

DK | Penguin Random House

Top 10 Paris Highlights

The Top 10 of Everything

CONTENTS

Paris Area by Area

Streetsmart

The information in this DK Eyewitness Top 10 Travel Guide is checked annually. Every effort has been made to ensure that this book is as up-to-date as possible at the time of going to press. Some details, however, such as telephone numbers, opening hours, prices, gallery hanging arrangements and travel information are liable to change. The publishers cannot accept responsibility for any consequences arising from the use of this book, nor for any material on third party websites, and cannot guarantee that any website address in this book will be a suitable source of travel information. We value the views and suggestions of our readers very highly. Please write to: Publisher, DK Eyewitness Travel Guides, Dorling Kindersley, 80 Strand, London WC2R 0RL, Great Britain, or email travelguides@dk.com.

Within each Top 10 list in this book, no hierarchy of quality or popularity is implied. All 10 are, in the editor's opinion, of roughly equal merit.

Front cover and spine *Eiffel Tower, illuminated*
Back cover *Avenue of trees in autumn leading to the Musée du Louvre*
Title page *Giant flag flies in the middle of the Arc de Triomphe*

Welcome to
Paris

Paris, City of Light. City of romance and revolution. A heady mix of café philosophers and Coco Chanel couture. A foodie paradise. A culture-lover's dream. The focus of a thousand iconic movie images. Paris is all these things and more... so who could deny that it's Europe's most magical destination? With Eyewitness Top 10 Paris, it's yours to explore.

We love Paris: its culture, its charm, its *je ne sais quoi*. What could be better than exploring the chic shops of the **Marais** district or sniffing out the best cheeses in **rue Montorgeuil**'s mouthwatering market; wandering through village-like **Montmartre** or browsing the bookstalls of the **Latin Quarter**; taking in a late-night cabaret show or strolling **boulevard St-Germain** for an early morning coffee at **Café de Flore** in the footsteps of Hemingway and Picasso? And what could be more fun than hopping on a Vélib' bike and cycling along the Seine from the **Eiffel Tower** to **Notre-Dame**?

Paris is a city made for strolling, along its leafy boulevards and through its parks, against a backdrop of elegant Haussmann buildings and soaring contemporary structures. There's history in these cobblestoned streets, but Paris is also a striking 21st-century city, where modern dancers perform in the ornate **Opéra Garnier**, and a new generation of acclaimed chefs is experimenting and building upon Paris' reputation for gastronomic excellence.

Whether you're coming for a weekend or a week, our Top 10 guide brings together the best of everything the city has to offer, from the world-famous glories of the **Louvre** to the hidden delights of pretty **Canal St-Martin**. The guide gives you tips throughout, from seeking out what's free to avoiding the crowds, plus 11 easy-to-follow itineraries, designed to help you visit a clutch of sights in a short space of time. Add inspiring photography and detailed maps, and you've got the essential pocket-sized travel companion. **Enjoy the book, and enjoy Paris.**

Top then clockwise: **Musée du Louvre, Sacré-Coeur, Versailles gardens, Centre Georges Pompidou, view from Pont Alexandre III, Galeries Lafayette interior, Moulin Rouge**

Exploring Paris

Paris has an inexhaustible wealth of things to see and do. Here are some ideas for how to make the most of your time. The city is relatively compact, so you should be able to do most of your sightseeing on foot, and you're never far from a metro station.

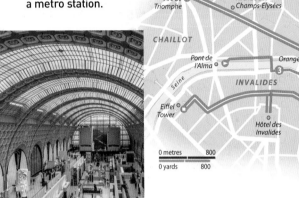

Musée d'Orsay is housed in a former railway station.

Key
— Two-day itinerary
— Four-day itinerary

Two Days in Paris

Day ❶
MORNING
Cross **Pont Neuf** *(see p80)* over the River Seine to the **Ile de la Cité** *(see pp78–81)* and visit the magnificent cathedral of **Notre-Dame** *(see pp20–23)* or lovely **Sainte-Chapelle** *(see pp36–7)*. Continue south into the lively **Latin Quarter** *(see p124–7)* and pause for lunch in a classic Left Bank bistro *(see p133)*.

AFTERNOON
Meander through stylish **St-Germain-des-Prés** *(see p124–7)* to the **Musée d'Orsay** *(closed Mon; see pp16–19)* and admire its collection of Impressionist paintings. From here it's a short walk to **Les Invalides** *(see pp38–9)* and the **Eiffel Tower** *(see pp24–5)*, stunningly lit up at night.

Day ❷
MORNING
Take in the views from atop the **Arc de Triomphe** *(see pp30–31)*, then stroll the lively **Champs-Elysées** *(see p111)* and leafy **Tuileries** *(see p103)* to the **Louvre** *(closed Tue; see pp12–15)*.

AFTERNOON
Explore the hip **Marais** *(see pp92–5)*, stopping en route at the **Pompidou Centre** *(closed Tue; see pp32–3)*. Take a metro to **Montmartre** *(see pp146–9)* and walk up to **Sacré-Coeur** *(see pp26–7)* for panoramic sunset views.

Four Days in Paris

Day ❶
MORNING
Visit Montmartre's dazzling **Sacré-Coeur** *(see pp26–7)*, then head down through **Pigalle** *(see pp146–9)* to the

Musée du Louvre's modern entrance is I M Pei's magnificent glass and steel pyramid.

Montmartre's leafy Place du Tertre is always crowded with artists at their easels or selling their work.

lavish **Opéra Garnier** *(see p104)* and elegant **Place Vendôme** *(see p104)*.

AFTERNOON
Wander through the **Tuileries** *(see p103)* and visit Monet's exquisite *Water Lilies* at the **Orangerie** *(closed Tue; see p52)*. Then stroll along the **Champs-Elysées** *(see p111)* to the **Arc de Triomphe** *(see pp30–31)*.

Day ❷
MORNING
Discover modern art at the **Pompidou Centre** *(see pp32–3)*, then learn the history of Paris at **Musée Carnavalet** *(closed Mon; see p50)*. Enjoy a bistro lunch on **Place des Vosges** *(see p93)*.

AFTERNOON
Check out the trendy **Marais** district *(see pp92–5)*, then tranquil **Ile St-Louis** *(see pp78–81)*. Marvel at **Notre-Dame** *(see pp20–23)* before a concert at **Sainte-Chapelle** *(see pp36–7)*.

Day ❸
MORNING
Take a boat trip along the River Seine *(see p170)* before a visit to the great Impressionists at the **Musée d'Orsay** *(closed Mon; see pp16–19)*.

AFTERNOON
Pay your respects to Napoleon at **Les Invalides** *(see pp38–9)* and then head off to the **Eiffel Tower** *(see pp24–5)*.

Day ❹
MORNING
You'll have time to see all the star exhibits of the **Louvre** *(closed Tue; see pp12–15)* before heading off for lunch in the **Latin Quarter** *(see pp124–7)*.

AFTERNOON
Visit France's great and good at the **Panthéon** *(see pp34–5)*, explore the lovely **Jardin des Plantes** *(see p135)* and end the day with live jazz at **Caveau de la Huchette** *(see p65)*.

Top 10 Paris Highlights

Magnificent vaulting and stained-glass windows, Sainte-Chapelle

🔟 Paris Highlights

From Notre-Dame to the Eiffel Tower, Paris holds some of the world's most famous sights. These ten attractions should be top of the list for any first-time visitor, and remain eternally awe-inspiring.

Musée du Louvre ①

The world's most visited museum also contains one of the world's finest collections of art and antiquities (up to 1848). To complete the superlatives, it was once France's largest royal palace *(see pp12–15)*.

② Musée d'Orsay

This former railway station is one of the world's leading art galleries and, for many, reason alone to visit Paris *(see pp16–19)*.

Notre-Dame ③

This great Gothic cathedral, founded on the site of a Gallo-Roman temple, is a repository of art and history. It is also the geographical "heart" of France *(see pp20–23)*.

④ Eiffel Tower

Nearly seven million visitors a year ascend to the top of this most famous Paris landmark for the spectacular views. It was erected for the Universal Exhibition of 1889 *(see pp24–5)*.

Sacré-Coeur ⑤

The terrace in front of this monumental white-domed basilica in Montmartre affords one of the finest free views over Paris *(see pp26–7)*.

6 Arc de Triomphe

Napoleon's triumphal arch, celebrating battle victories, stands proudly at the top of the Champs-Elysées and, along with the Eiffel Tower, is one of the city's most enduring images *(see pp30–31)*.

7 Centre Georges Pompidou

Home to France's National Museum of Modern Art, the building itself is a fascinating work of contemporary art *(see pp32–3)*.

Panthéon 8

The great and the good of France, including Voltaire, are buried in the Panthéon *(see pp34–5)*.

9 Sainte-Chapelle

Called "a gateway to heaven", this exquisite church was built to house relics collected by St Louis on his Crusades *(see pp36–7)*.

10 Hôtel des Invalides

The glowing golden dome of the Hôtel des Invalides church is unmistakable across the rooftops of Paris. It houses Napoleon's tomb *(see pp38–9)*.

Map labels: MONTMARTRE, BLVD DE CLICHY, BLVD DE ROCHECHOUART, BOULEVARD JSSMANN, RUE LA FAYETTE, BOULEVARD POISSONNIERE, VD DES CAPUCINES, BEAUBOURG, RUE ST MARTIN, BLVD DE SEBASTOPOL, PLACE DE LA REPUBLIQUE, Jardin des Tuileries, DE RIVOLI, QUAI DU LOUVRE, MARAIS, RUE DE RIVOLI, BLVD BEAUMARCHAIS, ST-GERMAIN, BLVD ST GERMAIN, Q. DE L'HOTEL DE VILLE, PLACE DE LA BASTILLE, Jardin du Luxembourg, BLVD ST MICHEL, QUARTIER LATIN, RUE MONGE, Seine, Jardin des Plantes

TOP 10 ⭐ Musée du Louvre

One of the world's most impressive museums, the Louvre contains some 35,000 priceless objects. It was built as a fortress by King Philippe-Auguste in 1190, but Charles V (1364–80) made it his home. In the 16th century François I replaced it with a Renaissance-style palace and founded the royal art collection with 12 paintings from Italy. Revolutionaries opened the collection to the public in 1793. Shortly after, Napoleon renovated the Louvre as a museum.

1 Venus de Milo
The positioning of this statue, dramatically lit at the end of a hallway, enhances its beauty. Believed to represent the goddess Aphrodite, it dates from the end of the 2nd century BC and was discovered on the Greek island of Milos in 1820.

2 Mona Lisa
Arguably the most famous painting in the world, Leonardo's portrait of the woman with the enigmatic smile *(see p15)* has been beautifully restored. Visit early or late in the day.

3 Marly Horses
Coustou's rearing horses being restrained by horse-tamers were sculpted in 1745 for Louis XIV's Château de Marly. Replicas stand near the Place de la Concorde.

4 Slaves
Michelangelo sculpted *Dying Slave* **(left)** and *Rebellious Slave* (1513–20) for the tomb of Pope Julius II in Rome. The unfinished figures seem to be emerging from their "prisons" of stone.

5 Glass Pyramid
The unmistakable glass pyramid, designed by I M Pei, became the Louvre's new entrance in 1989. Stainless steel tubes make up the 21-m-high (69-ft) frame **(above)**.

6 Medieval Moats
An excavation in the 1980s uncovered the remains of the medieval fortress. You can see the base of the towers and the drawbridge support under the Cour Carrée.

7 The Winged Victory of Samothrace
This Hellenistic treasure (3rd–2nd century BC) stands atop a stone ship radiating grace and power. It was created to commemorate a naval triumph at Rhodes.

8 The Raft of the Medusa

The shipwreck of a French frigate three years earlier inspired this gigantic early Romantic painting (left) by Théodore Géricault (1791–1824) in 1819. The work depicts the moment when the survivors spot a sail on the horizon.

9 Perrault's Colonnade

The majestic east façade by Claude Perrault (1613–88), with its paired Corinthian columns, was part of an extension plan commissioned by Louis XIV.

10 The Lacemaker

The Winged Victory of Samothrace **7**

The Raft of the Medusa **8**

Mona Lisa **2**

Marly Horses **3**

Dying Slave **4**

Glass Pyramid **5**

Perrault's Colonnade **9**

Key
- Ground floor
- First floor
- Second floor

Venus de Milo **1**

Medieval Moats **6**

10 The Lacemaker

Jan Vermeer's masterpiece (above), painted around 1665, gives a simple but beautiful rendering of everyday life and is the highlight of the Louvre's Dutch collection.

NEED TO KNOW

MAP L2 ■ Musée du Louvre, 75001 ■ 01 40 20 53 17 ■ www.louvre.fr

Open 9am–6pm Mon, Thu, Sat & Sun, 9am–9:45pm Wed & Fri; closed Tue & public hols

Admission €12 (subject to change); free 1st Sun of month (except Apr–Sep); under-18s free; under-26s (EU only) free

Partial disabled access

■ For a light lunch, try out Le Café Marly in the Richelieu Wing or the food court in Carrousel du Louvre. For a more special option make a reservation at the Grand Louvre restaurant below the pyramid.

■ Beat the queues and buy tickets in advance online or at machine kiosks at the Porte des Lions entrance at the west end of the Denon Wing (except Friday).

Gallery Guide
The foyer is under the pyramid. Visitors who have tickets are given priority access at the pyramid. Alternatively, buy tickets at the Carrousel du Louvre entrance (99 rue de Rivoli) or Porte des Lions. The Sully, Denon and Richelieu wings lead off from the foyer. Painting and sculpture are displayed by country, plus galleries for *objets d'art*, antiquities, prints and drawings.

Louvre Collections

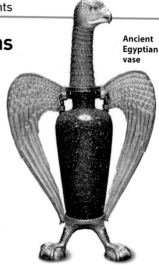

Ancient Egyptian vase

1 French Paintings
This superb collection ranges from the 14th century to 1848 and includes works by such artists as Jean Watteau, Georges de la Tour and J H Fragonard.

2 French Sculpture
Highlights include the Tomb of Philippe Pot by Antoine le Moiturier, the Marly Horses (see p12) and works by Pierre Puget.

3 Egyptian Antiquities
The finest collection outside Cairo, featuring a Sphinx in the crypt, the Seated Scribe of Sakkara, huge sarcophagi, mummified animals, funerary objects and intricate carvings depicting everyday life in Ancient Egypt.

4 Greek Antiquities
The wondrous art of Ancient Greece here ranges from a Cycladic idol from the third millennium BC to Classical Greek marble statues (c.5th century BC) to Hellenistic works (late 3rd–2nd century BC).

5 Oriental Antiquities
A stunning collection includes a recreated temple of an Assyrian king and the Codex of Hammurabi (18th-century BC), mankind's oldest written laws.

6 Italian Paintings
French royalty adored the art of Italy and amassed much of this collection (1200–1800). It includes many works by Leonardo da Vinci.

7 Italian Sculpture
Highlights of this collection, dating from the early Renaissance, include a 15th-century Madonna and Child by Donatello and Michelangelo's Slaves (see p12).

8 Dutch Paintings
Rembrandt's works are hung alongside domestic scenes by Vermeer and portraits by Frans Hals.

9 Objets d'Art
The ceramics, jewellery and other items in this collection span history and the world.

10 Islamic Art
This exquisite collection, which spans 13 centuries and 3 continents, is covered by an ultra-modern glass veil.

Collections Floorplan

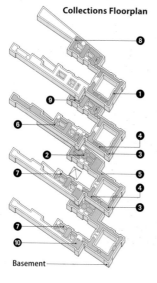

Basement

LEONARDO DA VINCI AND THE MONA LISA

Leonardo da Vinci, Renaissance man extraordinaire, was not only an artist but also a sculptor, engineer, architect and scientist. His many interests included the study of anatomy and aerodynamics.

Born in Vinci to a wealthy family, Leonardo da Vinci (1452–1519) took up an apprenticeship under Florentine artist Andrea del Verrocchio, then served the Duke of Milan as an architect and military engineer, during which time he painted the *Last Supper* mural (1495). On his return to Florence, to work as architect to Cesare Borgia, he painted his most celebrated portrait, the *Mona Lisa* (1503–06). It is also known as *La Gioconda*, allegedly the name of the model's aristocratic husband, although there is ongoing speculation regarding the identity of the subject. The work, in particular the sitter's mysterious smile, shows mastery of two techniques: *chiaroscuro*, the contrast of light and shadow, and *sfumato*, subtle transitions between colours. It was the artist's own favourite painting and he took it with him everywhere. In 1516 François I brought them both to France, giving da Vinci the use of a manor house in Amboise in the Loire Valley, where he died three years later.

Mona Lisa, da Vinci's enigmatic portrait

TOP 10
LOUVRE RESIDENTS

1 Charles V (1364–80)

2 Henri II (1547–49)

3 Catherine de' Medicis (1519–89)

4 Henri IV (1589–1610)

5 Louis XIII (1610–43)

6 Louis XIV (1643–1715)

7 Anne of Austria (1601–66)

8 Guillaume Coustou, sculptor (1677–1746)

9 Edmé Bouchardon, sculptor (1698–1762)

10 François Boucher, artist (1703–70)

🔟 ⭐ Musée d'Orsay

This wonderful collection covers a variety of art forms from the 1848–1914 period, and includes a superb Impressionists section. Its setting, in a converted railway station, is equally impressive. Built in 1900, in time for the Paris Exposition, the station was in use until 1939, when it was closed and largely ignored, bar acting as the location for Orson Welles' 1962 film, The Trial. It was later used as a theatre and as auction rooms, and in the mid-1970s was considered for demolition. In 1977, the Paris authorities decided to save the imposing station building by converting it into this striking museum.

1 The Building

The former railway station that houses this museum **(left)** is almost as stunning as the exhibits. The light and spacious feel on stepping inside, after admiring the magnificent old façade, takes one's breath away.

2 Van Gogh Paintings

The star of the collection is Vincent van Gogh (1853–90) and the most striking of the canvases on display is the 1889 work showing the artist's Bedroom at Arles **(right)**. Also on display are some of the artist's self-portraits, painted with his familiar intensity (Middle level).

3 Le Déjeuner sur l'Herbe

Edouard Manet's (1832–83) controversial painting (1863) was first shown in an "Exhibition of Rejected Works". Its bold portrayal of a classically nude woman enjoying the company of 19th-century men in suits brought about a wave of criticism (Room 29).

4 Olympia

Another Manet portrayal (1865) of a naked courtesan, receiving flowers sent by an admirer, was also regarded as indecent, and shocked the public and critics, but it was an important influence on later artists (Room 14).

5 Blue Waterlilies

Claude Monet (1840–1926) painted this stunning canvas (1919) on one of his favourite themes. His love of water-lilies led him to create his own garden at Giverny in order to paint them in a natural setting. This work inspired many abstract painters later in the 20th century (Room 36).

6 Degas' Statues of Dancers

The museum has an exceptional collection of works by Edgar Degas (1834–1917). Focusing on dancers and the world of opera, his sculptures range from innocent to erotic. Young Dancer of Fourteen (1881) was the only one exhibited in the artist's lifetime **(left)** (Room 31).

7 Jane Avril Dancing

Toulouse-Lautrec's (1864–1901) paintings define Paris's *belle époque*. Jane Avril was a famous Moulin Rouge dancer and featured in several of his works, like this 1895 canvas **(left)**, which Toulouse-Lautrec drew from life, in situ at the cabaret (Room 10).

8 Dancing at the Moulin de la Galette

One of the best-known paintings of the Impressionist era (1876), this work was shown at the Impressionist exhibition in 1877. The exuberance of Renoir's (1841–1919) work captures the look and mood of Montmartre and is one of the artist's masterpieces (Room 32).

9 La Belle Angèle

This portrait of a Brittany beauty (1889) by Paul Gauguin (1848–1903) shows the influence of Japanese art on the artist. It was bought by Degas, to finance Gauguin's first trip to Polynesia (Room 72).

10 Café Campana

Offering a rest from all the impressive art, the museum's café, renovated by the Campana Brothers, is delightfully situated behind one of the former station's huge clocks. A break here is an experience in itself and the food is good too.

NEED TO KNOW

MAP J2 ■ 1 Rue de la Légion d'Honneur, 75007 ■ 01 40 49 48 14 ■ www. musee-orsay.fr

Open 9:30am–6pm Tue–Sun (Thu till 9:45pm); closed 1 Jan, 1 May, 25 Dec

■ Admission €11 (under-18s free, under-26s EU only free), €8.50 for 18–25s non-EU. Tickets can be bought online.

■ The busy restaurant is open for lunch, plus dinner on Thursdays; closed Monday. For a snack or a drink try the upper level café (Café Campana) or the self-service mezzanine café just above.

■ Music concerts are often held. Call 01 40 49 47 50.

Museum Guide

As soon as you enter the gallery, collect a map. The ground floor houses fine works from the early to mid-19th century, as well as striking Oriental works, decorative arts and a bookshop. The middle level includes Naturalist, Symbolist and Post-Impressionist paintings, and sculpture terraces. The upper level is home to the Impressionist galleries. The museum also features temporary exhibitions focusing on 19th-century artists, such as Manet, Renoir and Degas.

Musée d'Orsay Collections

1 The Impressionists
One of the best Impressionist collections in the world. Admirers of Manet, Monet and Renoir will not be disappointed.

2 The Post-Impressionists
The artists who moved on to a newer interpretation of Impressionism are equally well represented, including Matisse, Toulouse-Lautrec and the towering figure of Van Gogh.

3 School of Pont-Aven
Paul Gauguin was at the centre of the group of artists associated with Pont-Aven in Brittany. His work here includes the carved door panels known as the *House of Pleasure* (1901).

4 Art Nouveau
Art Nouveau is synonymous with Paris, with many metro stations retaining entrances built in that style. Pendants and glassware by René Lalique (1860–1945) are among the examples on display here.

5 Symbolism
This vast collection includes works by Gustav Klimt (1862–1918) and Edvard Munch (1863–1944), and

Blue Dancers (1890), Edgar Degas

Collections Floorplan

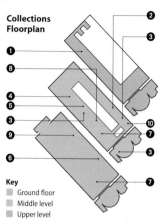

Key
- Ground floor
- Middle level
- Upper level

James Whistler's (1834–1903) famous portrait of his mother, dating from 1871.

6 Romanticism
The Romantics wanted to heighten awareness of the spiritual world. One striking example is *The Tiger Hunt* (1854) by Eugène Delacroix (1798–1863).

7 Sculpture
The collection includes pieces by Rodin (*see p120*) and satirical carvings of politicians by Honoré Daumier (1808–79).

8 Naturalism
Naturalist painters intensified nature in their work. *Haymaking* (1877) by Jules Bastien-Lepage (1848–84) is a fine example.

9 Nabis
The Nabis Movement made art into a more decorative form. Pierre Bonnard (1867–1947) is one of its founding members.

10 Photography Collection
Some 10,000 early photographs include work by Bonnard, Degas and British photographer Julia Margaret Cameron (1815–79).

THE IMPRESSIONIST MOVEMENT

Regarded as the starting point of modern art, the Impressionist Movement is probably the best-known and best-loved art movement in the world – certainly if prices at auction and the crowds in the Musée d'Orsay are anything to go by. It began in France, and almost all its leading figures were French. Impressionism was a reaction against the formality and Classicism insisted upon by the Académie des Beaux-Arts in Paris, which was very much the art establishment, deciding what would or would not be exhibited at the Paris Salon. The term "impressionism" was actually coined by a critic of the style, who dismissed the 1872 Monet painting *Impression: Sunrise*, now on display at the Musée Marmottan (*see p157*).

The artists themselves then adopted the term. The style influenced painters such as Van Gogh and was to have a lasting influence on 19th- and 20th-century art.

Cathedral at Rouen (1892–3), Claude Monet

On the Beach (1873), **Edouard Manet**

TOP 10 ⭐ **Notre-Dame**

The "heart" of the country, both geographically and spiritually, the Cathedral of Notre-Dame (Our Lady) stands on the Ile de la Cité. After Pope Alexander III laid the foundation stone in 1163, an army of craftsmen toiled for 170 years to realize Bishop Maurice de Sully's magnificent design. Almost destroyed during the Revolution, the Gothic masterpiece was restored in 1841–64 by architect Viollet-le-Duc. At 130 m (430 ft) in length with a high-vaulted nave and double side aisles, it is home to one of France's largest organs.

Notre-Dame

1 Flying Buttresses
The striking flying buttresses supporting the cathedral's east façade are by Jean Ravy. The best view is from Square Jean XXIII.

2 The Towers
The towers are 69 m (226 ft) high; climb the 387 steps of the north tower for great views. In 2013, new bells rang here to celebrate the cathedral's 850th birthday.

3 West Front
The glorious entrance to the cathedral **(above)** is through three elaborately carved portals. Biblical scenes, sculpted in the Middle Ages, depict the Life of the Virgin, the Last Judgment and the Life of St Anne. Above is the Gallery of Kings of Judaea and Israel.

4 Portal of the Virgin
The splendid stone tympanum **(right)** was carved in the 13th century and shows the Virgin Mary's death and coronation in heaven. However, the statue of the Virgin and Child that stands between the doors is a modern replica.

5 Galerie des Chimères
Lurking between the towers are the famous gargoyles (chimères) **(above)**, placed here to ward off evil.

6 Rose Windows

Three great rose windows adorn the north, south and west façades, but only the north window **(left)** retains its 13th-century stained glass, depicting the Virgin surrounded by figures from the Old Testament. The south window shows Christ encircled by the Apostles.

7 The Spire

The 96-m (315-ft) spire was added by Viollet-le-Duc. Next to the Apostles statues is one of the architect, admiring his work.

8 Statue of the Virgin and Child

Also known as Notre-Dame de Paris (Our Lady of Paris), this beautiful 14th-century statue was brought to the cathedral from the chapel of St Aignan. It stands against the southeast pillar of the transept, at the entrance to the chancel.

Cathedral Floorplan

9 Treasury

Ancient manuscripts, reliquaries and religious garments are housed in the sacristy. The Crown of Thorns is on public view on the first Friday of every month.

10 Choirstalls

More than half of the original stalls commissioned by Louis XIV survive. Among the beautifully carved work on the 78 stalls are scenes from the Life of the Virgin.

NEED TO KNOW

MAP N4 ■ 6 Parvis Notre-Dame – Place Jean-Paul II, 75004 ■ 01 53 10 07 00 (towers); 01 42 34 56 10 (cathedral)

Open Cathedral daily 8am–6:45pm (to 7:15pm Sat & Sun); towers Apr–Sep 10am–6:30pm daily (to 11pm Fri–Sat Jul–Aug); Oct–Mar: 10am–5:30pm daily

Admission (towers): €8.50 (€5.50 18–25s, under-18s free), free 1st Sun of month

■ There are cafés opposite Square Jean XXIII.

■ Free organ recitals on Sunday afternoons.

Cathedral Guide
Enter through the West Front. The stairs to the towers are outside to your left. Ahead, the central nave soars to a height of 35 m (115 ft), while 24 side chapels line the walls. These contain the "May" paintings by Charles le Brun, donated by the goldsmiths' guild each May

in the 17th and 18th centuries. The fine transept across the nave is the best place to admire the three rose windows. Remnants of the 14th-century stone screen can be seen on the north and south bays of the chancel. Nicolas Coustou's *Pietà* stands behind the high altar, flanked by statues of Louis XIII by Coustou and Louis XIV by Antoine Coysevox.

Famous Visitors to Notre-Dame

1 Joan of Arc
The patriot Jeanne d'Arc (1412–31), who defended France against the invading English, had a posthumous trial here in 1455, despite having been burned at the stake 24 years earlier. She was found to be innocent of heresy.

2 François II and Mary Stuart
Mary Stuart (Mary Queen of Scots; 1542–87) had been raised in France and married the Dauphin in 1558. He ascended the throne as François II in 1559 and the king and queen were crowned in Notre-Dame.

3 Napoleon
The coronation of Napoleon (1769–1821) in Notre-Dame in 1804 saw the eager general seize the crown from Pope Pius VII and crown himself emperor and his wife, Josephine, empress.

4 Josephine
Josephine's (1763–1814) reign as Empress of France lasted only five years; Napoleon divorced her in 1809.

5 Pope Pius VII
In 1809 Pope Pius VII (1742–1823), who oversaw Napoleon's Notre-Dame coronation, was taken captive when the emperor declared the Papal States to be part of France.

The pope was imprisoned at Fontainebleau, 50 km (30 miles) south of Paris.

6 Philip the Fair
In 1302 the first States General parliament was formally opened at Notre-Dame by Philip IV (1268–1314), otherwise known as Philip the Fair. He greatly increased the governing power of the French royalty.

7 Henry VI of England
Henry VI (1421–71) became King of England at the age of one. Like his father, Henry V, he also claimed France and was crowned in Notre-Dame in 1430.

Statue of Joan of Arc inside Notre-Dame

8 Marguerite of Valois
In August 1572, Marguerite (1553–1589), sister of Charles IX, stood in the Notre-Dame chancel during her marriage to the Protestant Henri of Navarre (1553–1610), while he stood alone by the door.

9 Henri of Navarre
As a Protestant Huguenot, Henri's marriage to the Catholic Marguerite resulted in uprising and massacres. In 1589 he became Henri IV, the first Bourbon king of France, and converted to Catholicism, stating that "Paris is well worth a Mass".

10 Charles de Gaulle
On 26 August 1944, Charles de Gaulle entered Paris and attended a Magnificat service to celebrate the liberation of Paris, despite the fact that hostile snipers were still at large outside the cathedral.

Charles de Gaulle visits Notre-Dame

THE MAN WHO SAVED NOTRE-DAME

Novelist Victor Hugo

By 1831, when Victor Hugo's novel *Notre-Dame de Paris (The Hunchback of Notre-Dame)* was published, the cathedral was already in a sorry state of decay. Even for the crowning of Napoleon in 1804, the setting for such ceremonial state occasions was crumbling and had to be disguised with wall hangings and ornamentation. During the Revolution, the cathedral was even sold to a scrap dealer, though fortunately not demolished. Hugo was determined to save France's spiritual heart and helped mount a successful campaign to restore Notre-Dame before it was too late; the man chosen to plan and oversee the restoration was Eugène Emmanuel Viollet-le-Duc (1814–79). He had already proved his skill in restoration work, on the cathedrals of Amiens and Laon, and the beautiful walled city of Carcassonne in southern France. Work began in 1841 and continued for 23 years until the building was completed more or less as it appears today.

TOP 10
EVENTS IN NOTRE-DAME HISTORY

1 Construction of the cathedral begins (1163)

2 St Louis places the Crown of Thorns here temporarily (1239)

3 Construction is completed (1334)

4 Retrial of Joan of Arc (1455)

5 Revolutionaries loot the cathedral and make it a Temple of Reason (1789)

6 Crowning of Emperor Napoleon (1804)

7 Restoration work is completed (1864)

8 Mass for the Liberation of Paris (1944)

9 De Gaulle's Requiem Mass is held (1970)

10 New bells with a medieval tone mark the 850th anniversary (2013)

The Hunchback of Notre-Dame, Hugo's 1831 novel, tells the story of Quasimodo, a hunchbacked bell-ringer at Notre-Dame, who falls in love with gypsy girl Esmeralda.

🔟 ⭐ Eiffel Tower

The most distinctive symbol of Paris, the Eiffel Tower (Tour Eiffel) was much maligned by critics when it appeared on the city's skyline in 1889 as part of the Universal Exhibition, but its graceful symmetry soon made it the star attraction. At 312 m (1,023 ft) high, it was the world's tallest building until it was surpassed by New York's Chrysler Building in 1930. Despite its delicate appearance, it weighs 10,100 metric tons and engineer Gustave Eiffel's construction was so sound that it never sways more than 9 cm (3.5 in) in strong winds.

Eiffel Tower

1 Lighting
A 200,000-watt lighting system makes the Eiffel Tower **(left)** a spectacular night-time sight. It sparkles like a giant Christmas tree for five minutes every hour from dusk until 1am.

2 View from the Trocadéro
Day or night, the best approach for a first-time view of the tower is from the Trocadéro *(see p142)*, which affords a monumental vista from the Chaillot terrace across the Seine.

3 Gustave Eiffel's Office
Located at the top of the tower is Gustave Eiffel's office, which has been restored to its original condition. It displays wax models of Thomas Edison and Eiffel himself.

4 First Level
You can walk the 345 steps up to the 57-m- (187-ft-) high first level and enjoy a meal at 58 Tour Eiffel. Renovated in 2014, this level includes glass floors and educational displays.

5 Viewing Gallery
At 276 m (906 ft), the stupendous view **(right)** stretches for 80 km (50 miles) on a clear day. You can also see Gustave Eiffel's sitting room on this level.

⑦ Champ-de-Mars

The long gardens of this former parade ground stretch from the base of the tower to the École Militaire (military school).

⑧ Ironwork

The complex pattern of the girders **(above)**, held together by 2.5 million rivets, stabilizes the tower in high winds. The metal can expand up to 15 cm (6 in) on hot days.

⑨ Bust of Gustave Eiffel

This bust of the tower's creator, by Antoine Bourdelle, was placed below his remarkable achievement, by the north pillar, in 1929.

⑩ Hydraulic Lift Mechanism

The 1899 lift mechanism is still in operation and travels some 103,000 km (64,000 miles) a year. The uniformed guard clinging to the outside is a model.

⑥ Second Level

At 116 m (380 ft) high, this level is the location of Le Jules Verne restaurant **(below)**, one of the finest in Paris for food and views *(see p123)*. It is reached by a private lift in the south pillar.

THE LIFE OF GUSTAVE EIFFEL

Born in Dijon, Gustave Eiffel (1832–1923) was an engineer and builder who made his name building bridges and viaducts, and helped in the design of the Statue of Liberty. Eiffel was famous for the graceful designs and master craftsmanship of his many wrought-iron constructions. He once said that his famous tower was "formed by the wind itself". In 1890 he became immersed in the study of aero-dynamics, and kept an office in the tower until his death, using it for experiments. In 1889, when the Eiffel Tower was erected, its creator was awarded the Légion d'Honneur.

MAP B4 ■ Champ de Mars, 7e ■ 08 92 70 12 39 ■ www.tour-eiffel.com

Open Lift 9:30am–11:45pm daily; last adm for top 10:30pm (mid-Jun–1 Sep: 9am–12:45am; last adm for top 11pm); Stairs 9:30am–6:30pm daily; last adm 6pm (mid-Jul–1 Sep: 9am–12:45am; last adm midnight) Admission: €5 (stairs); €9–€15.50 (lift) Disabled access to first and second levels only

■ There are restaurants and snack bars on levels 1 and 2, along with a Champagne bar on level 3, plus food kiosks around the base.

■ Beat the queues by booking your visit in advance, either by phone or online.

TOP10 ⭐ Sacré-Coeur

One of the most photographed images of the city, the spectacular white basilica of Sacré-Coeur (Sacred Heart) watches over Paris from its highest point. The basilica was built as a memorial to the 58,000 French soldiers killed during the Franco-Prussian War (1870–71). It took 46 years to build and was finally completed in 1923 at a cost of 40 million francs (6 million euros). Priests still pray for the souls of the dead here, 24 hours a day, as they have since 1885. People flock here for the breathtaking panoramic views – at sunset, in particular, there are few sights in Paris more memorable.

1 Great Mosaic of Christ

A glittering Byzantine mosaic of Christ, created by Luc Olivier Merson between 1912 and 1922, decorates the vault over the chancel. It represents France's devotion to the Sacred Heart.

3 Bronze Doors

The doors of the portico entrance are beautifully decorated with bronze relief sculptures depicting the Last Supper and other scenes from the life of Christ.

2 Crypt Vaults

The arched vaults of the crypt (above) house a chapel that contains the heart of Alexandre Legentil, one of the advocates of Sacré-Coeur.

4 The Dome

The distinctive egg-shaped dome of the basilica is the second-highest view-point in Paris after the Eiffel Tower. Reached via a spiral staircase, vistas can stretch as far as 48 km (30 miles) on a clear day.

5 Statue of Christ

The basilica's most important statue shows Christ giving a blessing. It is symbolically placed in a niche over the main entrance, above the two bronze equestrian statues.

6 Stained-Glass Gallery

One level of the great dome is encircled by stained-glass windows **(right)**. From here there is a grand view over the whole interior.

7 Bell Tower

The *campanile*, designed by Lucien Magne and added in 1904, is 80 m (262 ft) high. One of the heaviest bells in the world, the 19-ton La Savoyarde hangs in the belfry. Cast in Annecy in 1895, it was donated by the dioceses of Savoy.

8 Façade

Architect Paul Abadie (1812–1884) employed a mix of domes, turrets and Classical features in his design. The Château-Landon stone secretes calcite when wet and so keeps the façade bleached white **(left)**.

9 Equestrian Statues

Two striking bronze statues of French saints stand on the portico above the main entrance, cast in 1927 by Hippolyte Lefèbvre. One is of Joan of Arc, the other is of Louis IX, later canonized as Saint Louis.

10 The Funicular

To avoid the steep climb up to Sacré-Coeur, take the *funiculaire* cable railway **(below)** and enjoy the views at leisure. It runs from the end of rue Foyatier, near Square Willette.

Following pages Notre-Dame illuminated at dusk

TOP10 ⭐ Arc de Triomphe

The best day to visit the world's most familiar triumphal arch is 2 December, the date that marks Napoleon's victory at the Battle of Austerlitz in 1805, when the sun, setting behind the Champs-Elysées and the Arc de Triomphe, creates a spectacular halo around the building. Work began on the 50-m (164-ft) arch in 1806 but was not completed until 1836, due, in part, to Napoleon's fall from power. Four years later, Napoleon's funeral procession passed beneath it, on its way to his burial in Les Invalides (see pp38–9). Today the arch is a focal point for numerous public events.

4 Tomb of the Unknown Soldier

In the centre of the arch flickers the eternal flame on the Tomb of the Unknown Soldier (left), a victim of World War I buried on 11 November 1920. It is symbolically reignited every day at 6:30pm.

1 Museum

Within the arch is a small but interesting museum which tells the history of its construction and gives details of various celebrations and funerals that the arch has seen over the years. The more recent of these are shown in a short video.

2 Departure of the Volunteers in 1792

One of the most striking sculptures is on the front right base. It shows French citizens leaving to defend their nation against Austria and Prussia.

3 Triumph of Napoleon

As you look at the arch from the Champs-Elysées, the relief on the left base shows the restored *Triumph of Napoleon*. It celebrates the Treaty of Vienna peace agreement signed in 1810, when Napoleon's empire was in its heyday.

5 Viewing Platform

Taking the elevator or climbing the 284 steps to the top of the Arc de Triomphe gives visitors a sublime view (below) of Paris and a sense of the arch's dominant position in the centre of the Place de l'Etoile. To the east is the magnificent Champs-Elysées (see p111) and to the west is the Grande Arche de La Défense (see p155). There are another 40 steps after the lift.

Arc de Triomphe

7 Battle of Austerlitz

Another battle victory is shown on a frieze on the arch's north side. It depicts Napoleon's heavily outnumbered troops breaking the ice on Lake Satschan in Austria, a tactic which drowned thousands of enemy troops.

6 Battle of Aboukir

Above the *Triumph of Napoleon* carving is this scene **(above)** showing Napoleonic victory over the Turks in 1799. The same victory was commemorated on canvas in 1806 by the French painter Antoine Gros and is now on display at the Palace of Versailles *(see p155)*.

8 Frieze

A frieze running around the arch shows French troops departing for battle (east) and their victorious return (west).

THE GREAT AXIS

The Arc de Triomphe is the central of three arches; together they create a grand vision of which even Napoleon would have been proud. He was responsible for the first two, placing the Arc de Triomphe directly in line with the Arc de Triomphe du Carrousel in front of the Louvre *(see pp12–15)*, which also celebrates the victory at Austerlitz. In 1989, the trio was completed with the Grande Arche de La Défense. The 8km-long (5-mile) *Grand Axe* (Great Axis) runs from here to the Louvre's Pyramid.

9 General Marceau's Funeral

Marceau died in battle against the Austrian army in 1796, after a famous victory against them the previous year. His funeral is depicted in a frieze located above the *Departure of the Volunteers in 1792*.

10 Thirty Shields

Immediately below the top of the arch runs a row of 30 shields, each carrying the name of a Napoleonic victory.

NEED TO KNOW

MAP B2 ■ Place Charles-de-Gaulle, 75008 ■ 01 55 37 73 77 (enquiries) ■ arc-de-triomphe. monuments-nationaux.fr

Open Apr–Sep: 10am–11pm daily (until 10:30pm Oct–Mar; last adm 45 mins before closing); closed 1 Jan, 1 May, 8 May (am), 14 Jul (am), 11 Nov (am), 25 Dec and events

Admission €9.50

■ Try to get here early, as the morning light shows the golden tone of the stonework at its best.

■ Enjoy a coffee and the old-world charm of Le Fouquet (99 Ave des Champs-Elysées). It's expensive, but worth the treat.

TOP 10 ⭐ Centre Georges Pompidou

Today one of the world's most famous pieces of modern architecture, when the Pompidou Centre opened in 1977, architects Richard Rogers and Renzo Piano startled everyone by turning the building "inside out", with brightly coloured pipes displayed on the façade. Designed as a cross-cultural arts complex, it houses the excellent Musée National d'Art Moderne (Modern Art Museum), as well as a cinema, library, shops and performance space. The outside forecourt is a popular gathering spot for tourists and locals alike.

1 Escalator
One of the building's most striking and popular features is the external escalator **(right)** which climbs, snake-like, up the front of the Centre in its plexiglass tube. The view gets better and better as you rise high above the activity in the Centre's forecourt, before arriving at the top for the best view of all.

4 Bookshop
The ground-floor bookshop sells a range of postcards, posters of major works in the Modern Art Museum and books on artists associated with Paris.

2 Pipes
Part of the shock factor of the Pompidou Centre is that the utility pipes are outside the building **(above)**. Not only that, they are vividly coloured: bright green for water, yellow for electricity and blue for air conditioning.

3 Top-Floor View
The view from the top of the Pompidou Centre is spectacular. The Eiffel Tower is visible, as is Montmartre in the north and the monolithic Tour Montparnasse to the south. On clear days views can stretch as far as La Défense (see p155).

5 The Piazza
Visitors and locals gather in the open space in front of the Centre to enjoy a variety of street performers and the changing installations of sculptures, which are often related to shows at the Centre.

6 Stravinsky Fountain
This colourful fountain in Place Igor Stravinsky was designed by Niki de Saint-Phalle and Jean Tinguely as part of the Pompidou Centre development. Inspired by composer Stravinsky's ballet *The Firebird* (1910), the bird spins and sprays water.

8 Violinist at the Window

The French artist Henri Matisse (1869–1964) was one of the proponents of the short-lived Fauvist Movement, which advocated the use of bold, strong colours. His *Violinist at the Window* was painted in 1917–18 and can be interpreted as a self-portrait.

7 Man with a Guitar

Within the Modern Art Museum, this 1914 work **(above)** by artist Georges Braque (1882–1963) is one of the most striking of the Cubist Movement.

NEED TO KNOW

MAP P2 ■ Place Georges Pompidou 75004 ■ 01 44 78 12 33 ■ www.centrepompidou.fr

Museum: 11am–10pm Wed–Mon (11pm Thu); closed 1 May. Admission €11–14. Free 1st Sun of the month, under-18s free, under-26s free (EU only)

Brancusi's Studio: 2–6pm Wed–Mon.
....
■ The centre's café is pleasant and has free Wi-Fi access. For something grander, head to Georges, the rooftop brasserie.

■ Buy tickets online to avoid the queues.
....

Centre Guide

The Centre is home to various institutions. The Museum of Modern Art (Mnam) is on levels 4 and 5, the cinema on level 1. Check at the information desk or on the website for details about the temporary shows, rehangs of works on level 5 and the contemporary art "happenings". Displays at the Mnam often change and some works are now shared with its sister institution in Metz.

9 Brancusi's Studio

The Romanian sculptor Constantin Brancusi (1876–1957) left his entire studio to the state. It has been reconstructed **(left)** in the Piazza, and displays his abstract works.

10 La Baigneuse

Joan Miró (1893–1983) was born in Barcelona but moved to Paris in 1920. His simplistic yet evocative *La Baigneuse (The Swimmer)* (1924) depicts an immense blue ocean, watched over by a crescent moon. The form of a woman is almost lost in the waves; tendrils of her yellow hair reflect their serpentine lines.

TOP 10 ⭐ The Panthéon

Paris's Panthéon is a fitting final resting place for the nation's great figures. Originally built as a church, at the behest of Louis XV, it was completed in 1790. It was intended to look like the Pantheon in Rome, but actually more closely resembles St Paul's Cathedral in London. During the Revolution it was used as a mausoleum. Napoleon returned it to the Church in 1806. It became a public building in 1885.

1 Crypt
The crypt **(above)** is eerily impressive in its scale, compared to most tiny, dark church crypts. Here lie the tombs and memorials to worthy French citizens, including the prolific French writer Emile Zola *(see p45)*.

2 Frescoes of Sainte Geneviève
Delicate murals by 19th-century artist Pierre Puvis de Chavannes, on the south wall of the nave, tell the story of Sainte Geneviève, the patron saint of Paris. She is believed to have saved the city from invasion in 451 by Attila the Hun and his hordes through the power of her prayers.

3 Façade
The Panthéon's façade **(right)** was inspired by Roman architecture. The 22 Corinthian columns support both the portico roof and bas-reliefs.

4 Dome
Inspired by Sir Christopher Wren's design for St Paul's Cathedral in London, as well as by the Dôme Church at Les Invalides *(see p38)*, this iron-framed dome **(right)** is made up of three layers. At the top, a narrow opening lets in only a tiny amount of natural light, in keeping with the building's sombre purpose.

5 Dome Galleries
A staircase leads to the galleries immediately below the dome itself, affording spectacular 360-degree panoramic views of Paris. The pillars surrounding the galleries are both decorative and functional, providing essential support for the dome.

6 Monument to Diderot
French philosopher Denis Diderot (1713–84) is honoured by this grand 1925 monument by Alphonse Terroir.

7 Foucault's Pendulum

In 1851 French physicist Jean Foucault (1819–68) followed up an earlier experiment to prove the Earth's rotation by hanging his famous pendulum from the dome of the Panthéon. The plane of the pendulum's swing rotated 11° clockwise each hour in relation to the floor, thereby proving Foucault's theory.

LOUIS BRAILLE

One of the most influential citizens buried in the Panthéon is Louis Braille (1809–52). Braille became blind at the age of three. He attended the National Institute for the Young Blind and was a gifted student. He continued at the Institute as a teacher and, in 1829, had the idea of adapting a coding system in use by the army, by turning words and letters into raised dots on card. Reading Braille has transformed the lives of blind people ever since.

Panthéon Floorplan

NEED TO KNOW

MAP N6 ■ Place du Panthéon, 75005 ■ 01 44 32 18 00 ■ pantheon.monuments-nationaux.fr

Open Apr–Sep: 10am–6:30pm daily; Oct–Mar: 10am–6pm daily; closed 1 Jan, 1 May, 25 Dec

Admission €7.50 (non EU under-25s €6, EU under-18s and under-26s free)

No disabled access

■ Crêpes à Gogo (12 rue Soufflot, open 7am–11pm) is an ideal pit stop for a crêpe or coffee.

■ Ticket sales stop 45 minutes before closing time, so arrive in plenty of time.

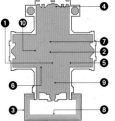

8 Pediment Relief

The bas-relief above the entrance shows a female figure, representing France, handing out laurels to the great men of the nation – the same way that Greeks and Romans honoured their heroes.

9 Tomb of Voltaire

A statue **(left)** of the great writer, wit and philosopher Voltaire (1694–1788) stands in front of his tomb.

10 Tomb of Victor Hugo

The body of the French author *(see p23)* was carried to the Panthéon in a pauper's hearse, at his own request.

TOP 10 ⭐ Sainte-Chapelle

This Gothic masterpiece, built by Louis IX (1214–70) as a shrine for his holy relics of the Passion and completed in 1248, is considered the most beautiful church in Paris, not least for its 15 stained-glass windows soaring 15 m (50 ft) to a star-covered vaulted ceiling. The church was damaged during the 1789 Revolution but restored in the mid-19th century.

1 Window of Christ's Passion

Located above the apse, this stained-glass depiction of the Crucifixion is the most beautiful window in the chapel.

2 Lower Chapel

Intended for use by the king's servants, and dedicated to the Virgin Mary, this chapel **(below)** is not as light and lofty as the Upper Chapel but is still a magnificent sight.

5 Upper Chapel Entrance

As you emerge, via a spiral staircase, into this airy space **(right)**, the effect of light and colour is utterly breathtaking. The 13th-century stained-glass windows, the oldest extant in Paris, separated by stone columns, depict biblical scenes from Genesis right through to the Crucifixion. To "read" the windows, start in the lower left panel and follow each row left to right, from bottom to top.

6 The Spire

The open latticework and pencil-thin shape give the *flèche* (spire) a very delicate appearance. In fact, three earlier church spires burned down – this one was erected in 1853 and rises 75-m (245-ft) into the air.

3 Main Portal

Like the Upper Chapel, the main portal has two tiers. Its pinnacles are decorated with a crown of thorns as a symbol of the relics within.

Rose Window 4

The Flamboyant rose window **(right)**, depicting St John's vision of the Apocalypse in 86 panels, was a gift from Charles VIII in 1485. The green and yellow hues are brightest at sunset.

7 **St Louis' Oratory**
In the late 14th century Louis XI added an oratory where he could watch Mass through a small grille in the wall. The chapel originally adjoined the Conciergerie, the former royal palace on the Ile de la Cité *(see p79)*.

9 **Seats of the Royal Family**
During Mass, the royal family sat in niches located in the fourth bays on both sides of the chapel, away from the congregation.

RELICS OF THE PASSION

Louis IX, later St Louis, was the only French king to be canonized. While on his first Crusade in 1239, he purchased the alleged Crown of Thorns from the Emperor of Constantinople, and subsequently other relics, including pieces of the True Cross, nails from the Crucifixion and a few drops of Christ's blood, paying almost three times more for them than for the construction of Sainte-Chapelle itself. The relics reside in Notre-Dame and are only displayed on religious holidays.

8 **Evening Concerts**
Sainte-Chapelle has excellent acoustics. From March until November, classical concerts are held here several evenings a week.

10 **Apostle Statues**
Beautifully carved medieval statues of 12 apostles stand on pillars along the walls. Badly damaged in the Revolution, most have been restored: the bearded apostle **(right)**, fifth on the left, is the only original statue.

NEED TO KNOW

MAP N3 ■ 6 Blvd du Palais, 75001 ■ 01 53 40 60 97 ■ sainte-chapelle. monuments-nationaux.fr

Open Mar–Oct: 9:30am–6pm daily (mid-May–mid-Sep: till 9pm Wed); Nov–Feb: 9am–5pm; closed 1 Jan, 1 May, 25 Dec

Admission €8.50, €5.50 for under-25s (free 1st Sun of month Nov–Mar). €12.50 joint adm to Conciergerie *(see p79)*. Temp exhibitions €1.50 extra. Ticket sales stop 30 mins before closing.

Restricted disabled access (48 hrs advance notice for wheelchairs)

■ For a little 1920s-style elegance, try Brasserie des Deux Palais on the corner of boulevard du Palais and rue de Lutèce.

■ A pair of binoculars comes in handy if you want to see the uppermost glass panels.

TOP 10 ★ Hôtel des Invalides

The *"invalides"* for whom this imposing Hôtel was built were wounded soldiers of the late 17th century. Louis XIV had the building constructed between 1671 and 1678, and veterans are still housed here, although only a dozen or so compared to the original 4,000. They share their home with arguably the greatest French soldier of them all, Napoleon Bonaparte, whose body rests in a crypt directly below the golden dome of the Dôme Church. Other buildings accommodate military offices, the Musée de l'Armée and smaller military museums.

1 Invalides Gardens

The approach to the Hôtel is across public gardens and then through a gate into the Invalides Gardens themselves. Designed in 1704, their paths are lined by 17th- and 18th-century cannons.

2 Golden Dome

The second church at the Hôtel was begun in 1677 and took 27 years to build. Its magnificent dome stands 107 m (351 ft) high and glistens as much now as it did when Louis XIV, the Sun King, had it first gilded in 1715.

3 Musée de l'Armée

The Army Museum is one of the largest collections of militaria in the world **(left)**. Enthusiasts will be absorbed for hours, and even the casual visitor will be fascinated by the exhibits. The Département Moderne, which traces military history from Louis XIV to Napoleon III, is especially worth a visit *(see p119)*.

Dôme Church Ceiling 4

The colourful, circular painting on the interior of the dome **(right)** above the crypt is the *Saint Louis in Glory* painted in 1692 by the French artist Charles de la Fosse. Near the centre is St Louis, who represents Louis XIV, presenting his sword to Christ in the presence of the Virgin Mary and angels.

7 Napoleon's Tomb

Napoleon's body was brought here from St Helena in 1840, some 19 years after he died. He rests in grandeur in a cocoon of six coffins **(left)**, almost "on the banks of the Seine" as was his last wish.

Hôtel des Invalides Floorplan

5 Hôtel des Invalides

One of the loveliest sights in Paris, the Classical façade of the Hôtel **(below)** is four floors high and 196 m (645 ft) end to end. Features include the dormer windows with their variously shaped shield surrounds.

8 Church Tombs

Encircling the Dôme Church are the imposing tombs of great French military men, such as Marshal Foch and Marshal Vauban, who revolutionized military fortifications and siege tactics.

9 St-Louis-des-Invalides

Adjoining the Dôme Church is the Invalides complex's original church, worth seeing for its 17th-century organ, on which the first performance of Berlioz's *Requiem* was given.

10 Musée des Plans-Reliefs

Maps and models of French forts and fortified towns are displayed here. Some of them are beautifully detailed, such as the oldest model on display, of Perpignan, dating from 1686.

6 Musée de l'Ordre de la Libération

The Order of Liberation, France's highest military honour, was created by Général de Gaulle in 1940 to acknowledge contributions during World War II. The museum details the history of the honour and the wartime Free French movement.

NEED TO KNOW

MAP D4 ■ 129 Rue de Grenelle, 75007 ■ 08 10 11 33 99 ■ www.invalides.org

Open Apr–Oct: 10am–6pm daily (Nov–Mar: 10am–5pm); closed first Mon of month (except Jul–Sep), 1 Jan, 1 May, 1 Nov, 25 Dec

Admission €9.50 adults; €7.50 concessions; under-18s free; under-26s (EU only) free

Limited disabled access

■ Le Café du Musée, between the Varenne metro station and the Musée Rodin *(see p120)*, is a lovely spot for a drink.

Hôtel Guide
Approach from the Seine for the best view, and then walk around to the ticket office on the south side. You will need a ticket for the museums and to see Napoleon's Tomb. If time is short, concentrate on the Musée de l'Armée, before walking through to the cobbled courtyard in front of the Dôme Church.

The Top 10 of Everything

Interior of the
Louvre's Pyramid

🔟 Historical Events in Paris

Ste Geneviève, patron saint of Paris

1 Arrival of the Parisii

Although the remains of Neolithic settlements have been found dating back to 4500 BC, the first inhabitants are considered to be a Celtic tribe called the Parisii, who settled on the Ile de la Cité in the 3rd century BC. Hunters and fishermen, they named their village Lutetia, meaning "boatyard on a river". The tribe minted their own gold coins and a pagan altar has been found beneath Notre-Dame.

2 Roman Settlement

The Romans conquered the Parisii in 52 BC and rebuilt their city as an administrative centre on the Left Bank. The baths in the Musée National du Moyen Age *(see p50)* and the amphitheatre in Rue Monge are the only remains of the city's Roman incarnation as Lutetia. In AD 360 the Roman prefect was declared emperor and Lutetia was renamed Paris, after its original inhabitants.

3 Founding of France

Roman rule weakened under barbarian attacks. In 450 the prayers of a young nun, Geneviève, were credited with saving the city from invasion by Attila the Hun. She became the patron saint of Paris. But in 476 the Franks captured the city, Christianity became the official religion and Paris the capital of their new kingdom, France.

4 Charlemagne, Holy Roman Emperor

In 751 the Carolingian dynasty became rulers of France when Pepin the Short ascended the throne. His heir Charlemagne was crowned Holy Roman Emperor in 800 and moved the capital to Aix-la-Chapelle (now the city of Aachen). Paris fell into decline until Hugues Capet became king in 987, moving the capital back to his home city.

St Bartholomew's Day Massacre

5 St Bartholomew's Day Massacre

Catherine de Médicis, Henri II's queen, bore three French kings and one queen, Marguerite de Valois, who married the Protestant Henri of Navarre in August 1572. Catherine plotted to massacre the Protestant nobles who attended the wedding. The killings began on 24 August and thousands died. Henri of Navarre survived and later became Henri IV, the first Bourbon king.

6 French Revolution

Following decades of royal excess and the growing gulf between rich and poor, Paris erupted into Revolution with the storming of the Bastille prison in 1789 *(see box)*.

7 Napoleon's Coronation

As Paris rose from the ashes of Revolution, a young general from Corsica, Napoleon Bonaparte, saved the city from a royalist revolt, then led military victories in Italy and Egypt. He crowned himself Emperor of France in Notre-Dame in 1804 (see p22).

8 The Second Empire

In 1851, Napoleon's nephew, Louis-Napoleon, seized power as Emperor Napoleon III. He appointed Baron Haussmann to oversee the massive building and public works projects that transformed Paris into the most glorious city in Europe. The wide boulevards, many public buildings, parks, the sewer system and the first department stores date from between 1852 and 1870.

9 The Paris Commune

Following France's defeat in the Franco-Prussian War in 1871 (see p27), many citizens rejected the harsh terms of the surrender and a left-wing group revolted, setting up the Paris Commune. But, after 72 days, government troops marched on the city. In a week of brutal street fighting (21–28 May), much of the city burned and thousands of rebellious citizens were killed.

10 Liberation of Paris

The occupation of France by Germany during World War II was a dark period for Paris. The city was the centre for the French Resistance. Allied forces liberated Paris on 25 August 1944; just two days earlier, the German commander Von Choltitz had ignored Adolf Hitler's order to burn the city to the ground.

The Liberation of Paris

TOP 10 EVENTS IN THE FRENCH REVOLUTION

Storming of the Bastille

1 14 July 1789
The storming of the Bastille prison, a symbol of repression, launches the Revolution.

2 4 August 1789
The abolition of feudalism, and the right of everyone to be a free citizen, is declared.

3 26 August 1789
Formal declaration of the Rights of Man and the Citizen, which incorporated the ideals of equality and dignity, later subsumed into the 1791 Constitution.

4 October 1789
Citizens march on Versailles and the royal family returns to Paris to be imprisoned in the Tuileries Palace.

5 20 June 1791
King Louis XVI and his family try to escape but are spotted in Varenne and return to Paris as captives.

6 10 August 1792
A mob storms the Tuileries and the royals are imprisoned in the Temple.

7 21 September 1792
The monarchy is formally abolished and the First Republic is proclaimed.

8 1792–4
"The Terror" reigns, under the radical Commune led by Robespierre, Danton and Marat. Thousands are executed by guillotine.

9 21 January 1793
Louis XVI is found guilty of treason and executed. His queen Marie-Antoinette follows him to the guillotine on 16 October.

10 28 July 1794
Robespierre is guillotined, marking the end of The Terror, and the Revolution draws to a close.

TOP 10 Historical Novels Set in Paris

Performance of *Les Misérables*

1 Les Misérables

The 1862 novel by Victor Hugo (1802–85) is an all too vivid portrayal of the poor and the dispossessed in early 19th-century Paris. At its centre is the tale of nobleman Jean Valjean, unfairly victimized by an unjust system. The character of Marius, the young idealist, is based on Hugo's own experiences as an impoverished student.

2 The Hunchback of Notre-Dame

Better known by its English title, which inspired a film of the same name, Victor Hugo's Gothic novel was published in France in 1831 as *Notre-Dame de Paris*. Set in the Middle Ages, it tells the strange and moving story of a hunchback bell-ringer, Quasimodo, and his love for Esmeralda *(see p23)*.

3 A Tale of Two Cities

The finest chronicler of 19th-century London life, Charles Dickens (1812–70) chose to set his 1859 novel in London and Paris, against the background of the French Revolution *(see p43)*. His description of conditions in the Bastille prison makes for grim reading.

4 Le Père Goriot

Honoré de Balzac (1799–1850) chronicled Parisian life masterfully in his 80-volume *La comédie humaine* series, and this novel of 1853 is certainly among his finest. Balzac's former home at 47 rue Raynouard in the 16th *arrondissement*, where he lived from 1840 to 1847, is open to the public *(see p143)*.

5 Sentimental Education

Gustave Flaubert (1821–80) studied law in Paris but illness disrupted his chosen career and he devoted himself to literature. This work (*L'education sentimentale* in French), first published in 1870 in two volumes, stands alongside his greatest work, *Madame Bovary* (1857), and marks the move away from Romanticism to Realism in French literature.

6 Bel-Ami

Guy de Maupassant (1850–93) published this, one of his best novels, in 1885, criticizing the get-rich-quick Parisian business world of the *belle époque*. Widely acknowledged as one of the world's greatest short-story writers, Maupassant is buried in the cemetery at Montparnasse in Greater Paris *(see p156)*.

Guy de Maupassant

7 A la Recherche du Temps Perdu

The master work of Marcel Proust (1871–1922) was written in 13 volumes, the first novel appearing in 1913. Proust lived on boulevard Haussmann, and his epic tale is the fictionalized story of his own life, and of Paris during the *belle époque*. Proust is buried in Père Lachaise cemetery in eastern Paris *(see p156)*.

8 ## Nana
Perhaps the greatest Parisian chronicler of them all, Emile Zola (1840–1902) was born, lived and died in the city, although he spent part of his youth in Aix-en-Provence in southern France. *Nana* was published in 1880 and tells a shocking tale of sexual decadence, through the eyes of the central character, a dancer and prostitute.

9 ## L'Assommoir
Published in 1877, Zola's *L'Assommoir* (The Drunkard) shows a side of Paris that many at the time would have preferred to ignore – the alcoholism of the working classes. It is one of the author's series of 20 linked books known as the *Rougon-Macquart* sequence, which depicts life in every quarter of society through the eyes of two branches of the same family.

10 ## Thérèse Raquin
Here Zola focuses on the secret passions that lurk behind a single Paris shopfront, opening up to reveal a tale of obsessive lust that ultimately leads to a brutal murder. It was published in 1867 and, only his second novel, shows the author's astonishing maturity and unflinching examination of all aspects of 19th-century life.

Painting of *Nana* by Edouard Manet

TOP 10 FOREIGN WRITERS WHO LIVED IN PARIS

Ernest Hemingway

1 Ernest Hemingway
The US author (1899–1961) wrote *A Moveable Feast* as an affectionate portrait of his time living in Paris from 1921 to 1926.

2 F. Scott Fitzgerald
Like Hemingway, US writer Fitzgerald (1896–1940) lived in Montparnasse and frequented La Coupole *(see p131)*.

3 George Orwell
The English novelist (1903–50) tells of his shocking experiences living in poverty in *Down and Out in Paris and London* (1933).

4 Samuel Beckett
The Irish-born playwright (1906–89) lived in Paris from 1928 until his death.

5 Anaïs Nin
US novelist Nin (1903–77) met her lover, fellow American Henry Miller, in Paris. Her *Diaries* tell of her time here.

6 Albert Camus
Algerian-born Camus (1913–60) moved to Paris in 1935 and lived here until his death.

7 Henry Miller
Miller (1891–1980) showed the seedier side of Paris in his novel *Tropic of Cancer* (1934).

8 Nancy Mitford
The author of *The Pursuit of Love* (1945) and other novels, Mitford (1904–73) lived in Paris from 1943 until her death.

9 James Joyce
Joyce (1882–1941) lived in Paris from 1920 to 1940. *Ulysses* was published here in 1922 by Shakespeare and Co.

10 Milan Kundera
Czech-born Kundera (b.1929) moved to Paris in 1978, writing *The Unbearable Lightness of Being* here.

🔟 Historic Buildings

① Hôtel des Invalides
See pp38–9.

② Versailles
Louis XIV turned his father's old hunting lodge into the largest palace in Europe and moved his court here in 1678. It was the royal residence for more than a century until Louis XVI and his queen Marie-Antoinette fled during the Revolution *(see p155).*

③ Conciergerie
Originally home to the keeper of the king's mansion and guards of the Palais de Justice, the Conciergerie was turned into a jail at the end of the 14th century. It took its place in history during the Revolution, when more than 4,000 citizens (including Marie-Antoinette) were held prisoner here, half of whom were guillotined. It remained a prison until 1914 *(see p79).*

④ Hôtel de Ville
MAP P3 ▪ 4 Pl de l'Hôtel de Ville, 75001 ▪ 01 42 76 40 40 ▪ **Open for group tours only (booking essential: 01 42 76 54 04)**
Paris's city hall sports an elaborate façade, with ornate stonework, statues and a turreted roof. It is a 19th-century reconstruction of the original town hall, which was burned down during the Paris

Hôtel de Ville façade

Central courtyard of the Hôtel Dieu

Commune of 1871 *(see p43)*. Though the pedestrianized square in front is pleasant now, it was once the site of gruesome executions: Ravaillac, assassin of Henri IV, was quartered alive here in 1610.

⑤ Hôtel Dieu
MAP N4 ▪ 1 Pl du Parvis Notre-Dame, 75004
The Hôtel Dieu, now the hospital for central Paris, was built on the site of a foundling home in 1866–78; the original 12th-century building on the Ile de la Cité was demolished during the urban renewal schemes of the 19th century. A monument in the courtyard commemorates a courageous battle here in 1944 when Paris police held out against the Nazis.

⑥ Palais de Justice
The enormous building that now houses the French law courts and judiciary dates back as far as Roman times and was the royal

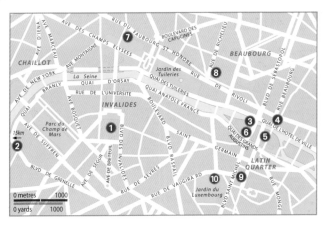

palace until the 14th century, when Charles V moved the court to the Marais. During the Revolution, thousands were sentenced to death in the Première Chambre Civile, allegedly the former bedroom of Louis IX *(see p80)*.

7 Palais de l'Elysée

This imposing palace has been the official residence of the President of the French Republic since 1873. It was built as a private mansion in 1718 and was owned by Madame de Pompadour, mistress of Louis XV, who extended the English-style gardens as far as the Champs-Elysées. After the Battle of Waterloo in 1815, Napoleon signed his second and final abdication here *(see p113)*.

8 Palais Royal

MAP L1 ■ Pl du Palais Royal, 75005 ■ Closed to the public

This former royal palace now houses State offices. It was built by Cardinal Richelieu in 1632, passing to the Crown on his death 10 years later, and was the childhood home of Louis XIV. The dukes of Orléans acquired it in the 18th century.

9 La Sorbonne

The city's great university had humble beginnings in 1253 as a college for 16 poor students to study theology. France's first printing

house was also established here in 1469. After suppression during the Revolution it became the University of Paris *(see p125)*.

10 Palais du Luxembourg

MAP L6 ■ 15 Rue de Vaugirard, 75006 ■ 01 44 54 19 49 ■ Open for reserved tours only; gardens open dawn–dusk daily

Marie de Médicis had architect Salomon de Brosse model this palace after her childhood home, the Pitti Palace in Florence. Shortly after its completion she was exiled by her son, Louis XIII. It was seized from the Crown during the Revolution to become a prison and it now houses the French Senate. Nearby is the Musée du Luxembourg.

Palais du Luxembourg

TOP 10 Places of Worship

(1) Notre-Dame
See pp20–23.

(2) Sacré-Coeur
See pp26–7.

(3) Sainte-Chapelle
Although this lovely chapel is no longer used for worship, the soaring stained-glass windows encourage reverence *(see pp36–7).*

(4) Eglise du Dôme
The final resting place of Napoleon Bonaparte is the beautiful Dôme Church in the Hôtel des Invalides complex – an elaborate monument in French Classical style. Built as the chapel for the resident soldiers of the Invalides, its ornate high altar is in stark contrast to the solemn marble chapels surrounding the crypt, which hold the tombs of French military leaders. Its golden dome can be seen for miles around *(see pp38–9).*

(5) The Panthéon
Modelled on the Pantheon in Rome, this domed late 18th-century church only served as a house of worship for two years, before becoming a monument

Façade of La Madeleine

and burial place for the great and the good of the Revolution era. Later distinguished citizens are also buried here *(see pp34–5).*

(6) La Madeleine
MAP D3 ■ Pl de la Madeleine, 75008 ■ Open 9:30am–7pm daily (services vary)
Designed in the style of a Greek temple in 1764, this prominent church in Paris's financial district, on the edge of the Opéra Quarter, is one of the city's most distinctive sights, spectacularly surrounded by 52 Corinthian columns. The church was consecrated to Mary Magdalene in 1845. The bronze doors, which include bas-reliefs of the Ten Commandments, and the Last Judgment on the south pediment are exterior highlights, while the ornate marble and gold interior has many fine statues, including François Rude's *Baptism of Christ*. It is also a popular venue for classical concerts.

(7) St-Eustache
For centuries, this monumental Gothic edifice was the market church serving the traders of Les Halles. Taking more than 100 years to build, it was finally completed in 1637 and its cavernous interior displays the architectural style of the early

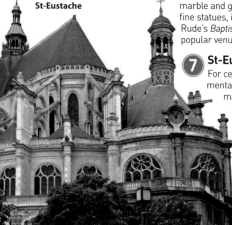

St-Eustache

Renaissance. Popular Sunday afternoon organ recitals and other classical concerts take place in this wonderfully atmospheric setting (see p85).

⑧ Grande Synagogue de la Victoire

MAP E2 ■ 44 Rue de la Victoire, 75009

Built in the late 19th century, this elaborate synagogue is the second largest in Europe. The building is open only to those wishing to attend services and to groups who have arranged a visit in advance. Other smaller synagogues can be found in the Marais, which has long had a large Jewish community, including one at 10 rue Pavée, built in 1913 by Hector Guimard, the architect who designed the city's magnificent Art Nouveau metro stations.

⑨ Mosquée de Paris

The city's Grand Mosque was built during the 1920s as a tribute to North African Muslims who gave military support to France during World War I. Its beautiful Hispano-Moorish architecture, including a minaret, was executed by craftsmen brought over from North Africa.

There is also a peaceful interior courtyard where visitors can sit and sip a glass of mint tea (see p136).

⑩ St-Sulpice

Outstanding frescoes in the Chapel of the Angels by Eugène Delacroix are the highlight of this 17th-century church's otherwise sober interior. With more than 6,500 pipes, its organ, designed by Jean-François Chalgrin in 1776, is one of the largest in the world. The novelist Victor Hugo married Adèle Foucher here in 1822 (see p125).

St-Sulpice church organ

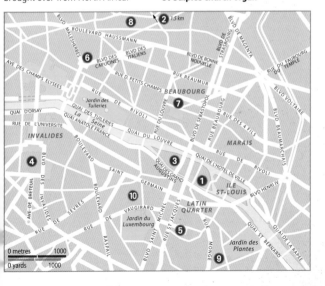

🔟 Museums

The Lady and the Unicorn,
Musée National du Moyen Age

1 Musée du Louvre

French and Italian sculpture, Greek and Roman antiquities and paintings from the 12th to the 19th centuries are just some of the highlights of the world's largest museum *(see pp12–15)*.

2 Musée Carnavalet

Housed in a grand Marais mansion, this museum showcases the history of Paris. The collection includes painting, sculpture and antique furniture, recreating private residences of the 16th and 17th centuries. There is also a poignant collection of mementoes from the Revolution, as well as a wonderful French garden *(see p94)*.

3 Musée des Arts Décoratifs

Set over nine levels, adjoining the west end of the Louvre's Richelieu Wing, this decorative arts museum showcases furniture and tableware from the 12th century to the present. The breathtaking anthology of pieces ranges from Gothic panelling and Renaissance porcelain to 1970s carpets and chairs by Philippe Starck. Also in the museum is the Musée de la Mode et du Textile, which mounts fashion exhibitions, and the Musée de la Publicité, which has exhibitions on advertising *(see p104)*.

4 Musée National du Moyen Age

This splendid museum dedicated to the art of the Middle Ages is known by several names, including the Musée de Cluny after the beautiful mansion in which it is housed, and the Thermes de Cluny after the Roman baths adjoining the museum. Highlights include the famous "Lady and the Unicorn" tapestries, medieval stained glass and exquisite gold crowns and jewellery *(see p126)*.

5 Musée du quai Branly

In a city dominated by Western art, this museum housing 300,000 artifacts (of which 3,500 are on display at any one time) tips the balance in favour of arts from Africa, Asia, Oceania and the Americas. Must-sees include the African instruments. The striking Jean Nouvel-designed building is an attraction in itself *(see p120)*.

6 Muséum National d'Histoire Naturelle

Paris's Natural History Museum in the Jardin des Plantes contains a fascinating collection of animal skeletons, plant fossils, minerals and gemstones. Its highlight is the magnificent Grande Galerie de l'Evolution, which depicts the changing interaction between man and nature during the evolution of life on Earth *(see p60 & p135)*.

Stegosaurus model, Muséum National d'Histoire Naturelle

Musée des Arts et Métiers

and other decorative arts, amassed by the founders of the Samaritaine department store, including paintings by Rembrandt, Reynolds and other masters (see p93).

9 Cité de l'Architecture et du Patrimoine

The Cité de l'Architecture and the Musée des Monuments Français showcase French architectural heritage and have become one of the world's great architectural centres. The Galeries des Moulages houses models of great French cathedrals (see p141).

10 Musée Jacquemart-André

Set in an elegant private mansion, this museum was once the home of Edouard André and his artist wife Nélie Jacquemart. The museum houses their spectacular personal art collection, which features works by Boucher, Botticelli, Rembrandt and Fragonard, as well as excellent temporary exhibits (see p113).

7 Musée des Arts et Métiers

MAP G3 ▪ 60 Rue Réaumur, 75003 ▪ Open 10am–6pm Tue–Sun (to 9:30pm Thu) ▪ Admission charge ▪ www.arts-et-metiers.net

Housed in the grand Abbaye de St-Martin-des-Champs, this industrial design museum is a fascinating repository of printing machines, vintage cars, music boxes, early flying machines, automatons and other inventions.

8 Musée Cognacq-Jay

The Hôtel Donon is a fine setting for this superb collection of 18th-century art, furniture, porcelain

Musée Jacquemart-André

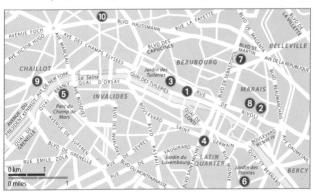

TOP 10 Art Galleries

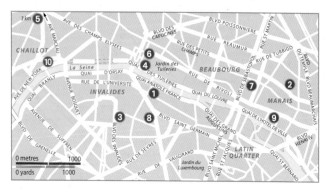

1 Musée d'Orsay
See pp16–19.

2 Musée Picasso
After a five-year renovation, the beautifully restored Hôtel Salé *(see p98)* was reopened in 2014 to showcase this extensive collection of paintings, sculptures, drawings and other masterpieces by Pablo Picasso (1881–1973). Large sculptures adorn the garden and courtyard while, inside the gorgeous 17th-century mansion, twice as much as before of the collection is now on display *(see p93)*. Be sure not to miss Picasso's own collection of paintings, including

The Thinker,
Musée Rodin

works by Cézanne, Renoir, Matisse and others of his contemporaries, located on the third floor.

3 Musée Rodin
On a sunny day, head straight for the gardens of the Musée Rodin, next to the Hôtel des Invalides complex, to enjoy some of the French sculptor's most famous works, including *The Thinker* and *The Burghers of Calais*, while strolling among the shady trees and rose bushes. Auguste Rodin (1840–1917) lived and worked for nine years in the beautiful 18th-century Hôtel Biron, where the rest of the collection is housed. The museum reopened in autumn 2015 following a three-year renovation project and a complete reorganization of the collection *(see p120)*.

4 Musée de l'Orangerie
MAP D3 ■ Jardin des Tuileries, 75001 ■ Open 9am–6pm Wed–Mon ■ Admission charge ■ www.musee-orangerie.fr

The prime exhibits here are eight of Monet's huge waterlily canvases *(see p16)* and the gallery, located in a corner of the Tuileries, was renovated in 2006 to improve their display. The Walter-Guillaume collection covers works by Matisse, Picasso, Modigliani and other modern masters from 1870 to 1930.

Fondation Louis Vuitton

⑤ Fondation Louis Vuitton
8 Ave du Mahatma Gandhi, Bois de Boulogne, 75116 ▪ Open **11am–8pm Mon, Wed & Thu, 11am–11pm Fri, 10am–8pm Sat & Sun** ▪ **Admission charge** ▪ www.fondationlouisvuitton.fr

Close to the Jardin d'Acclimatation in the Bois de Boulogne (see p159), Frank Gehry's dramatic glass structure contains a gallery and event space hosting contemporary arts exhibitions. A shuttle to the arts centre leaves Place Charles de Gaulle every 15 minutes (tickets €1).

⑥ Jeu de Paume
MAP D3 ▪ **1 Pl de la Concorde, 75008** ▪ Open **11am–9pm Tue, 11am–7pm Wed–Sun** ▪ Closed **1 Jan, 1 May, 25 Dec** ▪ **Admission charge**

This gallery is one of the finest exhibition spaces in the city, set within a 19th-century real-tennis court (jeu de paume). It has a strong reputation for showcasing outstanding photography, film and video installations.

⑦ Musée National d'Art Moderne
MAP P2 ▪ **Pl Georges Pompidou, 75004** ▪ Open **11am–10pm Wed–Mon** ▪ **Admission charge**

The revolutionary Pompidou Centre is the perfect home for France's outstanding Modern Art Museum. It features 1,400 works on two levels, one focusing on artists and movements of the first half of the 20th century, the other featuring art from the 1960s to the present (see pp32–3).

⑧ Musée Maillol
Works of the French artist Aristide Maillol, including his drawings, engravings, paintings and plastercasts, are the focal point of this museum, which was created by his model, Dina Vierny. Other major artists feature in temporary exhibitions (see p127).

⑨ Maison Européenne de la Photographie
If you're a photography fan, don't miss this splendid gallery in the Marais. Its exhibitions range from portraits to documentary work, retrospectives to contemporary photographers (see p95).

⑩ Palais de Tokyo
MAP B4 ▪ **13 Ave du Président Wilson, 75116** ▪ Open **noon–midnight Wed–Mon** ▪ **Admission charge** ▪ www.palaisdetokyo.com

Dedicated to contemporary art, this lively museum in the Chaillot Quarter, hosts regularly changing exhibitions and installations by international artists.

Palais de Tokyo, built for the World's Fair in 1937

🔟 Riverfront Sights

Eiffel Tower and the Seine, viewed from Pont Alexandre III

1 Eiffel Tower

Although the top of the Eiffel Tower can be seen above rooftops across the city, one of the best views of this Paris landmark is from the Seine. The Pont d'Iéna lies at the foot of the tower, bridging the river to link it to the Trocadéro Gardens. The tower, illuminated at night, is a highlight of a dinner cruise on the Seine *(see pp24–5)*.

2 Palais de Chaillot

The curved arms of the Palais de Chaillot encircling the Trocadéro Gardens can be seen from the Seine. In the centre of the gardens magnificent fountains spout from the top of a long pool lined with statues, while two huge water cannons spray their charges back towards the river and the Eiffel Tower on the opposite bank *(see p141)*.

3 Liberty Flame
MAP C3

A replica of the New York Statue of Liberty's torch was erected here in 1987 by the *International Herald Tribune* to mark their centenary and honour the freedom fighters of the French Resistance during World War II. It is located on the right bank of the Pont de l'Alma, the bridge over the tunnel where Diana, Princess of Wales, was killed in an automobile crash in 1997. The Liberty Flame has now become her unofficial memorial and is often draped with notes and flowers laid in her honour.

4 Grand Palais and Petit Palais

Gracing either side of the magnificent Pont Alexandre III are these two splendid exhibition halls, built for the Universal Exhibition of 1900. The iron Art Nouveau skeleton of the Grand Palais is topped by an enormous glass roof, which is most impressive when illuminated at night. The Petit Palais is smaller but similar in style, with a dome and many Classical features *(see p111)*.

Liberty Flame by Pont de l'Alma

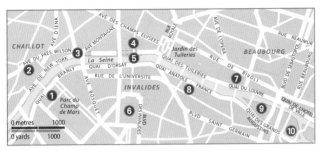

5 Pont Alexandre III

The most beautiful bridge in Paris is the Pont Alexandre III, a riot of Art Nouveau decoration including cherubs, wreaths, lamps and other elaborate statuary. Built for the Universal Exhibition of 1900, it leads to the Grand Palais and Petit Palais. There are wonderful views of the Invalides complex and the Champs-Elysées from the bridge (see p112).

6 Dôme Church

An impressive view of the Eglise de Dôme in the Hôtel des Invalides complex can be had from the Pont Alexandre III. The golden dome beckons visitors down the long parkway lined with streetlamps and statues (see pp38–9).

7 Musée du Louvre

This grand museum stretches along the river from the Pont Royal to the Pont des Arts. The Denon Wing, which can be seen from the Seine, was largely built during the reigns of Henri IV and Louis XIII in the late 16th and early 17th centuries (see pp12–15).

8 Musée d'Orsay

The view of this exceptional modern art gallery from the Right Bank of the Seine is one of its finest angles, showing off the arched terminals, great clock faces and grand façade of this former railway station, built in 1898–1900. Architect Victor Laloux designed it specifically to harmonize with the Louvre and Tuileries Quarter across the river (see pp16–19).

9 Conciergerie

This huge and imposing building, which served as a notorious prison during the French Revolution, commands the western end of the Ile de la Cité. The magnificent building retains some of the few medieval features on the island, including a torture chamber, kitchens, a clock and the twin towers that rise above the Quai de l'Horloge (see p79).

10 Notre-Dame

The great cathedral is never more majestic than when viewed from the Left Bank of the Seine. It rises at the eastern end of the Ile de la Cité above the remains of the ancient tribes who first settled Paris in the 3rd century BC (see pp20–23).

Notre-Dame viewed from the Seine

🔟 Parks and Gardens

View from the terrace of the Jardin du Luxembourg

1 Jardin du Luxembourg

Parisians love this centrally located park, set around the Palais du Luxembourg. The sweeping terrace is a great place for people-watching, while locals sunbathe around the Octagonal Lake or sail toy boats in the water. Statues are dotted throughout the grounds, and there is a café (see p125).

2 Jardin des Tuileries

Now officially part of the Louvre, these gardens were laid out in the 17th century as part of the old Palais de Tuileries. They stretch along the Seine between the Louvre and Place de la Concorde. The walkways are lined with lime and chestnut trees. Statues include bronze figures by Aristide Maillol (see p103).

3 Jardin des Plantes

Established as a medicinal herb garden for the king in 1635, these vast botanical gardens are a wonderfully tranquil spot. Paths are lined with statuary and mature trees, including the oldest in Paris, grown from the stump of an *Acacia robinia* dating from 1636 (see p135).

4 Bois de Boulogne

At the weekends, Parisians head for this vast park on the western edge of the city, which has a boating lake and paths for cycling, jogging and strolling. There are three formal gardens, lakes and waterfalls, and even two horse-racing tracks. It's a good spot for a break from the city bustle (see p156).

5 Bois de Vincennes

Another great escape from the city, this park is to the east of Paris what the Bois de Boulogne is to the west. A former royal hunting ground, it was landscaped in the 1860s. Now it features ornamental lakes and waterfalls, a zoo, a funfair and horse-racing tracks (see p156).

6 Parc Monceau

The most fashionable green space in Paris, full of well-heeled residents of the nearby mansions and apartments. The lush landscaping dates from the 18th

Classical colonnade in Parc Monceau

century, and some architectural follies, such as the Classical colonnade, survive *(see p157)*.

7 Jardins du Palais Royal
MAP L1 ■ Pl du Palais Royal, 75001

These lovely gardens are enclosed by the 18th-century arcades of the Palais Royal *(see p104)*. Modern sculptures include Daniel Buren's controversial striped columns.

8 Parc Clichy-Batignolles
147 Rue Cardinet, 75017 ■ Metro Brochant

Away from the tourist crush, this park in the heart of the laid-back Batignolles neighbourhood was developed with an eye to ecology and biodiversity. Locals come to skate, play *pétanque*, tend the community gardens and laze on the lawns, while wildlife and rare flora thrive in the wetlands-like environment.

9 Parc Montsouris
Blvd Jourdan, 75014 ■ Metro Cité Universitaire

Located south of Montparnasse, this large park in central Paris is very popular with city residents. It was laid out in the English style, atop an old granite quarry, by landscape architect Adolphe Alphand between 1865 and 1878. Hemingway *(see p45)* and other writers and artists frequented the park in the mid-20th century. It has a jogging path, lake and a bandstand.

10 Parc des Buttes Chaumont
Rue Manin, 75019 ■ Metro Buttes-Chaumont

The great city planner Baron Haussmann created this wonderful retreat northeast of the city centre in 1867, from what was formerly a rubbish dump. His architects built artificial cliffs, waterfalls, streams and a lake complete with an island crowned by a Roman-style temple. There is a café and lovely views of Sacré-Coeur. The park is currently being renovated *(see p61)*.

TOP 10 FOUNTAINS

Observatory Fountain

1 Agam Fountain
La Défense ■ RER La Défense
Jewish architect Yaacov Agam designed this fountain of water and lights.

2 Four Seasons Fountain
MAP C4 ■ Rue de Grenelle
Paris in female form looks down on figures representing the Seine and Marne rivers, designed in 1739 by sculptor Edme Bouchardon.

3 Fontaine des Innocents
MAP N2 ■ Square des Innocents
Carved by Jean Goujon in 1547, this is Paris's only Renaissance fountain.

4 Medici Fountain
MAP L6 ■ Jardin du Luxembourg
This ornate 17th-century fountain with a pond was built for Marie de Médicis.

5 Molière Fountain
MAP E3 ■ Rue de Richelieu
This 19th-century fountain honours the French playwright.

6 Observatory Fountain
MAP L6 ■ Jardin du Luxembourg
Four bronze statues representing the continents hold aloft a globe.

7 Châtelet Fountain
MAP N2 ■ Pl du Châtelet
The two sphinxes of this 1808 fountain are appropriate to commemorate Napoleon's victory in Egypt.

8 Stravinsky Fountain
Birds squirt water from this colourful Pompidou Centre fountain *(see p32)*.

9 Trocadéro Fountains
Spouting towards the Eiffel Tower, these fountains are illuminated at night *(see p24)*.

10 Versailles Fountains
The fountains at Versailles *(see p155)* flow to music at weekends in spring and in summer.

 Off the Beaten Track

Wall of skulls and bones, Catacombs

1 Catacombs

MAP E4 ■ 1 Ave du Colonel Henri Rol-Tanguy, 75014 ■ 01 43 22 47 63 ■ Open 10am–8pm Tue–Sun, ■ Admission charge ■ www.catacombes.paris.fr

The catacombs are an underground warren of tunnels, filled with the bones of some six million Parisians, brought here from 1785 to 1865 as a solution to the problem of overflowing cemeteries. Aside from the macabre sight of walls lined with skulls and bones, it's a thrill to enter the tunnels, part of a vast quarry network that underlies the whole city. Come early, as there's often a queue – only 200 visitors are allowed in at a time.

2 Promenade Plantée

MAP H5

Starting near the Bastille Opera House (see p65) and ending at Bois de Vincennes, this 4-km (2.5-mile) walkway, much of it high above the streets on a former railway viaduct, is a wonderful way to see a little-visited part of the city. Planted all along with trees and flowers, the path runs past tall mansion blocks, whose decorative mouldings and balconies (not to mention smart interiors) are a treat to see close up.

3 Little-visited Louvre

While the crowds flock to the *Mona Lisa* and *Venus de Milo*, canny visitors set out to discover other parts of the Louvre's collections, such as the Islamic arts section. Opened in 2012, it includes beautiful Iznik tiles and exquisite glass, gold and ivory objects from Andalusia, Iraq and India – all under a stunning gold filigree roof (see pp12–15).

4 Pinacothèque de Paris

MAP D3 ■ 28 Pl de la Madeleine and 8 rue Vignon, 75008 ■ 01 42 68 02 01 ■ 10:30am–6:30pm daily (to 8:30pm Wed & Fri) ■ Admission charge ■ www.pinacotheque.com

This privately run gallery puts on much-acclaimed exhibitions and also has a permanent collection of around one hundred paintings, including works by Rembrandt and Picasso. Unusually, the artworks are hung by theme, such as "landscape", just as a private collector might display his or her paintings.

5 Canal Barge Cruise

MAP J2 ■ 12 Port de Solferino, 75007 ■ Cruises daily ■ Admission charge ■ www.pariscanal.com

A great way to get away from the city bustle and see a different side of Paris is to take a barge along the

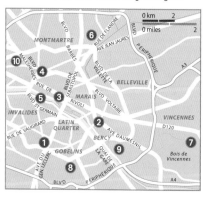

pretty Canal St-Martin. Paris Canal boats depart from the quay outside the Musée d'Orsay *(see pp16–19)* and make their leisurely way past the Ile de la Cité and Notre-Dame, and through several locks and a tunnel, to Parc de la Villette *(see p156)*.

Barge on Canal St-Martin

6 Le Centquatre-Paris
5 Rue Curial, 75019 ▪ 01 53 35 50 00 ▪ Metro Riquet ▪ Open noon–7pm Tue–Fri, 11am–7pm Sat & Sun ▪ Admission charge ▪ www.104.fr

The "104" is a huge arts centre, housed in a converted 19th-century funeral parlour with a lofty glass roof. It contains numerous artists' studios and workshops, and puts on excellent exhibitions and installations, as well as music, dance, cinema and theatre.

7 Parc Floral de Paris
Route de la Pyramide, 94300 ▪ Metro Chateau de Vincennes ▪ 9.30am–8pm daily, winter till dusk ▪ Admission charge Jun–Sep: Wed, Sat & Sun, otherwise free ▪ www. parcfloraldeparis.com

Set within the Bois de Vincennes, this lovely park has wonderful displays of camellias, rhododendrons, ferns and irises. It hosts horticultural exhibitions and free jazz concerts in summer and has plenty to appeal to children, including an adventure park.

8 Buttes-aux-Cailles
Metro Corvisart

The Butte-aux-Cailles quarter, in the southeast of the city, is a bit like a mini-Montmartre, with its pretty cobbled streets and old-fashioned streetlamps. The main Rue de la Butte-aux-Cailles with its restaurants and bohemian bars buzzes well into the night.

9 Bercy Village
28 Rue François Truffaut, 75012 ▪ Metro Cour St-Emilion ▪ www. bercyvillage.com

The district of Bercy is where barges from all over France used to deliver wine to the capital. The former warehouses, a handsome ensemble of ochre-coloured stone buildings, have been converted into shops, restaurants and, fittingly, wine bars. It's well worth a wander, especially on Sundays when shops in most other parts of Paris are closed.

10 Musée Nissim de Camondo
MAP C2 ▪ 63 Rue de Monceau, 75008 ▪ 01 45 63 26 32 ▪ Open 10am–5:30pm Wed–Sun ▪ Admission charge

Wealthy art collector Count Moïse de Camondo had this grand mansion built to house his superb collection of 18th-century art. The rooms are full of tapestries, paintings, gilded furniture and Sèvres porcelain. As interesting as the artworks is the portrait that emerges of a well-to-do family, beset by tragedy (it is named for his son, killed in World War I) and ultimately fell victim to Auschwitz.

Musée Nissim de Camondo

🔟 Children's Attractions

Musée de la Magie et des Automates

① Disneyland® Paris
The French offspring of America's favourite theme park is a clone of its parent, and has now been joined by the Walt Disney Studios® complex. Both have big queues, so arrive early. There are rides for children of all ages and most adults are equally enchanted *(see p155)*.

② Parc Astérix
Plailly, 60128 ▪ RER B to Roissy CDG1, then shuttle from A3 ▪ Open May–Aug: 10am–6pm Mon–Thu, 10am–7pm Fri, Sat & Sun; Sep–Oct: 10am–6pm Sat & Sun ▪ Admission charge ▪ www.parcasterix.fr
There's not just the Gaul of Asterix and Obelix to discover here, but six worlds, including ancient Greece and Rome, and all with the zany spin and charm of Goscinny and Uderzo's beloved comic books. Dozens of great attractions include one of Europe's longest roller coasters.

③ Eiffel Tower
A trip to the top is one of the most memorable activities for children in Paris *(see pp24–5)*.

④ Grande Galerie de l'Evolution
The most exciting and imaginatively designed section in the Natural History Museum is the Great Gallery of Evolution. Elephants, giraffes and other stuffed animals rise out of a recreated savannah, and a huge whale skeleton hangs from the ceiling, while special displays help tell the story of the development of life on Earth. Nature workshops are also held for children during school holidays *(see p135)*.

⑤ Musée de la Magie et des Automates
MAP R4 ▪ 11 Rue St-Paul, 75004 ▪ 01 42 72 13 26 ▪ Open 2–7pm Wed, Sat, Sun (daily during school holidays, except Jul & Aug) ▪ Admission charge ▪ www.museedelamagie.com
Kids are enchanted by this museum of magic, located in the cellars of the former home of the Marquis de Sade. Magicians conjure up shows every half hour involving optical illusions, card tricks and lots of audience participation. Exhibits include working automata and memorabilia of master magicians such as Houdini (1874–1926).

⑥ Parc de la Villette
One of the city's top children's attractions, with activities for all ages. The Cité des Sciences et de l'Industrie, a high-tech hands-on science museum, gets star billing, while the Cité des Enfants is a science and nature attraction for younger children. Kids also love the Argonaute, a real 1950s submarine that voyaged around the world 10 times, the Géode with its IMAX screen and the futuristic outdoor playground *(see p156)*.

Parc de la Villette

⑦ Jardin d'Acclimatation
MAP A2 ■ Bois de Boulogne, 75016 ■ Open 10am–7pm daily (6pm Sep–Apr) ■ Admission charge ■ www.jardindacclimatation.fr

This amusement park at the north end of the Bois de Boulogne (see p156) has roller coasters, pony rides and puppet shows. An electric train, "le Petit Train", runs to the park from Porte Maillot.

⑧ Musée des Arts Forains
Pavillons de Bercy, 53 Ave des Terroirs de France, 75012 ■ Metro Cour Saint-Emilion ■ See website for opening dates ■ 01 43 40 16 22 ■ Admission charge ■ www.arts-forains.com

This private museum in a former wine warehouse in Bercy Village (see p59) is a secret wonderland filled with vintage fairground attractions, automata, theatre props, antique merry-go-rounds and a 1920s hall of mirrors. It is open by appointment for guided tours all year round, but visitors are welcome without prior reservations for 10 days over the Christmas and New Year period to try out the traditional fairground games and ride on the carousels.

⑨ Jardin du Luxembourg
MAP L6 ■ Jardin du Luxembourg, 75006 ■ Open dawn–dusk daily

The park has tennis courts, puppet shows, donkey rides and a good playground (for a fee). But most fun of all is the traditional Parisian pastime of sailing model boats in the large Octagonal Lake and riding the 19th-century carousel.

⑩ Parc des Buttes Chaumont
Rue Manin, 75019 ■ Open 7am–10pm daily (9pm Sep–Apr)

The highest park in Paris is great for a family picnic. Kids will enjoy exploring the rugged terrain with its cliffs, beaches, suspended bridges and waterfalls, as well as the boating facilities, pony rides and puppet shows.

TOP 10 MERRY-GO-ROUNDS

Carousel by the Eiffel Tower

1 Jardin des Plantes
The curious Dodo Manège features extinct animals including horned, giraffe-like sivatherium (see p135).

2 Jardin du Luxembourg
Children can play the traditional French game of rings on this historic 1879 merry-go-round.

3 Montmartre
At the foot of Sacré-Coeur (see pp26–7), this grand double-decker merry-go-round has gorgeous painted horses and carriages.

4 Parc de la Villette
An airplane, a hot-air balloon and a Tintin-style space rocket join the wooden horses on this two-storey merry-go-round.

5 Jardin d'Acclimatation
A traditional carousel with wooden horses is just one of the collection of merry-go-rounds here.

6 Jardins du Trocadéro
A wonderful hot-air balloon graces this dual-platform merry-go-round (see p142).

7 Hôtel de Ville
Lucky riders jump on whenever this seasonal merry-go-round appears in the heart of the town (see p46).

8 Eiffel Tower
The Parisian icon (see pp24–5) provides a dramatic backdrop to this solar-powered merry-go-round.

9 Parc Monceau
This charming little carousel is much loved by the local children (see p157).

10 Jardin des Tuileries
Set among the trees, antique wooden horses spin round this enchanting merry-go-round (see p103).

Following pages Interior of the Opéra National de Paris Garnier

TOP 10 Entertainment Venues

1 Opéra National de Paris Garnier

Going to the opera here is not just a night out, but a whole experience. The theatre has returned to hosting opera after a spell as a dance-only venue. The vast stage can hold a cast of 450, and the building itself is an example of excessive opulence, complete with grand staircase, mirrors and marble *(see p104)*.

2 Folies-Bergère
MAP F2 ▪ 32 Rue Richer, 75009 ▪ 08 92 68 16 50 ▪ www. foliesbergere.com

The epitome of Parisian cabaret, the Folies were, for a time, little more than a troupe of high-kicking, bare-breasted dancers.

Poster for the Folies Bergère

Today, the musical shows reflect the days when Maurice Chevalier and Josephine Baker performed here.

3 The Lido
MAP D3 ▪ 116 Bis, Ave des Champs-Elysées, 75008 ▪ 01 40 76 56 10 ▪ www.lido.fr

Home to world-famous troupe of long-legged dancers the Bluebell Girls, the fabulous special effects here include aerial ballets and an on-stage skating rink. There are many who regard this dinner-cabaret as an essential Parisian experience.

4 Le Crazy Horse Paris
MAP C3 ▪ 12 Ave George V, 75008 ▪ 01 47 23 32 32 ▪ www. lecrazyhorseparis.com

More risqué than the other big-name cabaret shows, the Saloon has a reputation for putting on the most professional as well as the sexiest productions. Striptease features, along with glamorous dancing girls and other cabaret acts. The computer-controlled lighting effects are spectacular.

5 Le Cirque d'Hiver
MAP H3 ▪ 110 Rue Amelot, 75011 ▪ 01 47 00 28 81 ▪ www. cirquedhiver.com

Worth visiting for the façade alone, this whimsical, circular listed building, dating from 1852, plays host to the traditional Cirque Bouglione, complete with acts such as trapeze artists, clowns, jugglers and tame tigers.

6 Moulin Rouge

The home of the Can-Can, Toulouse-Lautrec immortalized the theatre's dancers on canvas during the *belle époque* and the results are on display in the Musée d'Orsay *(see p17)*. The show still has all the

Exterior of the Moulin Rouge

razzamatazz that has been dazzling audiences since 1889. The pre-show dinner is optional *(see p148)*.

7 Comédie Française
MAP L1 ▪ 1 Pl Colette, 75001 ▪ 08 25 10 16 80 (+33 1 44 58 15 15 from abroad) ▪ www.comedie-francaise.fr

Paris's oldest theatre was founded in 1680 and is still the only one with its own repertory company, staging both classical and modern drama (in French). The theatre has been based in the current building since 1799. Around the corner from the main box office, a special window opens 45 minutes before curtain-up, selling reduced-price under-27 and concessions tickets.

8 Opéra National de Paris Bastille
MAP H5 ▪ Pl de la Bastille, 75012 ▪ 08 92 89 90 90 (+33 1 71 25 24 23 from abroad) ▪ www.operadeparis.fr

Opened in 1992 as the largest opera house in the world, this modern building was heavily criticized, not least for its acoustics and poor facilities. However, this is still the best place to see opera in Paris.

9 Théâtre du Châtelet
MAP N2 ▪ 1 Pl du Châtelet, 75001 ▪ 01 40 28 28 40 ▪ www.chatelet-theatre.com

The city's largest concert hall and fourth largest auditorium was built in 1862. Its repertoire covers classical music, ballet and opera, as well as Broadway shows and popular Sunday morning chamber music concerts.

10 Théâtre de la Ville
MAP N2 ▪ 2 Pl du Châtelet, 75004 ▪ 01 42 74 22 77 ▪ www.theatredelaville-paris.com

Once known as the Sarah Bernhardt Theatre, in honour of the great Parisian actress who performed here and managed the theatre in the 19th century, today it puts on an eclectic range of modern dance, music shows and some classical theatre.

TOP 10 JAZZ CLUBS

Performance at New Morning

1 Sunset-Sunside
MAP N2 ▪ 60 Rue des Lombards
A double serving of late-night jazz: acoustic and modern at street level; electric, fusion and groove in the cellar.

2 Au Duc des Lombards
MAP N2 ▪ 42 Rue des Lombards
The best overseas jazz artists come here to play with home-grown talent.

3 Baiser Salé
MAP N2 ▪ 58 Rue des Lombards
Jazz, blues and World Music are the mainstays at this tiny cellar club.

4 Caveau des Oubliettes
MAP F5 ▪ 52 Rue Garlande
Jazz in an ex-dungeon, with a gig at 10pm every night except Mondays.

5 Autour de Midi de Minuit
MAP E1 ▪ 11 Rue Lepic
Mostly swing but some modern jazz as well, below an excellent bistro.

6 Jazz Club Etoile
MAP A2 ▪ 81 Blvd Gouvion-St-Cyr
Features visiting African-American musicians. Jazzy Brunch on Sunday.

7 New Morning
MAP F2 ▪ 7–9 Rue des Petites Ecuries
An eclectic mix of music, with jam sessions and impromptu performances.

8 Le Petit Journal Montparnasse
MAP D6 ▪ 13 Rue du Commandant Mouchotte
Doors close at 2am, but open again five hours later, mainly for big band jazz.

9 Le Petit Journal St-Michel
MAP M5 ▪ 71 Blvd St-Michel
New Orleans-style swinging jazz in a lively Latin Quarter cellar.

10 Caveau de la Huchette
MAP N4 ▪ 5 Rue de la Huchette
Ignore the tourist-trap setting – it's worth every penny of the entrance fee.

TOP 10 Fine Dining

Elegant interior of Taillevent

1 L'Astrance
MAP B4 ▪ 4 Rue Beethoven, 75016 ▪ 01 40 50 84 40 ▪ Closed Sat–Mon, Feb, Aug, 1 week Oct (call to check) ▪ No disabled access ▪ €€€

There is probably no table in Paris that is more coveted than one in this sober 25-seat dining room, with its set menus at €70 (for lunch) or €230 (for dinner), orchestrated by young culinary genius Pascal Barbot. You'll need to book a month ahead for lunch, two months for dinner.

2 Guy Savoy
Artichoke and truffle soup is one of star chef Guy Savoy's signature dishes, in his chic and smart restaurant (jacket and tie required for male diners). One of the city's best dining experiences. To sample Savoy's cooking at more affordable prices, try the bistro-style Les Bouquinistes in the St-Germain Quarter *(see p133)*.

3 Septime
80 Rue de Charonne, 75011 ▪ 01 43 67 38 29 ▪ Closed Mon L, Sat & Sun ▪ €€

Chef Bertrand Grébaut trained with Passard before setting up this Michelin-starred bistro serving excellent seasonal dishes. Good-value set menus at lunch and dinner.

4 Taillevent
Taillevent's atmospheric oak-panelled dining room is frequented by a mix of businessmen and romantic couples. Dishes such as rex rabbit with Cremona mustard and black radish feature on the seasonal menu and there's an exceptional wine list. You need to book well ahead to dine here *(see p117)*.

5 Le Jules Verne
Now in the perfectionist hands of world-famous chef Alain Ducasse, this restaurant on the second floor of the Eiffel Tower has entered the 21st century. It has been revamped with a futuristic brown decor and there is a suitably luxurious menu, replete with truffles in winter. Service is excellent and the panoramic views are simply breathtaking, but you will need to book in advance *(see p123)*.

Stylish bistro Septime

(6) Alain Ducasse au Plaza Athénée

MAP C3 ■ 25 Ave Montaigne, 75008 ■ 01 53 67 65 00 ■ Closed Mon–Wed L, Sat & Sun ■ €€

The star chef's interpretation of modern haute cuisine – based on fish, vegetables and grains – is served in this glamorous restaurant.

(7) Le Chateaubriand

MAP H3 ■ 129 Ave Parmentier, 75011 ■ 01 43 57 45 95 ■ €€€

One of the best restaurants in Paris, Le Chateaubriand provides a relaxed setting for its reasonably affordable gastronomic cuisine. Basque chef Iñaki Aizpitarte creates innovative and award-winning dishes for a daily changing menu. Book in advance.

(8) Pierre Gagnaire

MAP B2 ■ 6 Rue Balzac, 75008 ■ 01 58 36 12 50 ■ No disabled access ■ Closed Sat, Sun, Aug ■ €€€

Famous French chef Pierre Gagnaire creates culinary magic at this formal restaurant. Try the foie gras, oysters and ginger served with tamarillo sorbet and Paris mushrooms.

(9) L'Arpege

MAP D4 ■ 84 Rue de Varenne, 75007 ■ 01 47 05 09 06 ■ No disabled access ■ Closed Sat & Sun ■ €€€

Alain Passard's three-Michelin-star restaurant is highly regarded in Paris. Dishes, using produce from

L'Atelier de Joël Robuchon

the biodynamic garden, might include beetroot in a hibiscus-salt crust with bitter orange.

(10) L'Atelier de Joël Robuchon

MAP E4 ■ 5 Rue de Montalembert, 75007 ■ 01 42 22 56 56 ■ €€€

Take a seat at the lacquered bar to experience a top French chef's take on contemporary cuisine. Signature dishes are the merlan Colbert (fried whiting), and carbonara with Alsatian cream and bacon.

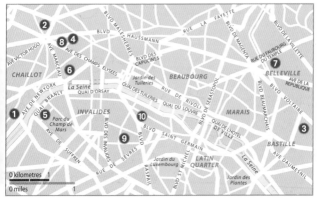

🔟 Cafés and Bars

1 Café de Flore

A hang-out for artists and intellectuals since the 1920s, its regulars have included Salvador Dalí and Albert Camus. During World War II Jean-Paul Sartre and Simone de Beauvoir "more or less set up house in the Flore". Although its prices have skyrocketed, its Art Deco decor hasn't changed and it's still a perennial favourite with French filmmakers and literati (see p131).

Café de Flore

2 Le Petit Vendôme

MAP E3 ▪ 8 Rue des Capucines, 75002 ▪ 01 42 61 05 88 ▪ €

The search for the best sandwiches in Paris stops here, with bread from the award-winning Julien bakery and just the right slathering of butter with cured ham or goat's cheese. Good hot dishes are served too.

3 Café Marly

MAP L2 ▪ 93 Rue de Rivoli, 75001 ▪ €€

Superbly situated in the Richelieu wing of the Louvre (see p13), this café offers simple but expertly prepared brasserie fare (steaks, salads, steak tartare, club sandwiches) as well as delicious desserts. The dining room has plush decor and velvet armchairs, but the best spot is under the arcade overlooking the glass pyramid and the cour Napoléon.

4 Les Deux Magots

Rival to the neighbouring Flore as a rendezvous for the 20th-century intellectual élite. Hemingway, Oscar Wilde, Djuna Barnes, André Breton and Paul Verlaine were all regulars, and Picasso met his muse Dora Maar here in 1937. Similarly pricey, with outside tables facing the boulevard and the square (see p131).

5 Café de la Paix

MAP E3 ▪ 5 Pl de l'Opéra, 75009 ▪ €€€

A grand Parisian café with prices to match, but it's worth a visit to enjoy the frescoed walls and sumptuous setting, designed by Charles Garnier, architect of the Opera House across the square (see p104). This is another Paris landmark with a string of famous past patrons, and arguably the best *millefeuille* cakes in town.

6 La Closerie des Lilas

The main restaurant here is expensive, but the bar is a good spot to soak up the atmosphere of this historic site where artists and writers from Baudelaire to Archibald MacLeish have drunk since 1808. Look out for the famous names of visitors etched on the tables in the bar. The busy brasserie also has live piano music in the evenings and attracts a chic crowd (see p161).

7 Le Fumoir

MAP F4 ▪ 6 Rue de l'Amiral de Coligny, 75001 ▪ 01 42 92 00 24 ▪ €€€

There are many reasons to drop into this café-bar-restaurant situated next to the Louvre, whether it be to

Pavement tables at Les Deux Magots

people-watch from the terrace out front or hide out with a martini and game of backgammon in the comfy library at the back. The hot chocolate is heavenly, cocktails are expertly made and the bistro cooking shows Italian and Swedish influences. They also serve a great Sunday brunch.

8 Chez Jeannette
MAP G2 ▪ 47 Rue du Faubourg St-Denis, 75010 ▪ 01 47 70 30 89 ▪ No disabled access ▪ €

Although the owners haven't touched the scruffy vintage decor, this café near Gare de l'Est has become one of the hottest hang-outs in Paris, with a crowd outside to prove it. Inside, the high ceilings, mirrors and old-fashioned booths, as well as reasonably priced food, create a lively atmosphere.

9 Caffè Sterne
MAP H5 ▪ 47 Passage des Panoramas, 75002 ▪ 01 75 43 63 10 ▪ €€–€€€

Within the characterful Passage des Panoramas, this wittily designed restaurant serves some of the best (and priciest) Venetian dishes around. There is as much to look at as there is to eat: at the entrance, a lynx and a wolf wear rhinestone necklaces; inside, a winged rabbit watches as waiters bring out Venetian *cichetti* (antipasti), fantastic fresh pastas and an excellent veal Milanese. To try what's on offer without busting the budget, book ahead for the reasonably priced set lunch menu.

10 Café de la Nouvelle Marie
MAP N6 ▪ 19 Rue des Fossés St-Jacques, 75005 ▪ 01 44 07 04 41 ▪ €

Quite possibly the quintessential Parisian café, this popular spot near the Sorbonne attracts locals and visitors who come for the lively atmosphere and reliably good, classic dishes written on the chalkboard. The solid wine list includes plenty by the glass or carafe.

TOP 10 WINE BARS

Clown Bar interior

1 Clown Bar
MAP R1 ▪ 114 Rue Amelot ▪ 01 43 55 87 35
Arguably the best wine list in Paris.

2 L'Avant Comptoir
MAP M5 ▪ 3 Carrefour de l'Odéon ▪ 01 44 27 07 97
Jostle around the zinc bar for delicious little bites, and glasses of natural wine.

3 Frenchie Bar à Vins
MAP F3 ▪ 6 Rue du Nil ▪ 01 40 39 96 19
A superb international wine list.

4 Le Barav
6 Rue Charles-François Dupuis ▪ MAP R1 ▪ 01 48 04 57 59
Well-priced wines in the upper Marais.

5 Le Garde Robe
MAP M2 ▪ 41 Rue de l'Arbre Sec ▪ 01 49 26 90 60
Cheeses, oysters and charcuterie round out the menu of natural wines here.

6 Le Cave
MAP H3 ▪ 129 Ave Parmentier ▪ 01 43 55 06 74
Wine store of Le Chateaubriand (see p67).

7 Verjus Bar à Vins
MAP E3 ▪ 47 Rue Montpensier ▪ 01 42 97 54 40
This cozy wine bar specializes in independent French winemakers.

8 Vivant Cave
MAP F2 ▪ 43 Rue des Petites Ecuries ▪ 01 42 46 43 55
Winemakers and chefs gather here.

9 Le Baron Rouge
MAP H5 ▪ 1 Rue Théophile Roussel ▪ 01 43 43 14 32
An unpretentious, long-time favourite.

10 Quedubon
MAP H2 ▪ 22 Rue du Plateau ▪ 01 42 38 18 65
A list of over 200 natural wines.

For a key to restaurant price ranges *see p83*

Shops and Markets

Galeries Lafayette

1 Galeries Lafayette
MAP E2 ■ 40 Blvd Haussmann, 75009

This expansive store opened in 1894 as a monument to Parisian style, topped by a glorious steel-and-glass dome. Along with designer clothes, there's a fabulous food hall. The seventh floor has great views.

2 Flower and Bird Markets
MAP P4 ■ Pl Louis-Lépine, 75004

Dating from 1808, the colourful Marché aux Fleurs (flower market) on the Ile de la Cité is the oldest and one of the largest flower markets in Paris. Its blooms brighten up the area between the stark walls of the Conciergerie and Hôtel Dieu from Monday to Saturday – everything from orchids to orange trees. On Sundays it is joined by the Marché aux Oiseaux (bird market).

3 Au Printemps
MAP E2 ■ 64 Blvd Haussmann, 75009

One of Paris's two top department stores, the iconic Printemps opened in 1864. Its goods range from designer clothing and accessories to mid-range labels and funky fashions, home decor and furniture. The sixth-floor brasserie is crowned with a lovely Art Nouveau stained-glass cupola.

4 Bastille Market
MAP H5 ■ Blvd Richard-Lenoir, 75011

Every Thursday and Sunday morning, this market stretches along the tree-lined boulevard that separates the Marais from the Bastille. Sunday is the best day, when locals come to socialize as well as shop for fish, meat, bread and cheese. Some stalls sell North African and other international food.

5 Place de la Madeleine
This is a gourmand's delight. Some of the most delectable speciality food shops in Paris are dotted around the edges of this square, including the famous

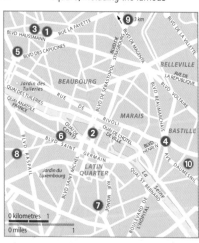

Fauchon food hall and the smaller but no less mouthwatering Hédiard. There's Maille for mustard, Kaspia for caviar, Marquise de Sévigné for chocolates and La Maison de la Truffe for truffles *(see p106)*.

Stall at Marché aux Puces de St-Ouen

6 Rue de Buci
MAP L4

The artist Picasso reputedly did his shopping at this daily morning market in the heart of St-Germain. The bountiful fruit and vegetable stalls are of high quality but of greater interest are the food shops opening on to the street, which sell specialist and regional fare. You can also buy freshly prepared Italian dishes and delicious pastries.

7 Rue Mouffetard
MAP F6

One of the oldest street markets in Paris winds downhill through the Latin Quarter every morning Tuesday to Sunday. Although this formerly cheap and bohemian market has been discovered as a tourist spot, it retains its charm, the narrow streets lined with food stalls and speciality shops. There are also plenty of good restaurants in the quieter side streets.

8 Le Bon Marché
MAP D5 ■ 22 Rue de Sèvres, 75007

Paris's first department store was founded on the Left Bank in 1852, its structure partially designed by Gustave Eiffel *(see p25)*. Today it's even more hip than its competitors, with an in-store boutique

featuring avant-garde fashions. It also has designer clothes, its own line of menswear and the enormous La Grande Epicerie food hall.

9 Marché aux Puces de St-Ouen
Porte de Clignancourt, 75018 ■ Metro Porte de Clignancourt

Every Saturday to Monday the largest antiques market in the world is held here. There are actually several markets here: the oldest, Marché Vernaison, is the most charming. Marché Malik sells vintage clothing, while others offer furniture, jewellery and paintings.

10 Marché d'Aligre
MAP H5 ■ Pl d'Aligre, 75012

Away from the tourist bustle, this market retains its authentic Parisian atmosphere. An indoor hall houses vendors selling cheese, artisan beer, olive oil and charcuterie among other high quality goods. Outside, inexpensive fruit, vegetables and flowers fill the street-side stands each morning from Tuesday to Sunday.

Le Bon Marché

TOP 10 Paris for Free

Musée Carnavalet paintings

1 Musée Carnavalet

The permanent collections at all of Paris's municipal museums are free, and few are more rewarding than those of the Carnavalet. This museum charts the history of the city of Paris from the Middle Ages up to the *belle époque* through an extraordinary collection of paintings, sculptures, decorative arts and archaeological finds *(see p94)*.

2 Festival de Cinéma en Plein Air

229 Ave Jean Jaurès, 75019 ▪ Metro Porte de Pantin ▪ www.cinema.arbo.com

Each summer a giant screen is erected in Parc de la Villette *(see p156)*, showing movies (in the original language, with French subtitles) in the open air every evening for a month. The films, which range from classics to the less well-known, are all free. Deckchairs and blankets are available for hire, and many people bring their own picnic to make an evening of it.

3 Musée des Beaux Arts de la Ville de Paris

The grand Neo-Classical Petit Palais is anything but "little", and is home to this fascinating collection of art

and artifacts, including some fine Art Nouveau pieces. Free lunchtime concerts are held once a month on a Thursday in its auditorium, and there's a charming inner garden with a café *(see p111)*.

4 Free Visits to Museums

On the first Sunday of every month admission to the permanent collections of most Paris museums, including the Louvre, Pompidou Centre, Musée Rodin and Musée d'Orsay, is free to everyone.

5 Hôtel de Ville

Paris's city hall hosts regular excellent, free exhibitions, usually on a Parisian theme; a recent exhibition focused on the Liberation of Paris. In addition, free events often take place on the square in front of the building, including concerts and live screenings of major sporting events *(see p46)*.

6 Berges de Seine

MAP B4–E4 ▪ www.lesberges.paris.fr

The Berges de Seine, the stretch of river between the Musée du quai Branly and Musée d'Orsay, is an attractive, lively promenade with loads of free activities, such as concerts and workshops, board games, a climbing wall and play spaces for children.

Berges de Seine

7 Les Journées du Patrimoine

www.journeesdupatrimoine.
culture.fr

On the third weekend of September, many buildings that are normally off-limits, such as the Elysée Palace, are opened up to the public for free.

8 Musée d'Art Moderne de la Ville de Paris

This museum of modern art, with a forecourt giving onto the Seine, may not rival the Pompidou's collection, but it's free and there aren't the crowds to contend with. Almost all of the major 20th-century artists who worked in France are represented, including Picasso, Braque, Chagall and Modigliani, along with some new modern artists (see p142).

9 Cimetière du Père Lachaise

It would be easy to while away an afternoon at Père Lachaise cemetery, tracking down celebrity graves including those of Oscar Wilde, Chopin and Jim Morrison.

With its moss-grown tombs and ancient trees, it's also an atmospheric and rather romantic place for a stroll (see p156).

Grave of Frédéric Chopin, Père Lachaise

10 Organ recitals

Free organ recitals are given at Notre-Dame cathedral (see pp20–21) at 8pm on Saturdays and 4:30pm on Sundays, and at 5:30pm on Sundays in the beautiful church of St-Eustache (see p85), which has one of the finest organs in France.

TOP 10 BUDGET TIPS

Lunch at the bar

1 Sightseeing by bus
The bus is a great way of sightseeing cheaply – for example, number 63 takes a scenic route along the Seine.

2 Set-price lunch
Fixed price (prix fixe) lunches are usually good value and almost always cost less than evening meals. They can be a great way of dining at a top restaurant without breaking the bank.

3 Cutting transport costs
Buying a carnet of tickets, a Mobilis or Paris Visite card will save on transport costs (see p165).

4 Lodgings for less
It's almost always cheaper to stay in an apartment, B&B or hostel than at a hotel (see p171).

5 Cut-price entertainment
Half-price same-day theatre and concert tickets are sold at kiosks on place de la Madeleine.

6 Sitting at the bar
In cafés, it's often cheaper to have a drink or a snack at the bar than when sitting at a table.

7 Museum pass
With so many museums to visit, the Carte Musées et Monuments offers savings (www.parismuseumpass.com).

8 Out for breakfast
Having breakfast at a café will cost considerably less than at a hotel.

9 Youth savings
State-run museums, including the Louvre, are free for anyone under 18 and EU citizens under 26.

10 Cheaper movies
Cinemas in the 5th arrondissement (around the Panthéon) are cheaper than those elsewhere.

🔟 Festivals and Events

The Tour de France speeding through the streets of Paris

 Tour de France
www.letour.fr

Don't miss this summer highlight if you really want to understand the French passion for cycling. Towards the end of July each year, the world's greatest and most gruelling cycle race approaches Paris. On the final laps the riders pass the Louvre, race along the banks of the Seine, hurtle down the rue de Rivoli and, of course, cross the finish line on the Champs-Elysées. Thousands of fans pack the streets to cheer the riders home and see who will win the Yellow Jersey.

 Nuit Blanche
First weekend Oct

Paris held its first Nuit Blanche in 2002 and the all-night contemporary art event now attracts more than 1,500,000 people each year. Its goal is to give a fresh perspective on Paris with installations and exhibitions in several different neighbourhoods, and to make contemporary art more accessible to all.

3 Fête de la Musique
21 Jun

To celebrate the summer equinox, professional and amateur musicians take to the streets of Paris. Major performances take place in Place de la République and other concert venues, but the most fun is to be had wandering through residential neighbourhoods and dropping into locals' bars.

 Fête du Cinéma
www.feteducinema.com

Film buffs should be sure to verify the exact dates of this annual event, held each June. For just three days, cinemagoers pay full price for the first film that they see, but can then see as many other films as they choose, for a few euros each.

 Grandes Eaux Nocturnes
Dates in Jun, Jul and Aug

This is a true midsummer night's dream, with superb illuminations and installations in the gardens of Versailles, plus a dazzling firework display over the Grand Canal.

Fête de la Musique street performers

Festival d'Automne à Paris

Mid-Sep–Dec ■ www.festival-automne.com

This major festival promotes contemporary arts across the board, encouraging people from all walks of life to performances of dance, music, film and drama.

 Fêtes des Vendanges

Oct: first Fri (for five days)

Paris was once a major wine producer but these days only the vineyards at Montmartre remain *(see p149)*. These yield just under 600 litres (5 barrels) of wine each autumn. Despite the small harvest, great fun is had at the Fêtes des Vendanges with wine, food stalls and a street parade.

 Paris Jazz Festival

Jun & Jul ■ www.parcfloraldeparis.com

Paris is home to jazz all year round *(see p65)*, but every summer there is a major jazz festival in the city. Acts from all over the world come to play in the Parc Floral de Paris in the Bois de Vincennes *(see p156)*. Many smaller venues are involved as well.

 Paris Plages

Jul & Aug ■ www.paris.fr

Launched in 2002 by the then mayor of Paris, Bertrand Delanoë, this hugely popular summer event transforms a stretch of the Seine *quais* and the Canal du l'Ourcq into a mini Cannes, with tons of soft sand, sunbeds, parasols and palm trees. There are also outdoor events and plenty of activities for children.

Mois de la Photo

Nov ■ www.mep-fr.org

Paris reveres the art of photography and every alternate November (in even-numbered years) it hosts the "Month of the Photo". Galleries, museums, shops, cultural centres and many other venues give space to exhibitions, workshops and lectures on all aspects of the art. For anyone interested in photography, it is an exciting time to visit Paris.

TOP 10 SPORTS EVENTS

Paris Marathon runners

1 Tour de France
This great cycle race ends in Paris.

2 Prix de l'Arc de Triomphe
Longchamp racecourse ■ Oct: first weekend
This world-renowned horse race attracts the city's *crème de la crème*.

3 French Tennis Open
Stade Roland Garros ■ end May–early Jun
This legendary clay-court tournament is part of the prestigious Grand Slam.

4 Gucci Masters
Paris Nord Villepinte ■ Dec
Show-jumping fans and competitors descend on Paris.

5 Six Nations Rugby
Stade de France ■ Feb–Mar
The French team plays England, Scotland, Ireland, Wales and Italy.

6 Paris Marathon
Apr
Runners start at the Champs-Elysées and end at Avenue Foch.

7 Football Cup Final
Stade de France ■ mid-May
Quite simply the biggest club event in French football.

8 Prix de Diane
Chantilly ■ Jun: second Sun
Parisian high society flocks to this up-market horse race.

9 Top 14 Rugby Final
Stade de France ■ May/Jun
Some of the world's finest rugby players take part in the final of the French Rugby league.

10 Ice-Skating Grand Prix
Palais Omnisports de Paris-Bercy ■ Nov
The Trophée Eric Bompard is the Paris leg of the International Grand Prix.

Paris
Area by Area

A Gothic gargoyle stares out over Paris
from Notre-Dame's western façade

TOP 10 Ile de la Cité and Ile St-Louis

Paris was born on the Ile de la Cité. The first settlers came to this island on the Seine in 300 BC and it has been a focus of church and state power over many centuries, home to the great cathedral of Notre-Dame and the Palais de Justice. This tiny land mass is also the geographical heart of the city – all distances from Paris are measured from Point Zéro, just outside Notre-Dame. While the Ile de la Cité bustles with tourists, the smaller Ile St-Louis, linked to its neighbour by a footbridge, has been an exclusive residential enclave since the 17th century. Its main street is lined with shops, galleries and restaurants and is a lovely place for a stroll.

Notre-Dame gargoyle

AREA MAP OF ILE DE LA CITE AND ILE ST-LOUIS

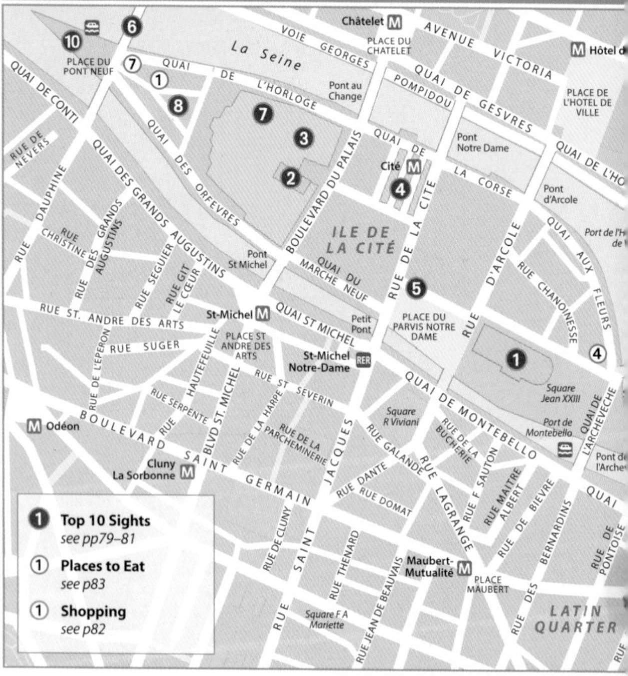

1 Top 10 Sights
see pp79–81

1 Places to Eat
see p83

1 Shopping
see p82

1 Notre-Dame
See pp20–23.

2 Sainte-Chapelle
See pp36–7.

3 Conciergerie
MAP N3 ■ 2 Blvd du Palais, 75001 ■ Open 9:30am–6pm daily ■ Admission charge

This imposing Gothic palace, built by Philippe le Bel (the Fair) in 1301–15, has a rich history. Parts of it were turned into a prison, controlled by the concierge, or keeper of the king's mansion, hence the name. Ravaillac, assassin of Henri IV, was tortured here, but it was during the Revolution that the prison became a place of terror, when thousands were held here awaiting execution by guillotine. Today you can see the Salle des Gardes and the magnificent vaulted Salle des Gens d'Armes (Hall of the

Marché aux Fleurs, Ile de la Cité

Men-at-Arms), medieval kitchens, a torture chamber, the Bonbec tower and the prison. The cell where Marie-Antoinette was held, and the history of other famous Revolution prisoners, is on display. Outside, look for the square Tour de l'Horloge, erected in 1370, which houses the city's first public clock, still ticking.

4 Marché aux Fleurs
MAP N3

One of the last remaining flower markets in the city centre, the beautiful Marché aux Fleurs is also the oldest, dating from the early 19th century. It is held year-round, Monday to Saturday, in place Louis-Lépine, filling the north side of the Ile de la Cité with dazzling blooms from 8am to 7pm. There is also a bird market here on Sundays, which sells some rare species *(see p70)*.

5 Crypte Archéologique
MAP P4 ■ Place du Parvis-Notre-Dame, 75004 ■ Open 10am–6pm Tue–Sun ■ Admission charge

Fascinating remnants of early Paris dating back to Gallo-Roman times were discovered in 1965, during an excavation of the square in front of Notre-Dame in order to build an underground car park. The archae-ological crypt displays parts of 3rd-century Roman walls, rooms heated by hypocaust, as well as remains of medieval streets and foundations. The scale models showing the evolution of the city from its origins as a Celtic settle-ment are particularly interesting.

Pont Neuf and the Ile de la Cité

⑥ Pont Neuf
MAP M3

The name – New Bridge – is somewhat incongruous for the oldest surviving bridge in Paris. Following its completion in 1607, Henri IV christened it by charging across on his steed; the bronze equestrian statue of the king was melted down during the Revolution but replaced in 1818. Decorated with striking carved heads, the bridge was unique for its time in that it had no houses built upon it. It has 12 arches and a span of 275 m (912 ft) extending to both sides of the island.

⑦ Palais de Justice
MAP M3 ■ 10 Blvd du Palais, 75001 ■ Open 8:30am–6pm Mon–Fri

Stretching across the west end of the Ile de la Cité from north to south, the Palais de Justice, along with the Conciergerie, was once part of the Palais de la Cité, seat of Roman rule and the home of the French kings until 1358. It took its present name during the Revolution and the buildings now contain the city's law courts. You can watch the courts in session from Monday to Friday and wander through the public areas, with their many ornate features. The Cour du Mai (May Courtyard) is the area through which prisoners passed on their way to execution during the Revolution.

⑧ Place Dauphine
MAP M3

In 1607, Henri IV transformed this former royal garden into a triangular square and named it after his son, the Dauphin and future King Louis XIII. Surrounding the square were uniformly built houses of brick and white stone; No. 14 is one of the few that retains its original features. One

Palais de Justice

THE GUILLOTINE

Dr Joseph Guillotine invented his "humane" beheading machine at his home near the Odéon and it was first used in April 1792. During the Revolution some 2,600 prisoners were executed on the places du Carrousel, de la Concorde, de la Bastille and de la Nation, after awaiting their fate in the Conciergerie prison.

side was destroyed to make way for the expansion of the Palais de Justice. Today this quiet, charming spot is a good place to relax over a drink or meal *(see p83)*.

⑨ St-Louis-en-l'Ile

MAP Q5 ▪ 19 bis Rue St-Louis-en-l'Ile, 75004 ▪ Open 9:30am–1pm, 2–7:30pm daily (until 7pm Sun)

This lovely Baroque church on Ile St-Louis was designed between 1664 and 1726 by the royal architect Louis Le Vau. The exterior features an iron clock (1741) at the entrance and an iron spire, while the interior, richly decorated with gilding and marble, has a statue of St Louis holding his Crusader's sword.

Square du Vert-Galant

⑩ Square du Vert-Galant

MAP M3

The tranquil western tip of the Ile de la Cité, with its verdant chestnut trees, lies beneath the Pont Neuf – take the steps behind Henri IV's statue. The king had a notoriously amorous nature and the name of this peaceful square recalls his nickname, meaning "old flirt". From here there is a wonderful view of the Louvre *(see pp12–15)* and the Right Bank. It is also the departure point for cruises on the Seine on Les Vedettes du Pont-Neuf *(see p171)*.

A DAY ON THE ISLANDS

▷ MORNING

Arrive at **Notre-Dame** *(see pp20–3)* by 8am to beat the crowds and appreciate its magnificence, then head for the fragrant Marché aux Fleurs. As well as flowers, you can buy all kinds of garden accessories and seeds. Return to Notre-Dame if you want to ascend the towers, which open at 10am. Take a coffee break at **Le Flore en l'Ile** *(see p83)*, with its views of the cathedral.

The fascinating Crypte Archéologique is worth a half-hour visit, then spend the late morning at **Sainte-Chapelle** *(see pp36–7)*, when the sun beams through the stained-glass windows.

There are plenty of places for lunch, but on a sunny day try **La Rose de France** *(see p83)*, which has terrace seating.

AFTERNOON

Spend a leisurely afternoon strolling the narrow streets of the **Ile St-Louis**, which are filled with characterful shops and galleries *(see p82)*.

Wind up with an afternoon treat by visiting **Berthillon**, considered the best ice-cream purveyor in all of France *(see p83)*. With at least 70 delicious varieties of ice cream on offer, ranging from plain vanilla to whisky, and including virtually any fruit you can think of, the hardest part will be choosing. There will be plenty of time to make your choice, however, as there will inevitably be a long queue, especially during the summer months.

See map on pp78–9 ←

Shopping

① Lafitte
MAP P4 ▪ 8 Rue Jean du Bellay, 75004 ▪ Closed Sun, Mon
Foie gras and other regional products from the southwest await shoppers looking to indulge in French gastronomy.

② Jean-Paul Gardil
MAP Q5 ▪ 44 Rue St-Louis-en-l'Ile, 75004 ▪ Closed Mon
This boucherie-charcuterie is a carnivore's palace, offering a fantastic choice of cured hams, pâtés and sausages, perfect for a picnic on pretty Ile St-Louis.

③ Librairie Ulysse
MAP Q5 ▪ 26 Rue St-Louis-en-l'Ile, 75004 ▪ Closed Sat–Mon
Today Paris, tomorrow the world. This eccentric travel bookshop will take you anywhere you want with thousands of titles, antiquarian and new, in French and English – including many on Paris itself.

④ Alain Carion
MAP Q5 ▪ 92 Rue St-Louis-en-l'Ile, 75004 ▪ Closed Sun, Mon
A wealth of meteorites, fossils and minerals. Some are made into imaginative jewellery.

⑤ Laguiole
MAP Q4 ▪ 35 Rue des Deux Ponts, 75004
Browse an exhaustive array of knives and cutlery sets from this iconic cutlery brand, which hails from the Aveyron region of southern France. Look for the famous bee motif on the handles.

⑥ Pylones Boutique
MAP Q5 ▪ 57 Rue St-Louis-en-l'Ile, 75004
Rubber and painted metal are used to create the whimsical jewellery and accessories sold here, along with a selection of novelty gifts.

⑦ Boulangerie des Deux Ponts
MAP Q5 ▪ 35 Rue des Deux Ponts, 75004 ▪ Closed Wed, Thu, Aug
Few passers-by are able to resist the freshly baked bread produced at this old-fashioned bakery.

⑧ Maison Moinet
MAP Q5 ▪ 45 Rue St-Louis-en-l'Ile, 75004 ▪ Closed Mon, Tue
A family-run confectioner from Vichy, this cute shops sells traditional French sweets and chocolates. Enticing for all ages.

⑨ La Ferme Saint Aubin
MAP Q5 ▪ 76 Rue St-Louis-en-l'Ile, 75004
Cheese in all shapes and sizes from all over France are sold at this *fromagerie*. An aromatic delight.

⑩ Clair de Rêve
MAP Q5 ▪ 35 Rue St-Louis-en-l'Ile, 75004
This interesting boutique sells original curiosities such as puppets, robots and miniature theatres making it an ideal shop if you're looking for a present with a difference.

Clair de Rêve boutique

Places to Eat

1 La Rose de France
MAP M3 ▪ 24 Pl Dauphine,
75001 ▪ 01 43 54 10 12 ▪ €
Dine on French classics on the lovely
terrace or in the cozy dining room.

2 Le Sergent Recruteur
MAP Q4 ▪ 41 Rue St-Louis-en-
l'Ile, 75004 ▪ 01 43 54 75 42
▪ Closed Tue–Thu L, Sun, Mon ▪ €€
Served in a stylishly refurbished
space, the tasting menus include
imaginative modern interpretations
of traditional dishes.

3 Les Fous de L'Ile
MAP Q4 ▪ 33 Rue des Deux
Ponts, 75004 ▪ 01 43 25 76 67
▪ Closed Tue L, Sat, Sun, end Feb,
Aug ▪ €
This modern Parisian bistro serves
typical dishes such as *entrecôte*
or steak tartare. It also hosts
exhibitions and live music.

4 Le Petit Plateau
MAP G5 ▪ 1 Quai aux Fleurs,
75004 ▪ 01 44 07 61 86 ▪ Closed Sun
▪ No disabled access ▪ €
This tearoom is a great lunch spot,
serving delicious home-made
salads, quiches and cakes.

**5 Brasserie de
l'Ile St-Louis**
MAP P4 ▪ 55 Quai de Bourbon, 75004
▪ 01 43 54 02 59 ▪ Closed Wed, Aug
▪ No disabled access ▪ €€
Wooden tables and a rustic look
complement hearty Alsace fare,
such as tripe in Riesling wine.

6 Isami
MAP P5 ▪ 4 Quai d'Orléans,
75004 ▪ 01 40 46 06 97 ▪ Closed Sun,
Mon, 3 weeks Aug, 2 weeks
Christmas ▪ No disabled access
▪ €€
This is consistently voted one of the
best Japanese restaurants in the city.
The sushi and sashimi platters are a
work of art but space is limited so be
sure to book ahead.

La Rose de France

7 Taverne Henri IV
MAP M3 ▪ 13 Pl du Pont-Neuf,
75001 ▪ 01 43 54 27 90 ▪ Closed Sun,
Aug ▪ €
A fine wine list and simple plates of
charcuterie or cheese.

8 Mon Vieil Ami
MAP Q5 ▪ 69 Rue St-Louis-en-
l'Ile, 75004 ▪ 01 40 46 01 35 ▪ Closed
Mon, Tue, Jan, Aug ▪ No disabled
access ▪ €€
A chic interior is the backdrop for
dishes such as pan-fried foie gras.

9 Le Flore en l'Ile
MAP P5 ▪ 42 Quai d'Orléans,
75004 ▪ 01 43 29 88 27 ▪ No disabled
access ▪ €
Go for the views as well as the food
at this bistro-cum-tearoom, open
from breakfast until 1am.

10 Berthillon
MAP G5 ▪ 31 Rue St-Louis-en-
l'Ile, 75004 ▪ 01 43 54 31 61 ▪ Closed
Mon, Tue, 1 week Feb, 1 week Easter,
Aug ▪ No credit cards ▪ €
There is always a queue outside this
legendary ice cream and sorbet shop
and tearoom but it is worth the wait.
Try the salted caramel ice cream.

PRICE CATEGORIES

For a three-course meal for one with half
a bottle of wine (or equivalent meal),
taxes and extra charges

€ under €30 €€ €30–€50 €€€ over €50

See map on pp78–9 ⬅

TOP 10 Beaubourg and Les Halles

The small but lively Beaubourg Quarter, brimming with art galleries and cafés, has become a major tourist attraction since the Centre Georges Pompidou opened in 1977.

Le Défenseur du Temps

Les Halles was the city's marketplace for 800 years – novelist Emile Zola called it "the belly of Paris". Its glass-roofed pavilions were demolished in 1969 but many of the surrounding bistros and speciality shops are still here.

AREA MAP OF BEAUBOURG AND LES HALLES

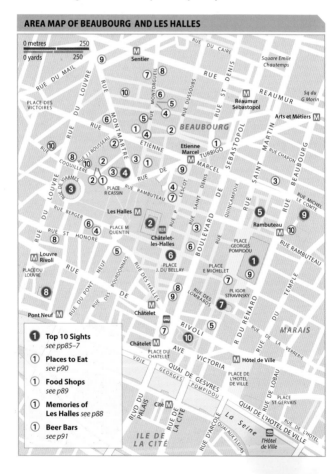

Legend
1 Top 10 Sights *see pp85–7*
1 Places to Eat *see p90*
1 Food Shops *see p89*
1 Memories of Les Halles *see p88*
1 Beer Bars *see p91*

1 Centre Georges Pompidou

See pp32–3.

2 Forum des Halles
MAP N2

Ten years after the original market was demolished, the so-called "largest urban hole in Europe" was filled with this controversial shopping complex. This largely underground maze caters mainly to the young with designer-name boutiques. Outside, buskers, young people and tourists throng the steps and gardens (not a place to linger at night). Today, it's more of a sore spot than a hotspot and French architect David Mangin has been commissioned to oversee its renovation, which will include a revamped shopping centre, gardens, metro and RER station. This is due to be completed by 2018.

3 Bourse du Commerce
MAP M1 ■ 2 Rue de Viarmes, 75001 ■ Open 9am–6pm Mon–Fri (ID required)

The circular building that houses the Commodities Exchange was erected as a grain market in 1767 and remodelled in the 19th century. It was first covered with a wooden dome, and then by subsequent structures of iron and copper. Under today's glass dome, activity in the world commodities market proceeds at a leisurely pace compared to the way other financial centres operate.

4 St-Eustache
MAP M1 ■ 2 Impasse St-Eustache, 75001 ■ Open 9:30am–7pm Mon–Fri, 9am–7pm Sat & Sun

With its majestic arches and pillars, St-Eustache is one of the most beautiful churches in Paris. Although Gothic in design, it took 105 years to build (1532–1637) and its interior decoration reflects the Renaissance style of this time. The church was modelled on Notre-Dame *(see pp20–23)*, with double side aisles and a ring of side chapels. The stained-glass windows made from sketches by Philippe de Champaigne (1631) and

The majestic St-Eustache

the ornate tomb of politician Jean-Baptiste Colbert (1619–83) are highlights. Don't miss the naïve sculpture in Chapelle St-Joseph, which recalls Les Halles' market days, or the Keith Haring triptych in the Chapelle des Charcutiers.

5 Le Défenseur du Temps
MAP P2 ■ Rue Bernard Clairvaux, 75003

The "Defender of Time", Paris's modern public clock, stands in the grim Quartier de l'Horloge (Clock Quarter) shopping area. This fantasy mechanical sculpture of brass and steel by Jacques Monastier is 4 m (13 ft) high and weighs 1 tonne. When the clock strikes the hour, the warrior fends off a savage cockerel, crab or dragon (representing air, water and earth) with his sword, with accompanying sound effects. At noon, 6pm and 10pm he vanquishes all three (when the clock is working).

Interior of the Bourse du Commerce

6 Fontaine des Innocents

MAP N2 ■ Rue St-Denis & Rue Berger, 75001

The Square des Innocents is a Les Halles crossroads and a hang-out for street performers and young people. It was built atop a cemetery in the 18th century, from which two million human remains were transferred to the Catacombs (see p58) at Denfert-Rochereau. The Renaissance fountain, the last of its era built in the city, was designed by Pierre Lescot and carved by sculptor Jean Goujon in 1547. It originally stood against a wall on rue St-Denis, and was moved to the new square, when the fourth side was added.

7 Eglise St-Merri

MAP P2 ■ 76 Rue de la Verrerie, 75004 ■ Open noon–12:45pm & 3–7pm Mon–Fri, 3–7pm Sat, 9:30am–7pm Sun

Formerly the parish church of the Lombard moneylenders, St-Merri was built between 1520 and 1612, and reflects the Flamboyant Gothic style. Its name is a corruption of St-Médéric, who was buried on this site in the early 8th century. The bell in the church's northwest turret, thought to be the oldest in Paris, dates from 1331. Other highlights include the decorative west front, the 17th-century organ loft, beautiful stained glass and carved wood panelling. There are free concerts at the weekends.

Stained glass in Eglise St-Merri

GEORGES POMPIDOU

Georges Pompidou (1911–74) **(below)** had the unenviable task of following Général de Gaulle as President of France, from 1969 until his death. During his tenure he initiated many architectural developments in Paris, including the controversial but ultimately successful Pompidou Centre, and the less popular scheme to demolish the Les Halles market.

8 St-Germain l'Auxerrois

MAP M2 ■ 2 Pl du Louvre, 75001 ■ Open 9am–7pm Tue–Sat, 9:30am–8:30pm Sun

When the Valois kings moved to the Louvre palace in the 14th century (see p12), this became the church of the royal family. On 24 August 1572, the tolling of its bell was used as the signal for the St Bartholomew's Day Massacre, when thousands of Huguenots who had come to Paris for the wedding of Henri of Navarre to Marguerite of Valois were murdered (see p22). The church features a range of architectural styles, from its Flamboyant Gothic façade to its Renaissance choir. Try to visit on Sunday afternoon, when there are organ recitals.

9 Musée de la Poupée

MAP P2 ■ Impasse Berthaud, 75003 ■ Open 1–6pm Tue–Sat ■ Closed public hols ■ Admission charge

This delightful museum exhibits a superb collection of 300 rare French dolls, including unglazed hand-painted porcelain dolls, which were manufactured between 1800 and 1945. The museum explores the history of the dolls, and their construction. It also features work by the main doll-makers of Germany and France. Another very special feature of the museum is its doll hospital, at which a specialist doll doctor works miracles on dolls and cuddly toys of all ages.

⑩ Tour St-Jacques
MAP N3 ■ 39 Rue de Rivoli, 75004

The late Gothic tower, dating from 1523, is all that remains of the church of St-Jacques-la-Boucherie, once the largest medieval church in Paris and a starting point for pilgrims on their journey to Santiago de Compostela in Spain. In the 17th century the mathematician and physicist Blaise Pascal used the tower for barometrical experiments. The church was pulled down after the Revolution. Visitors can explore the lower floors of the tower and visit the gardens around the base.

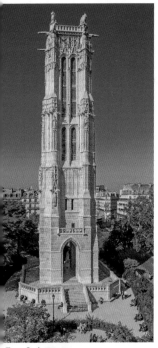

Tour St-Jacques

A DAY IN LES HALLES

rue Montorgueil
St-Eustache
Forum des Halles
Défenseur du Temps
Chez Denise
Centre Georges Pompidou
Fontaine des Innocents
Le Zimmer Café
Bistro Benoit

▶ **MORNING**

Start your day with breakfast at **Le Zimmer Café** *(1 Pl du Châtelet • 01 42 36 74 03)* before exploring the Museum of Modern Art at the **Centre Georges Pompidou** *(see pp32–3)*, where the temporary exhibits are also well worth a look.

If you need refreshment after all that art, it has to be **Georges** *(see p90)*, the chic brasserie at the top of the Centre Pompidou, which offers great views along with drinks, snacks or main meals.

On leaving the Centre, turn right into the Quartier de l'Horloge to catch the noon battle of the **Défenseur du Temps** clock.

If you have booked ahead, take your seat at Michelin-starred bistro **Benoit** *(see p90)*, whose lunchtime menu is far cheaper than in the evening.

AFTERNOON

Pass the **Fontaine des Innocents** as you head for Les Halles, but first pay a visit to the church of **St-Eustache** *(see p85)*, where the workers of the old Les Halles market worshipped.

Skirt the vast **Forum des Halles** *(see p85)* and head for charming **rue Montorgueil** and the little streets surrounding it – there are plenty of food shops and cafés to explore *(see p89)*.

Stop for a drink at **Chez Denise** *(see p90)*. It is packed at meal-times, but by late afternoon you might be lucky enough to get a table and to try their famous gâteau Marguerite with strawberries and cream.

See map on p84 ←

Memories of Les Halles

Sumptuous interior of Au Pied de Cochon

1 Au Pied de Cochon
This 24-hour brasserie still serves dishes that used to appeal to the earthy tastes of market workers, including the eponymous pigs' trotters *(see p90)*.

2 Le Christ Inn's Bistrot
MAP F3 ■ 15 Rue Montmartre, 75001
Dating back to the early 20th century, this ornate former working men's café/bar, decorated with historic tiles and murals, has only a small dining room, so book in advance.

3 St-Eustache Sculpture
The lively naïve sculpture by Raymond Mason in the church's Chapelle St-Joseph is a tribute to the beloved market. Its colourful figures depict *The Departure of Fruit and Vegetables from the Heart of Paris, 28 February 1969*.

4 Rue Montorgueil
MAP N1
The colourful market (Tuesday to Sunday) along this cobbled street is a reminder of the old Les Halles and is frequented by many Paris chefs.

5 Stöhrer
MAP N1 ■ 51 Rue Montorgueil, 75002
One of the loveliest old-fashioned patisseries in the city, founded in 1730 by a pastry chef who had worked for Louis XV.

6 Bistrot d'Eustache
MAP N2 ■ 37 Rue Berger, 75001
A visit here is like stepping back into the jazz spots of Paris in the 1930s–40s. It offers good, reasonably priced brasserie fare and live music on Friday and Saturday.

7 La Fresque
MAP N1 ■ 100 Rue Rambuteau, 75001
This wonderful restaurant used to be a fishmongers. Original tiles and a fresco of a fishing scene still decorate the back room.

8 Dehillerin
MAP M1 ■ 18 Rue Coquillière, 75001
Since 1820, everyone from army cooks to gourmet chefs has come here for copper pots, cast-iron pans and cooking utensils.

9 Duthilleul et Minart
MAP P1 ■ 14 Rue de Turbigo, 75001
For more than 100 years this shop has sold French work clothes and uniforms, such as chef's hats and watchmaker's smocks.

10 A La Cloche des Halles
MAP M1 ■ 28 Rue Coquillière, 75001
This wine bar literally chimes with history. The "cloche" is the bronze bell whose peal once signalled the beginning and end of the market day.

Food Shops

1 **G. Detou**
MAP N1 ■ 58 Rue Tiquetonne, 75002
The shelves at this chef's paradise are laden with chocolates, teas, artisanal mustards and more.

2 **L'Etpicerie de Bruno**
MAP N1 ■ 30 Rue Tiquetonne, 75002
This little store literally spices things up, with speciality peppers, salts and sugars, unusual rices and, yes, spices from all over the world.

3 **Charles Chocolatier**
MAP N1 ■ 15 Rue Montorgueil, 75001
On a cold day, stop in at this family-run chocolate shop for a take-out cup of their luscious hot chocolate; the ice creams in summer are delectable, too.

4 **A la Mère de Famille**
MAP N1 ■ 82 Rue Montorgueil, 75002
This branch of the oldest confectionery shop in Paris stocks regional French candies, all in the brand's vintage-inspired packaging.

5 **La Fermette**
MAP N1 ■ 86 Rue Montorgueil, 75002
The enthusiastic cheese-mongers here are ready with tips and tastings to help visitors make the perfect choice from the piles of cheese on display.

6 **Boulangerie Collet**
MAP N1 ■ 100 Rue Montorgueil, 75002
Run by the same family for two generations, this traditional boulangerie is particularly known for its viennoiseries and light-as-air meringues.

7 **Delitaly**
MAP F3 ■ 5 Rue des Petits Carreaux, 75002
You'll find fresh and dried pastas, gourmet olive oils and a mouth-watering selection of salami and other cured meats at this Italian deli.

8 **Eric Kayser**
MAP F3 ■ 16 Rue des Petits Carreaux, 75002
Beyond excellent baguettes, choose from all manner of pastries and other baked goods to stock up on for tea.

9 **Librairie Gourmande**
MAP F3 ■ 92–96 Rue Montmartre, 75002
This fabulous bookshop has an extensive collection of books on wine and cooking, some in English.

10 **L'Atelier de l'Eclair**
MAP F3 ■ 16 Rue Bachaumont, 75002
The home of the enticing éclair in all its guises, from simple chocolate and cream to Nutella, fig or foie gras.

Pastries at L'Atelier de l'Eclair

See map on p84

Places to Eat

PRICE CATEGORIES
For a three-course meal for one with half a bottle of wine (or equivalent meal), taxes and extra charges

€ under €30 €€ €30–€50 €€€ over €50

1 Aux Tonneaux des Halles

MAP N1 ■ 28 Rue Montorgueil, 75002 ■ 01 42 33 36 19 ■ Closed Sun ■ €

Authentic French dishes and well-priced wines are served at this friendly bistro, where the daily specials are written on the chalkboard. Regulars sing the praises of the *steak-frites*.

2 Au Pied de Cochon

MAP M1 ■ 6 Rue Coquillière, 75001 ■ 01 40 13 77 00 ■ €€

Long-time Les Halles favourite. If your taste is not for offal, there are other options, such as oysters and steak. Open 24 hours a day.

3 L'Ambassade d'Auvergne

MAP P1 ■ 22 Rue du Grenier St-Lazare, 75003 ■ 01 42 72 31 22 ■ Limited disabled access ■ €

Auvergne cooking, with lots of pork and cabbage dishes. Shared tables; good for solo diners.

4 Tour de Montlhéry, Chez Denise

MAP M2 ■ 5 Rue des Prouvaires, 75001 ■ 01 42 36 21 82 ■ Closed Sat, Sun mid-Jul–mid-Aug ■ €€

A Les Halles legend for its huge portions and convivial atmosphere. Book in advance.

5 Benoit

MAP P1 ■ 20 Rue St-Martin, 75004 ■ 01 42 72 25 76 ■ Closed Aug ■ €€€

First opened in 1912, this Michelin-starred location is, justifiably, the most expensive bistro in Paris. Try the lunchtime menu to keep the cost down.

6 Le Tambour

MAP N1 ■ 41 Rue Montmartre, 75002 ■ 01 42 33 06 90 ■ €€€

This 24-hour bistro draws a lively crowd with its friendly service and hearty French fare.

7 Café Beaubourg

MAP P2 ■ 43 Rue St-Merri, 75001 ■ 01 48 87 63 96 ■ €€€

The terrace here overlooks the Pompidou Centre. Steak tartare is a house special.

8 Spring

MAP M2 ■ 6 Rue Bailleul, 75004 ■ 01 45 96 05 72 ■ Closed Sun, Mon ■ €€€

American chef Daniel Rose offers a fixed menu, which includes dishes made with fresh ingredients from the market. Book in advance.

9 Restaurant Georges

MAP G4 ■ Centre Georges Pompidou, 19 Rue Beaubourg, 75004 ■ 01 44 78 47 99 ■ Closed Tue ■ €€€

Sleek design and a great view make this museum restaurant a superb choice for a glamorous night out.

10 Le Hangar

MAP G4 ■ 12 Impasse Berthaud, 75003 ■ 01 42 74 55 44 ■ Closed Sun, Mon ■ €€

Close to the Pompidou, this small, friendly bistro is no secret to the locals, who keep returning for the fabulous food, such as steak tartare, foie gras and moelleux au chocolat.

Interior of Benoit bistro

Beer Bars

1 The Frog and Rosbif
MAP F3 ■ 116 Rue St-Denis, 75002

For homesick Brits or Anglophiles, this is the place to find real ale (brewed downstairs) and fish and chips, play pub quizzes, read English newspapers and watch live football and rugby matches.

2 Quigley's Point
MAP M1 ■ 5 Rue du Jour, 75001

Right in front of Eglise St-Eustache, this friendly Irish pub serves beer from Holland, Germany, Ireland and Britain.

3 Hall's Beer Tavern
MAP N2 ■ 68 Rue St-Denis, 75001

Although situated in a fairly touristy street, this is a relaxed and friendly place with a good selection of draught beers on offer, including La Chouffe and Duvel.

4 Le Bogman
MAP N1 ■ 2 Rue de la Petite Truanderie, 75001

Formerly the Goblet d'Argent, this bar may have changed name and location, but it retains an Irish pub feel, with a dartboard and live music on Tuesdays.

5 Le Sous-Bock
MAP M2 ■ 49 Rue St-Honoré, 75001

A good place for *moules-frites* (mussels and French fries), with a choice of 20 beers on tap and over 300 bottled varieties to wash them down. There are also 40 different whiskies to sample.

6 McBride's
MAP F3 ■ 54 Rue St-Denis, 75001

A popular place to watch football or play a game of pool, this friendly Irish sports bar attracts homesick expats with its fried breakfasts. Enjoy live music on Sunday nights.

The Frog and Rosbif

7 Au Trappiste
MAP F3 ■ 4 Rue St-Denis, 75001

Calling itself "the kingdom of beer", this bar specializes in Belgian brews, including, of course, Trappist beers. Hearty Flemish and Alsace food such as *choucroute* is served.

8 Guinness Tavern
MAP N2 ■ 31 Rue des Lombards, 75004

Fourteen beers are on tap in this Irish bar, which has live music every night and a concert once a month. The party really kicks off after 10pm.

9 Café Oz
MAP F3 ■ 18 Rue St-Denis, 75001

A range of Australian beers and wines, combined with archetypal Outback decor, makes this rowdy bar popular with antipodean expatriates and French patrons alike.

10 La Taverne de Maître Kanter
MAP F3 ■ 16 Rue Coquillière, 75001

Part of a chain of Alsace-style taverns, this is a good place to relax over a pint of French beer. Alsatian dishes are also served.

See map on p84

TOP 10 Marais and the Bastille

For many, the Marais is one of the most enjoyable quarters of Paris, with chic shops, galleries and dining, as well as fine museums and atmospheric medieval lanes, but the district was little more than a muddy swamp until Henri IV built the Place Royale (now Place des Vosges) in 1605. Following its notoriety as the birthplace of the Revolution, the Bastille district sank into oblivion, until artists and designers arrived in the 1990s. Its streets are now home to the city's liveliest nightspots.

**Statue,
Musée
Carnavalet**

AREA MAP OF MARAIS AND THE BASTILLE

① Musée Picasso

MAP R2 ▪ 5 Rue de Thorigny, 75003 ▪ Open 11:30am–6pm Tue–Fri, 9:30am–6pm Sat & Sun ▪ Closed 1 Jan, 1 May, 25 Dec ▪ Admission charge (free first Sun of month) ▪ www.museepicassoparis.fr

When the Spanish-born artist Pablo Picasso died in 1973, his family donated thousands of his works to the French state in lieu of estate taxes. Thus Paris enjoys the largest collection of Picassos in the world. Housed in the grand Hôtel Salé (see p98), which emerged from extensive renovations in late 2014, the collection displays the range of his artistic

Elegant Place de Vosges

development, from his Blue and Pink periods to Cubism, and reveals his proficiency in an astonishing range of techniques and materials. Larger sculptures are housed in the garden and courtyard (see p52).

② Musée Cognacq-Jay

MAP Q3 ▪ 8 Rue Elzévir, 75003 ▪ Open 10am–6pm Tue–Sun ▪ www.museecognacqjay.paris.fr

This small but excellent museum illustrates the sophisticated French lifestyle in the so-called Age of Enlightenment, which centred on Paris. The 18th-century art and furniture on display were once the private collection of Ernest Cognacq and his wife, Louise Jay, founders of the former Samaritaine department store by Pont Neuf. It is superbly displayed in the Hôtel Donon, an elegant late 16th-century town mansion (see p51).

③ Place des Vosges

MAP R3

Paris's oldest square is also one of the most beautiful in the world. The square was commissioned by Henri IV. Its 36 houses with red-gold brick and stone façades, slate roofs and dormer windows were laid out with striking symmetry in 1612. Originally built for silk workers, the likes of Cardinal Richelieu (1585–1642) and playwright Molière (1622–73) quickly moved in and it remains an upper-class residential address. However, everyone can enjoy a stroll around the area and visit the art galleries under the arcades.

4 Musée Carnavalet

MAP R3 ■ 16 Rue des Francs Bourgeois, 75003 ■ Open 10am–6pm Tue–Sun ■ www.carnavalet.paris.fr

Devoted to the history of Paris, this museum sprawls through two mansions, the 16th-century Carnavalet and 17th-century Le Peletier de Saint-Fargeau. The former was the home of Madame de Sévigné, the famous letter-writer, from 1677 to 1696 and a gallery here is devoted to her life. The extensive museum contains period rooms filled with art and portraits, plus Revolutionary artifacts and memorabilia of 18th-century philosophers Rousseau and Voltaire *(see p50)*.

5 Place de la Bastille

MAP H5

Today this notorious square is not much more than a busy traffic circle. Originally, the Bastille was a fortress built by Charles V to defend the eastern edge of the city, but it soon became a jail for political prisoners. Angry citizens, rising up against the excesses of the monarchy, stormed the Bastille on 14 July 1789 *(see p43)* and destroyed this hated symbol of oppression sparking off the French Revolution. In its place is the bronze Colonne de Juillet (July Column), 52 m (171 ft) high and crowned by the Angel of Liberty, which commemorates those who died in the revolutions of 1830 and 1848. Looming behind it is the Opéra Bastille, once the largest opera house in the world, which opened on the bicentennial of the Revolution in 1989.

THE JEWISH QUARTER

The Jewish Quarter, centred on rues des Rosiers and des Écouffes, was established in the 13th century and has attracted immigrants since the Revolution. Many Jews fled here to escape persecution in Eastern Europe, but were arrested during the Nazi Occupation. Since World War II, Sephardic Jews from North Africa have found new homes here.

Passage de l'Homme

6 The Passages

MAP H5

The Bastille has been the quarter of working-class artisans and craft guilds since the 17th century and many furniture makers are still located in these small alleyways, called *passages*. Rue du Faubourg St-Antoine is lined with shops selling a striking array of traditional period furniture and modern designs, but don't miss the narrow *passages*, such as Passage de l'Homme, that run off this and other streets in the Bastille. Many artists and craftspeople have their *ateliers* (workshops) in these atmospheric alleys.

7 Musée de la Chasse et de la Nature

MAP Q2 ■ 62 Rue des Archives, 75003 ■ Open 11am–6pm Tue–Sun (to 9:30pm Wed) ■ Closed public hols ■ Admission charge (free first Sun of month) ■ www.chassenature.org

Occupying two well-preserved 17th- and 18th-century mansions, this intriguing museum explores the history of hunting, and humanity's relationship with the natural world. Curated to resemble the home of a rich collector, the museum displays tapestries and gilt-framed period paintings alongside taxidermy animals, and fascinating curiosity cabinets. There are surprises in each elegantly organized room, from the astonishing Jan Fabre-designed ceiling of owl feathers to the sleepy fox curled up on a chair.

Rue de Lappe
MAP H5

Once famous for its 1930s dance halls (*bals musettes*), rue de Lappe is still the Bastille's after-dark hotspot. This short, narrow street is filled with bars, clubs, restaurants and cafés, and positively throbs with music. Crowds of hip night-owls trawl the cobblestones looking for action, and spill into the adjoining rue de la Roquette and rue de Charonne, where there are even more trendy bars and restaurants.

 Maison Européenne de la Photographie
MAP Q3 ■ 5–7 Rue de Fourcy, 75004 ■ Open 11am–8pm Wed–Sun ■ Admission charge (free Wed after 5pm) ■ www.mep-fr.org

This excellent gallery showcases contemporary European photography. It is housed in an early 18th-century mansion, Hôtel Hénault de Cantorbre, a mix of historic features and modern spaces that shows off a permanent collection and changing exhibitions of items from its archives.

 Maison de Victor Hugo
MAP R4 ■ 6 Pl des Vosges, 75004 ■ Open 10am–6pm Tue–Sun ■ Closed public hols ■ Admission charge for exhibitions ■ www.maisonsvictorhugo.paris.fr

French author Victor Hugo (1802–85) lived on the second floor of the Hôtel de Rohan-Guémenée, the largest house on the place des Vosges, from 1832 to 1848. He wrote most of *Les Misérables* here *(see p44)* among other works. In 1903, the house became a museum covering his life.

Busts, Maison de Victor Hugo

A DAY IN THE MARAIS

 MORNING

Begin at the **Musée Carnavalet**, with its impressive collections and lovely garden courtyard. Afterwards, walk to the **Place des Vosges**: take in the whole square from the fountains in the centre.

Have a coffee at **Ma Bourgogne** *(19 Pl des Vosges • 01 42 78 44 64)*, right on the square. Revitalized, tour the **Maison de Victor Hugo**, then go to the southwest corner of the square, through a wooden door to the pretty garden of the **Hôtel de Béthune-Sully** *(see p98)*.

AFTERNOON

If the weather is nice, join the queue at **L'As du Falafel** *(see p101)* for a hearty falafel wrap to eat in the nearby square Charles-Victor Langlois. Otherwise, for shelter and a greater choice, head for the lively **Marché des Enfants Rouges** *(39 Rue de Bretagne)* and its international food stalls.

Spend a leisurely afternoon exploring the Marais, with its narrow, picturesque streets lined with shops and cafés. Pop into the fashionable boutiques along the **Rue des Francs Bourgeois** and **Rue Vieille du Temple**; bite into a slice of *babka* in the Jewish Quarter on **Rue des Rosiers**; then explore the ultra-hip Upper Marais, where concept store **Merci** *(see p96)* holds court.

Walk through **Place de la Bastille** – once the site of the city's dreaded prison – on the way to dinner in style beneath the chandeliers of **Le Train Bleu** *(20 Blvd Diderot • 01 43 43 09 06)*.

See map on pp92–3

Fashion and Accessory Shops

Shoes in the window of Anatomica

women are inspired by Tzigane and Asian styles, and made using vibrant natural fabrics. They sell children's clothes and home furnishings too.

5 **Home Autour du Monde**

MAP G4 ■ 8 Rue des Francs Bourgeois, 75003 ■ 01 42 77 16 18

French designer Bensimon's concept store stocks the brand's classic canvas sneakers in bright colours and Liberty prints for kids and adults.

6 **Monsieur**

MAP R1 ■ 53 Rue Charlot, 75003

This small store sells delicate gold and silver jewellery. Designer Nadia Azoug is often at work in the on-site *atelier*.

7 **Sessùn**

MAP H5 ■ 34 Rue de Charonne, 75011

This is the flagship store of the young, French womenswear label, which produces chic, edgy clothes and accessories.

8 **K. Jacques**

MAP Q3 ■ 16 Rue Pavée, 75004

The classic Saint-Tropez sandal, given iconic status by Brigitte Bardot and never out of fashion, is stocked here, in some 60 styles and colours.

9 **Isabel Marant**

MAP H5 ■ 16 Rue de Charonne, 75011

This designer is starting to get a lot of recognition outside France, her pieces are hip but elegant.

10 **Bonton**

MAP R1 ■ 5 Blvd des Filles du Calvaire, 75003

A gorgeous store for kids, this has three levels of clothes, accessories, toys and even a vintage photo booth.

1 **Anatomica**

MAP P3 ■ 14 Rue du Bourg Tibourg, 75004

One of the best men's stores in the city, carrying perfectly tailored clothes, and leather shoes from cult brand Alden.

2 **Merci**

MAP R2 ■ 111 Blvd Beaumarchais, 75003 ■ 01 42 77 00 33

This trendy multi-brand store stocks clothes and accessories alongside stylish homewares.

3 **Eric Bompard**

MAP R3 ■ 14 Rue de Sévigné, 75004

Everything is soft at this cashmere specialist – sweaters, scarves, gloves and much more.

4 **Antoine et Lilli**

MAP Q2 ■ 51 Rue des Francs Bourgeois, 75004

Behind the bright pink shopfront, chic and easy-to-wear clothes for

Specialist Shops

1 Mariage Frères
MAP Q3 ▪ 30 Rue du Bourg Tibourg, 75004
This famous tea house was founded in 1854 and sells all kinds of blends, as well as tea-making paraphernalia.

2 Jacques Genin
MAP G3 ▪ 133 Rue de Turenne, 75003
This trendy chocolatier is adored for his caramels and fruit jellies. He also bakes a fantastic *millefeuille*.

3 La Manufacture de Chocolat
MAP H4 ▪ 40 Rue de la Roquette, 75011
The *chocolaterie* of Michelin-starred chef Alain Ducasse smells divine – and has the taste to back it up.

4 Fragonard
MAP Q2 ▪ 51 Rue des Francs Bourgeois, 75004
If you can't visit this perfume-maker's factory in the south of France, pick up some soaps and scents in this fragrant boutique.

Soaps and scents at Fragonard

5 Goumanyat
MAP R1 ▪ 3 Rue Charles-François Dupuis, 75003
Paris's top chefs stock up on herbs, spices and teas here. Great for an interesting food gift or souvenir.

6 L'Arbre à Lettres
MAP H5 ▪ 62 Rue du Faubourg St-Antoine, 75012
This beautiful little bookshop specializes in fine arts, literature and human sciences.

L'Arbre à Lettres

7 A l'Olivier
MAP H5 ▪ 23 Rue de Rivoli, 75004
Opened in 1822, this shop specializes in sourcing the finest Provençal and Mediterranean olive oils, along with other culinary delights.

8 Papier Tigre
MAP R1 ▪ 5 Rue des Filles du Calvaire, 75003
Stylish graphic notebooks, greeting cards and other quirkily designed paper products are on offer at this modern stationery store.

9 Izraël
MAP P3 ▪ 30 Rue François Miron, 75004
Also called the "World of Spices", this tiny store is a treasure trove of cheese, wine, rum, honey, mustard and myriad other delights.

10 Village Saint Paul
MAP R4 ▪ Between Rue St-Paul and Rue des Jardins St-Paul, 75004
A secret maze of art galleries, fine antiques and design shops, tucked away behind Eglise St-Paul.

See map on pp92–3 ←

Mansions

Orangery, Hôtel de Béthune-Sully

1 Hôtel de Coulanges
MAP Q2 ■ 35 Rue des Francs Bourgeois, 75004 ■ Open only for concerts

This mansion boasts beautiful early 18th-century architecture; the right wing dates back to the early 1600s.

2 Hôtel Salé
Built in 1656–9 for Aubert de Fontenay, a salt-tax collector, this mansion is now the home of the Musée Picasso (see p93).

3 Hôtel Guénégaud
MAP P3 ■ 60 Rue des Archives, 75003 ■ Open 11am–6pm Tue–Sun ■ Admission charge

Designed by the architect François Mansart in the mid-17th century, this splendid mansion is now home to the Musée de la Chasse et de la Nature (see p94).

4 Hôtel de Beauvais
MAP P3 ■ 68 Rue François Miron, 75004 ■ Closed to the public

The young Mozart performed at this 17th-century mansion. Notice the balcony decorated with goats' heads.

5 Hôtel de St-Aignan
MAP P2 ■ 71 Rue du Temple, 75003 ■ Open 11am–6pm Mon–Fri, 10am–6pm Sun ■ Admission charge ■ www.mahj.org

The plain exterior hides an enormous mansion within. It is now the Museum of Jewish Art and History.

6 Hôtel de Béthune-Sully
MAP R4 ■ 62 Rue St-Antoine, 75004 ■ Closed to the public, except the gardens

This 17th-century mansion was home to the Duc de Sully, chief minister to Henri IV. It now houses the French National Monuments administration.

7 Hôtel de Soubise
MAP Q2 ■ 60 Rue des Francs Bourgeois, 75003 ■ Open 10am–5:30pm Mon, Wed, Fri, 2–5:30pm Sat & Sun ■ Admission charge

Along with the adjacent Hôtel de Rohan, this mansion houses the national archives.

8 Hôtel de Lamoignon
MAP Q3 ■ 24 Rue Pavée, 75004 ■ Closed to the public

This mansion was built in 1584 for the daughter of Henri II.

9 Hôtel de Marle
MAP G4 ■ 11 Rue Payenne, 75003 ■ Open noon–6pm Tue–Sun ■ Closed mid-Jul–end Aug

The Swedish Institute is located here.

10 Hôtel de Sens
MAP Q4 ■ 1 Rue Figuier, 75004 ■ Closed to the public

One of Paris's few medieval mansions. Henri IV's wife Marguerite de Valois (see p22) lived here after their divorce. It is now home to a fine arts library.

Medieval façade of Hôtel de Sens

Galleries

1 Galerie Marian Goodman
MAP P2 ■ 79 Rue du Temple,
75003 ■ Open 11am–7pm Tue–Sat
■ Closed Aug

Housed in a 17th-century mansion, this gallery is a slice of New York style. Artists include Jeff Wall and video-maker Steve McQueen.

2 Galerie Akié Arichi
MAP H5 ■ 26 Rue Keller, 75011
■ Open 2:30–7pm Tue–Sat
■ www.galeriearichi.com

Eclectic exhibitions covering photography, sculpture and painting, often with an Asian influence.

3 Galerie Alain Gutharc
MAP H4 ■ 7 Rue St-Claude, 75003 ■ Open 11am–1pm, 2–7pm Tue–Sat ■ www. alaingutharc.com

Alain Gutharc devotes his space to the work of young, contemporary French artists.

4 Galerie Daniel Templon
MAP P2 ■ 30 Rue Beaubourg, 75003 ■ Open 10am–7pm Mon–Sat
■ www.danieltemplon.com

A favourite among the French contemporary art establishment, exhibiting big international names as well as talented newcomers.

5 Galerie Karsten Greve
MAP R2 ■ 5 Rue Debelleyme, 75003 ■ Open 10am–7pm Tue–Sat

A leading international gallery with top names in modern and contemporary art and photography.

6 Galerie Patrick Seguin
MAP H4 ■ 5 Rue des Taillandiers, 75011 ■ Open 10am–7pm Tue–Sat

This gallery features stylish 20th-century furniture and architecture.

7 Galerie Thaddeus Ropac
MAP Q1 ■ 7 Rue Debelleyme, 75003 ■ Open 10am–7pm Tue–Sat
■ www.ropac.net

A major contemporary gallery showcasing new international artists.

8 Galerie Lavignes-Bastille
MAP H5 ■ 27 Rue de Charonne, 75011 ■ Open 2–7pm Tue–Sat
■ www.lavignesbastille.com

Narrative figuration, Op Art and new artists are featured here.

Galerie Lavignes-Bastille

9 Galerie Yvon Lambert
MAP Q1 ■108 Rue Vieille du Temple, 75003 ■ Open 10am–7pm Tue–Sat, 2–7pm Sun
■ www.yvon-lambert.com

Associated with gallery in Avignon, this shop displays art books, posters, limited edition prints and art objects.

10 Galerie Nikki Diana Marquardt
MAP R3 ■ 9 Pl des Vosges, 75004
■ Open 11am–7pm Mon–Sat ■ www. galerienikkidianamarquardt.com

This gallery shows politically motivated artworks executed in all types of media.

See map on pp92–3 ←

Fashionable Hang-outs

Kitsch decor in Andy Wahloo

1 Andy Wahloo
MAP Q1 ■ 69 Rue des Gravilliers, 75003

Located in one of Henri IV's former mansions, pop art and Oriental decor form a backdrop for some of the city's most fashionable soirées.

2 Zéro Zéro
MAP H4 ■ 89 Rue Amelot, 75011

It doesn't get much cooler than this den-like bar with wood panelling and flowered wallpaper. Though not listed on the menu, cocktails are a speciality.

3 La Perle
MAP Q2 ■ 78 Rue Vieille du Temple, 75003 ■ 01 42 72 69 93

This bistro is one of Paris' most famous hang-outs. Its straightforward menu draws a fashionable crowd in the evenings.

4 Bataclan
MAP H4 ■ 50 Blvd Voltaire, 75011

This venerable *salle de spectacle* concert hall attracts a wide range of international artists as well as French household names. The adjoining café serves drinks and light meals, along with a list of daily specials on the chalkboard.

5 Pop In
MAP H4 ■ 105 Rue Amelot, 75011

This shabby-chic bar and nightclub has cheap drinks, friendly staff, a cool crowd and funky DJs. It's open seven days a week until late.

6 Café de l'Industrie
MAP H4 ■ 16 Rue St-Sabin, 75011

A fashionable and sizable café that has three rooms where the walls are lined with paintings and old-fashioned artifacts. The food is cheap but pretty good, and the later it gets the better the buzz.

7 Grazie
MAP H4 ■ 91 Blvd Beaumarchais, 75003 ■ 01 42 78 11 96

Italian pizzeria with an industrial loft-style decor attracts a hip crowd. Authentic pizzas and classy cocktails.

8 Le Panic Room
MAP H4 ■ 101 Rue Amelot, 75011

Top Parisian DJs set the tone at this quirky bar offering fancy cocktails, a smoking room and cellar dance floor.

9 Le Square Trousseau
MAP H5 ■ 1 Rue Antoine Vollon, 75012

This charming Bastille district brasserie, with its lovely heated terrace, is something of a media haunt, serving good food from breakfast into the early hours.

10 Le Progrès
MAP R2 ■ 1 Rue de Bretagne, 75003 ■ 01 42 72 01 44

The pavement terrace of this corner café in the trendy Northern Marais fills up during Paris Fashion Week.

Places to Eat

1 L'Ambroisie
MAP R3 ▪ 9 Pl des Vosges, 75004 ▪ 01 42 78 51 45 ▪ Closed Sun, Mon ▪ €€€

The finest service matches the finest of food. The wine list is renowned and the chocolate tart is out of this world. Reserve in advance.

2 Café des Musées
MAP R2 ▪ 49 Rue de Turenne, 75003 ▪ 01 42 72 96 17 ▪ No disabled access ▪ €

A traditional bistro, which serves classic French dishes such as steak tartare and *crème brûlée*.

3 Patisserie Carette
MAP G4 ▪ 25 Pl des Vosges, 75003 ▪ 01 48 87 94 07 ▪ €

Salads and sandwiches, as well as delicious cakes, feature at this patisserie and tea room on the picturesque place des Vosges.

4 Au Vieux Chêne
7 Rue Dahomey, 75011 ▪ 01 43 71 67 69 ▪ Closed Sat, Sun, Aug ▪ €€

Hidden down a side street, this atmospheric bistro is a treat. Expect updated French classics such as duck *pot-au-feu* with foie gras.

Interior of Chez Paul

PRICE CATEGORIES

For a three-course meal for one with half a bottle of wine (or equivalent meal), taxes and extra charges

€ under €30   €€ €30–€50   €€€ over €50

5 La Gazzetta
MAP H5 ▪ 29 Rue de Cotte, 75012 ▪ 01 43 47 47 05 ▪ Closed Mon ▪ €€€

Inventive, contemporary dishes, such as venison, polenta, dried figs and dandelion leaves are served in an Art Deco-style setting.

6 Breizh Café
MAP G4 ▪ 109 Rue Vieille du Temple, 75003 ▪ 01 42 72 13 77 ▪ Closed Mon, Tue ▪ €

An award-winning crêperie with a contemporary take on both savoury and sweet Breton pancakes. Try the healthier buckwheat crêpes.

7 Le Baron Rouge
MAP H5 ▪ 1 Rue Théophile Roussel, 75012 ▪ 01 43 43 14 32 ▪ Closed Mon ▪ €

Cold meats, cheeses and oysters are served in an authentic setting next to Marché d'Aligre (see p71).

8 Chez Paul
MAP H5 ▪ 13 Rue de Charonne, 75011 ▪ 01 47 00 34 57 ▪ €

This old-style bistro has a simple but delicious menu. Book ahead.

9 Septime
MAP H5 ▪ 80 Rue de Charonne, 75011 ▪ 01 43 67 38 29 ▪ €

This modern restaurant serves dishes such as cress and sorrel risotto and veal tartare. Book ahead.

10 L'As du Fallafel
MAP Q3 ▪ 34 Rue des Rosiers, 75004 ▪ 01 48 87 63 60 ▪ Closed Fri dinner, Sat ▪ €

This is the best falafel joint in the city. The "special" with aubergine and spicy sauce is a must.

See map on pp92–3 ←

TOP 10 Tuileries and Opéra Quarters

These two quarters were once the province of the rich and the royal, and there's still an air of luxury about them. Adjoining the lovely Tuileries Gardens is the largest museum in the world, the Louvre, while the grand Opera House gives the second quarter its name. The place de la Concorde is one of the most historic sites in the city.

**Statue of Medea,
Jardin des Tuileries**

AREA MAP OF TUILERIES AND OPERA QUARTERS

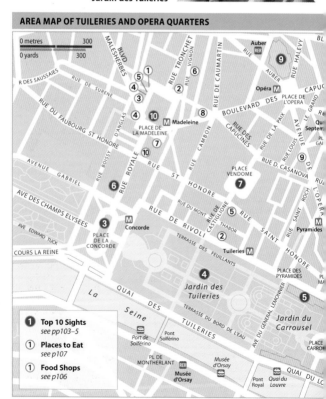

1 Top 10 Sights *see pp103–5*	
① Places to Eat *see p107*	
① Food Shops *see p106*	

1 Musée du Louvre
See pp12–15.

2 Rue de Rivoli
MAP M2

Commissioned by Napoleon and named for his victory over the Austrians at Rivoli in 1797, this grand street links the Louvre with the Champs-Elysées *(see p111)*. It was intended as a backdrop for his victory marches but was not finished until the 1850s, long after the emperor's death. Along one side, railings replaced the old Tuileries walls, opening up the view, while opposite, Neo-Classical apartments sit atop the long arcades. These are now lined with a mix of shops that sells everything from luxury goods to tourist souvenirs.

Obelisk in Place de la Concorde

3 Place de la Concorde
MAP D3

This historic octagonal square, covering more than 8 ha (20 acres), was built between 1755 and 1775 as the grand setting for a statue of Louis XV; by 1792 it had become the place de la Révolution and its central monument was the guillotine. Louis XVI, Marie-Antoinette and more than 1,000 others were executed here *(see p43)*. In 1795, in the spirit of reconciliation, it received its present name. The central obelisk, 23-m (75-ft) tall and covered in hieroglyphics, is from a 3,300-year-old Luxor temple, and was a gift from Egypt, erected in 1833. Two fountains and eight statues represent French cities. On the north side of the square are the Hôtel de la Marine and Hôtel Crillon.

4 Jardin des Tuileries
MAP J2

These gardens *(see p56)* were first laid out as part of the old Tuileries Palace, which was built for Catherine de Médicis in 1564 but burned down in 1871. André Le Nôtre redesigned them into formal French gardens in 1664. At the Louvre end is the Arc de Triomphe du Carrousel, erected by Napoleon in 1808. Also here is the entrance to an underground shopping centre, the Carrousel du Louvre. Nearby, sensuous nude sculptures by Aristide Maillol (1861–1944) adorn the ornamental pools and walkways. At the far end are the Jeu de Paume gallery *(see p53)* and the Musée de l'Orangerie *(see p52)*, famous for its giant canvases of Monet waterlilies.

STORMING OF THE TUILERIES

Visiting the Tuileries Gardens now, where children play and lovers stroll, it is hard to imagine the scenes that took place here on 20 June 1792. The palace and gardens were invaded by French citizens seeking to overthrow the monarchy. This was finally achieved on 10 August, when the Tuileries Palace was sacked and Louis XVI overthrown.

5 Musée des Arts Décoratifs

MAP M2 ■ 107 Rue de Rivoli, 75001 ■ Open 11am–6pm Tue–Sun (to 9pm Thu) ■ Admission charge ■ www.lesartsdecoratifs.fr

This huge collection covers the decorative arts from the Middle Ages to the 20th century. With over 100 rooms, its many highlights include the Medieval and Renaissance rooms, the Art Deco rooms and a superb jewellery collection. Also in the same building is the Musée Nationale de la Mode et du Textile, with displays of fashion, textiles, posters and advertising ephemera in changing temporary exhibitions.

6 Art Nouveau Museum

MAP D3 ■ 3 Rue Royale, 75008 ■ Open 2–5:30pm Wed–Sun, guided tours 2pm (in English) and 3:15pm ■ Admission charge ■ www.maxims-musee-artnouveau.com

This small museum (which is part of the famous Maxim's restaurant) houses Pierre Cardin's impressive Art Nouveau collection. The 750 works of art, by big names such as Tiffany, Toulouse-Lautrec, Galle Massier and Marjorelle, are set in a recreated 1900s apartment. A guided visit can be combined with dinner in the glamorous restaurant.

7 Place Vendôme

MAP E3

Jules Hardouin-Mansart, the architect of Versailles (see p155), designed the façades of this elegant royal square for Louis XIV in 1698. Originally intended for foreign embassies, bankers soon moved in and built lavish dwellings. It remains home to jewellers and financiers today. The world-famous Ritz hotel was established here at the turn of the 20th century. It underwent extensive renovations in 2015. The column, topped by a statue of Napoleon, is a replica of the one destroyed by the Commune in 1871.

8 Palais Royal

MAP L1 ■ Pl du Palais Royal, 75001 ■ Open Oct–Mar: 7am–8:30pm daily; Apr–Aug: 7am–10:15pm daily; Sep: 7am–9:30pm daily ■ Public access to gardens and arcades only

In the late 18th century extensive changes were made under the dukes of Orléans. The architect Victor Louis was commissioned to build 60 uniformly styled houses around three sides of the square and the adjacent theatre, which now houses the Comédie Française (see p65). Today the arcades house specialist shops, galleries and restaurants, and the courtyard and gardens contain modern works of art (see p47).

9 Opéra National de Paris Garnier

MAP E2 ■ Pl de l'Opéra, 75009 ■ 01 71 25 24 23 ■ Open 10am–5pm daily (closes at 1pm on day of matinee performances; closed public hols) ■ Admission charge ■ www.operadeparis.fr

Designed by Charles Garnier for Napoleon III in 1862,

Place Vendôme and Vendôme column

Performance at Opéra Garnier

Paris's opulent opera house took 13 years to complete. A range of styles from Classical to Baroque incorporates stone friezes and columns, statues and a green copper cupola. The ornate interior has a grand staircase, mosaic domed ceiling over the grand foyer and an auditorium with a ceiling by Marc Chagall. There's even an underground lake – the inspiration for Gaston Leroux's *Phantom of the Opera* – sadly closed to visitors (*see p64*).

⑩ Place de la Madeleine
MAP D3

Surrounded by 52 Corinthian columns, the huge, Classical-style Madeleine church (*see p48*) commands this elegant square. On the east side a colourful flower market takes place from Tuesday to Saturday. Around the square are some of the most upmarket *épiceries* (food stores) and speciality shops in the city (*see p70*).

A DAY IN THE TUILERIES

▶ MORNING

Visiting the **Louvre** (*see pp12–15*) takes planning, and you should get there at least 15 minutes before opening (unless you've already bought your ticket). Spend the whole morning there and pick up a map as you enter so that you can be sure to see the main highlights. Have a morning coffee in the elegant Richelieu, Denon or Mollien cafés within the museum.

From the Louvre, either visit the Carrousel du Louvre's underground shops or walk along **Rue de Rivoli** towards **Place de la Concorde** (*see p103*). This end of the street is filled with souvenir shops and overpriced cafés so turn right onto rue Mondovi for a good lunch at **Lescure**, a little rustic bistro (*7 Rue de Mondovi • 01 42 60 18 91 • Closed Sat, Sun*).

AFTERNOON

After being indoors all morning, get some fresh air in the **Jardin des Tuileries** (*see p103*) then walk down to **place de la Madeleine** to spend the afternoon browsing in its many gourmet stores, or visit the **Art Nouveau Museum** and be dazzled by its decorative arts collection. Later, take tea in the restaurant of one of the best shops, **Hédiard** (*see p106*).

Spend the evening attending a classical music concert at **La Madeleine** (*see p48*) or watching a performance at **Opéra National de Paris Garnier**. Finish the day with a delicious gastronomic dinner at three-Michelin-starred **Le Meurice** (*see p107*).

See map on pp102–3

Food Shops

Fresh fruit outside Hédiard

1 Hédiard
MAP D3 ▪ 21 Pl de la Madeleine, 75008

Founded in 1854, this world food emporium features a cornucopia of fruits and vegetables, teas, truffles and a host of other gourmet delights.

2 Fauchon
MAP D3 ▪ 26–30 Pl de la Madeleine, 75008

The king of Parisian *épiceries* (grocers). The mouthwatering window displays are works of art and tempt you inside for pastries, exotic fruits and some 3,500 other items.

3 Au Verger de la Madeleine
MAP D3 ▪ 4 Blvd Malesherbes, 75008

Rare vintage wines are the speciality here. The owner will help you find a wine to match the year of any special occasion.

4 Caviar Kaspia
MAP D3 ▪ 17 Pl de la Madeleine, 75008

The peak of indulgence. Caviars from around the world, plus smoked eel, salmon and other fishy fare, along with a wide range of vodkas. Try an amazing baked potato with caviar in the upstairs dining room.

5 La Maison de la Truffe
MAP D3 ▪ 19 Pl de la Madeleine, 75008

France's finest black truffles are sold here during the winter. Preserved truffles and other delicacies can be savoured in the shop or at home.

6 La Maison du Miel
MAP D3 ▪ 24 Rue Vignon, 75009

The "house of honey", family-owned since 1908, is the place to try speciality honeys, to spread on your toast or your body in the form of soaps and oils.

7 Boutique Maille
MAP D3 ▪ 6 Pl de la Madeleine, 75008

The retail outlet for one of France's finest mustard-makers. Fresh mustard served in lovely ceramic jars and seasonal limited edition mustards are available.

Fauchon biscuit tin

8 La Maison du Chocolat
MAP E3 ▪ 8 Blvd Madeleine, 75009

A superb chocolate shop, which offers fine chocolates and exquisite patisserie including eclairs, tarts and mouthwatering macarons.

9 Pierre Hermé
MAP E3 ▪ 39 Ave de l'Opéra, 75002

A rainbow of exquisite *macarons* in every flavour you can imagine is yours for the picking.

10 Ladurée
MAP D3 ▪ 16 Rue Royale, 75008

A splendid *belle époque* tea salon that has been serving some of the best *macarons* in Paris since 1862.

Places to Eat

(1) Bistrot Victoires
MAP F3 ■ 6 Rue de la Vrillière, 75001 ■ 01 42 61 43 78 ■ €€
With its vintage décor and exemplary duck confit, this much-loved neighbourhood bistro is often packed.

(2) Le Meurice
MAP E3 ■ 228 Rue de Rivoli, 75001 ■ 01 44 58 10 55 ■ Closed Sat, Sun ■ €€€
Try the sea bream with beetroot and caviar at Alain Ducasse's three-Michelin-starred establishment.

(3) Le Grand Véfour
MAP E3 ■ 17 Rue de Beaujolais, 75001 ■ 01 42 96 56 27 ■ Closed Sat, Sun, Aug, some of Dec ■ No disabled access ■ €€€
Guy Martin's beautiful 18th-century restaurant has two Michelin stars and is a gourmet treat.

(4) Lucas Carton
MAP D3 ■ 9 Pl de la Madeleine, 75008 ■ 01 42 65 22 90 ■ Closed Aug, public hols ■ No disabled access ■ €€€
Chef Julien Dumas takes the reigns at one of Paris's oldest gourmet restaurants. Superb quality food.

(5) Café Castiglione
MAP E3 ■ 235 Rue St-Honoré, 75001 ■ 01 42 60 68 22 ■ €€
The burgers at this classic brasserie are so popular that even the style gurus of Fashion Week will indulge.

Café Castiglione

PRICE CATEGORIES
For a three-course meal for one with half a bottle of wine (or equivalent meal), taxes and extra charges
....
€ under €30   €€ €30–€50   €€€ over €50

---

(6) Kunitoraya
MAP E3 ■ 1 Rue Villedo, 75001 ■ 01 47 03 33 65 ■ €
There's often a queue at this bustling udon bar serving perfect noodles in a rich broth. A larger sister restaurant is along the road at No. 5.

(7) A Casaluna
MAP E3 ■ 6 Rue Beaujolais, 75001 ■ 01 42 60 05 11 ■ No disabled access ■ €€
Traditional Corsican specialities such as baked aubergine with goat's cheese are served at this charming restaurant. Round off the meal with a chestnut or myrtle *digestif*.

(8) Willi's Wine Bar
MAP E3 ■ 13 Rue des Petits Champs, 75001 ■ 01 42 61 05 09 ■ Closed Sun, 10 days Aug ■ €€
This cozy bar and adjacent dining room – Macéo – is a popular haunt for lovers of modern French food and wines from small producers.

(9) Restaurant du Palais Royal
MAP E3 ■ 110 Galerie de Valois, 75001 ■ 01 40 20 00 27 ■ No disabled access ■ €€€
Contemporary French food is served in the bucolic setting of the Palais Royal gardens (see p57).

(10) Verjus
MAP E3 ■ 52 Rue de Richelieu, 75001 ■ 01 42 97 54 40 ■ Closed Sat, Sun ■ €€–€€€
You need to book in advance for the set six-course gourmet dinner in the intimate dining room, but you can simply turn up to enjoy a lighter bite in the wine bar, which doesn't accept bookings.

See map on pp102–3

TOP10 Champs-Elysées Quarter

The Champs-Elysées is the most famous street in Paris and the quarter that lies around it radiates wealth and power. It is home to the president of France, embassies and *haute couture* fashion houses, as well as five-star hotels and fine restaurants. The Champs-Elysées runs from place de la Concorde to place Charles de Gaulle, and it's here that France celebrates national events or mourns at the funeral cortèges of the great and good.

Petit Palais

AREA MAP OF CHAMPS-ELYSEES QUARTER

1 **Top 10 Sights**
see pp111-13

1 **Places to Eat**
see p117

1 **Designer Shops**
see p116

1 **International Connections** *see p114*

Previous pages The Louvre viewed from the Jardin des Tuileries

1 Arc de Triomphe
See pp30–31.

2 Avenue des Champs-Elysées
MAP C3

One of the most famous avenues in the world came into being when the royal gardener André Le Nôtre planted an arbour of trees beyond the border of the Jardin des Tuileries in 1667 *(see p103)*. First called the Grand Cours (Great Way), it was later renamed after the Elysian Fields. In the mid-19th century it acquired pedestrian paths, fountains, gas lights and cafés, and became the fashionable place for socializing and entertainment. Since the funeral of

Avenue des Champs-Elysées

Napoleon in 1840, it has also been the route for state processions, victory parades and other city events. The Rond-Point des Champs-Elysées is the prettiest part, with chestnut trees and flowerbeds. Formerly touristy parts have been revamped but flagship stores of international brands have made for less interesting shopping. A walk along the avenue is still an essential Paris experience.

3 Grand Palais
MAP D3 ■ 3 Ave du Général-Eisenhower, 75008 ■ 01 44 13 17 17 ■ Opening hours vary according to exhibition ■ Closed 1 May ■ Admission charge depending on exhibition ■ www.grandpalais.fr

This immense *belle époque* exhibition hall was built for the Universal Exhibition in 1900. Its splendid glass roof is a landmark of the Champs-Elysées. The façade is a mix of Art Nouveau ironwork, Neo-Classical stone columns and a mosaic frieze, with bronze horses and chariots at the four corners of the roof. The Galleries du Grand Palais host temporary art exhibitions.

4 Petit Palais
MAP D3 ■ Ave Winston Churchill, 75008 ■ 01 53 43 40 00 ■ Open 10am–6pm Tue–Sun (to 9pm Fri for temporary exhibitions) ■ www.petitpalais.paris.fr

The "little palace" echoes its neighbour in style. Set around a semicircular courtyard with Ionic columns and a dome, the building now houses the Musée des Beaux Arts de la Ville de Paris *(see p72)*.

Palais de la Découverte

in the sciences, from biology and chemistry to astronomy and physics, with interactive exhibits and demonstrations (the magnetism show is especially spectacular). There is also a planetarium, while the Planète Terre (Planet Earth) rooms examine global warming.

Rue du Faubourg St-Honoré
MAP D3

Running roughly parallel to the Champs-Elysées, this is Paris's equivalent of Fifth Avenue, Bond Street or Rodeo Drive. From Christian Lacroix and Versace to Gucci and Hermès, the shopfronts read like a *Who's Who* of fashion. Even if the prices may be out of reach, window-shopping is fun. There are also elegant antiques and art galleries. Look out for swallows that nest on many of the 19th-century façades.

Avenue Montaigne
MAP C3

In the 19th century the Avenue Montaigne was a nightlife hotspot. Parisians danced the night away at the Mabille Dance Hall until it closed in 1870 and Adolphe Sax made music with his newly invented saxophone in the Winter Garden. Today this chic avenue is a rival to the rue Faubourg-St-Honoré as the home to more *haute couture* houses, such as Christian Dior and Valentino. There are also luxury hotels, top restaurants, popular cafés, and the Comédie des Champs-Elysées and Théâtre des Champs-Elysées.

Pont Alexandre III
MAP D3

Built for the 1900 Universal Exhibition to carry visitors over the Seine to the Grand and Petit Palais, this bridge is a superb example of the steel architecture and ornate Art Nouveau style popular at the time. Named after Alexander III of Russia, who laid the foundation stone, its decoration displays both Russian and French heraldry. The bridge creates a splendid thoroughfare from the Champs-Elysées to the Hôtel des Invalides *(see p55)*.

Palais de la Découverte
MAP D3 ▪ Ave Franklin-D-Roosevelt, 75008 ▪ Open 9:30am–6pm Tue–Sat, 10am–7pm Sun ▪ Closed 1 Jan, 1 May, 14 Jul, 22 Jul, 25 Dec ▪ Admission charge

Set in a wing of the Grand Palais, this museum showcasing scientific discovery was created by a Nobel Prize-winning physicist for the World's Fair of 1937. The exhibits focus on invention and innovation

9 Palais de l'Elysée

MAP D3 ▪ 55 Rue du Faubourg St-Honoré, 75008 ▪ Closed to the public

Built in 1718, after the Revolution this elegant palace was turned into a dance hall, then, in the 19th century, became the residence of Napoleon's sister Caroline Murat, followed by his wife Empress Josephine. His nephew, Napoleon III, also lived here while plotting his 1851 coup. Since 1873 it has been the home of the president of France. For this reason, it is worth noting that the palace guards don't like people getting too close to the building (see p47).

Musée Jacquemart-André

10 Musée Jacquemart-André

MAP C2 ▪ 158 Blvd Haussmann, 75008 ▪ 01 45 62 11 59 ▪ Open 10am–6pm daily (to 8:30pm Mon for temporary exhibits) ▪ Admission charge ▪ www. musee-jacquemart-andre.com

This fine display of art and furniture, once belonging to avid collectors Edouard André and his wife Nélie Jacquemart, is housed in a late 19th-century mansion. It is best known for its Italian Renaissance works, including frescoes by Tiepolo and Paolo Uccello's *St George and the Dragon* (c.1435). The reception rooms feature the art of the 18th-century "Ecole française", with paintings by François Boucher and Jean-Honoré Fragonard. Flemish masters are to be found in the library.

A DAY OF SHOPPING

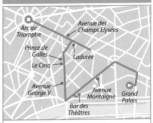

▶ MORNING

The Champs-Elysées quarter is a good area for leisurely walks. Start the morning strolling the grounds of the *belle époque* **Grand Palais** (see p111). The galleries host excellent exhibitions.

Make your way to the **Avenue Montaigne** for exquisite window-shopping – Prada and Dior, among others, have their flagship stores here. Take a break in the **Bar des Théâtres** (*44 Rue Jean Goujon • 01 47 23 34 63*), where fashion names and the theatre crowd from the Comédie des Champs-Elysées hang out.

Call ahead for a table at **Le Cinq** (see p117) to splurge on lunch, and head up the elegant **Avenue Georges V**, which is lined with luxury boutiques including Armani and Hermès, and grande-dame hotels such as legendary **Prince de Galles** (see p173).

AFTERNOON

Walk to and along the **Champs-Elysées** (see p111), with French chanteur Joe Dassin's jaunty 1969 tune in mind. The flagship stores of lots of high-end brands are here, along with luxury car show-rooms and fast-food outlets – housed in some notable buildings.

For tea and cakes en route, **Ladurée** (*75 Ave des Champs-Elyseés • 01 40 75 08 75*) is a wonderfully elegant experience.

Take the underpass to the **Arc de Triomphe** (see pp30–31) and climb to the top for the views, which are superb at dusk when the avenues radiating out from here light up.

See map on p110–11 ←

International Connections

1 **Avenue de Marigny**
MAP C3

American author John Steinbeck lived here for five months in 1954 and described Parisians as "the luckiest people in the world".

2 **8 Rue Artois**
MAP C2

Here, in September 2001, legendary Belgian mobster François Vanverbergh – godfather of the French Connection gang – fell victim to a drive-by assassin as he took his afternoon mineral water.

3 **37 Avenue Montaigne**
MAP C3

Having wowed Paris with her come-back performances, iconic German actress and singer Marlene Dietrich spent her reclusive final years in a luxury apartment here.

4 **Pont de l'Alma**
MAP C3

Diana, Princess of Wales, was killed in a tragic accident in the underpass here in 1997. Her unofficial memorial nearby attracts thousands of visitors each year *(see p54)*.

5 **31 Avenue George V, Hôtel George V**
MAP C3

A roll-call of rockers – from the Rolling Stones and Jim Morrison to J-Lo and Madonna – have made this hotel their regular Paris home-from-home.

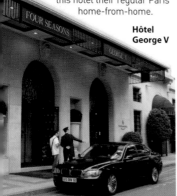

Hôtel George V

Marcel Proust

6 **102 Boulevard Haussmann**
MAP D2

Hypochondriac author Marcel Proust lived in a soundproofed room here, turning memories into a masterwork – *In Search of Lost Time*.

7 **37 Avenue George V**
MAP C3

Franklin D. Roosevelt and his new bride Eleanor visited his aunt's apartment here in 1905. He was later commemorated in the name of a nearby avenue.

8 **49 Avenue des Champs-Elysées**
MAP C3

Author Charles Dickens may well have had "the best of times and the worst of times" when he resided here during the winter of 1855–6. Ten years earlier he had also lived at 38 Rue de Courcelles.

9 **114 Avenue des Champs-Elysées**
MAP C2

Brazilian aviation pioneer Alberto Santos-Dumont planned many of his amazing aeronautical feats – notably that of circling the Eiffel Tower in an airship in 1901 – from this address.

10 **Hôtel d'Elysée-Palace**
MAP C3

Mata Hari, the Dutch spy and exotic dancer, set up her lair in Room 113 before finally being arrested outside 25 Avenue Montaigne.

Events on the Champs-Elysées

1 **1616**
Paris's grand avenue was first laid out when Marie de Médicis, wife of Henri IV, had a carriage route, the Cours-la-Reine (Queen's Way), constructed through the marshland along the Seine.

2 **1667**
Landscape gardener Le Nôtre lengthened the Jardin des Tuileries to meet the Cours-la-Reine, and opened up the view with a double row of chestnut trees, creating the Grand Cours.

3 **1709**
The avenue was renamed the Champs-Elysées (Elysian Fields). In Greek mythology, the Elysian Fields were the "place of ideal happiness", the abode of the blessed after death.

4 **1724**
The Duke of Antin, overseer of the royal gardens, extended the avenue to the heights of Chaillot, the present site of the Arc de Triomphe *(see pp30–31)*.

5 **1774**
Architect Jacques-Germain Soufflot lowered the hill of the Champs-Elysées by 5 m (16 ft) to reduce the steep gradient, therefore making an easier and safer passage for residents' horses and carriages.

6 **26 August 1944**
Parisians celebrated the liberation of the city from Nazi Occupation with triumphant processions and festivities.

7 **30 May 1968**
The infamous demonstrations of May 1968, when student protests against state authority spilled over into massive gatherings and riots. De Gaulle and his supporters held a huge counter-demonstration on the Champs-Elysées, marking a turning point in the uprising.

8 **12 November 1970**
The death of President Charles de Gaulle was an immense event in France, as he had been the single most dominant French political figure for 30 years. He was honoured by a silent parade along the Champs-Elysées.

9 **14 July 1989**
The parade on Bastille Day marking the bicentennial of the Revolution was a dazzling display of folk culture and avant-garde theatre. It was a distinct change from the usual military events, and was organized by Mitterand's Culture Minister, Jack Lang.

Crowds celebrate a World Cup win

10 **12 July 1998**
Huge, ecstatic crowds packed the Champs-Elysées to celebrate France's football team, "Les Bleus", winning the World Cup. People came from all over Paris and beyond to join in the festivities that captured the nation's imagination.

See map on p110–11

Designer Shops

Chanel boutique window

1 Chanel
MAP C3 ▪ 51 Ave Montaigne, 75008

Chanel classics, from the braided tweed jackets to two-toned shoes, as well as Lagerfeld's more daring designs, are displayed in this branch of the main rue Cambon store.

2 Christian Dior
MAP C3 ▪ 30 Ave Montaigne, 75008

The grey and white decor, with silk bows on chairs, makes a chic backdrop for fashions from lingerie to evening wear.

3 Givenchy
MAP C3 ▪ 28 Rue du Faubourg St-Honoré, 75008 ▪ 01 42 68 31 00

This fashion house has been synonymous with Parisian style since the 1930s. Shop for women's and men's ready-to-wear outfits here.

4 Balenciaga
MAP C3 ▪ 10 Ave George V, 75008 ▪ 01 47 20 21 11

This world-famous label is known for its modern creations, which are now designed by Alexander Wang.

5 Boutique Prada
MAP C3 ▪ 10 Ave Montaigne, 75008

The iconic Italian designer's stylish boutique displays clothes and accessories from the latest collection.

6 Joseph
MAP C3 ▪ 14 Ave Montaigne, 75008

Renovated by the leading architect Raed Abilama, this shop stocks the Joseph brand and a selection of other designer labels.

7 Jil Sander
MAP C3 ▪ 56 Ave Montaigne, 75008

A minimal and modern store, just like the clothes it sells. Sander's trouser suits, cashmere dresses and overcoats in neutral colours are displayed on two floors.

8 Chloé
MAP C3 ▪ 44 Ave Montaigne, 75008

Simple, classy, ready-to-wear designer women's clothes and accessories are sold in this minimalist temple to feminine chic.

9 Eres
MAP C3 ▪ 40 Ave Montaigne, 75008 ▪ 01 47 23 07 26

A range of luxury but understated swimwear and lingerie, in subtle colours, is beautifully displayed in this elegant boutique. Everything has a certain Parisian sensuality.

10 Barbara Bui
MAP C3 ▪ 50 Ave Montaigne, 75008 ▪ 01 42 25 05 25

High-end Parisian fashion designer Barbara Bui has been creating elegant womenswear and accessories since the 1980s. Her collection is made from colourful, luxury fabrics.

Barbara Bui bag

Places to Eat

PRICE CATEGORIES
For a three-course meal for one with half
a bottle of wine (or equivalent meal),
taxes and extra charges
....
€ under €30 ■ €€ €30–€50 ■ €€€ over €50

Interior of Epicure

1 **Alain Ducasse au Plaza Athénée**
MAP C3 ■ Hôtel Plaza Athénée, 25 Ave Montaigne, 75008 ■ 01 53 67 65 00 ■ Closed Mon–Wed L, Sat, Sun, Aug, some of Dec ■ €€€

Superchef Alain Ducasse's flagship restaurant. Langoustines with caviar is just one of the mouthwatering, three-Michelin-starred dishes.

2 **Le Mini Palais**
MAP D3 ■ Grand Palais, Ave Winston Churchill, 75008 ■ 01 42 56 42 42 ■ €€€

A modern French restaurant with a beautiful terrace. Try the duck fillet and foie gras burger, complete with a truffle sauce.

3 **Le Café Artcurial**
MAP C3 ■ 7 Rond-Point des Champs-Elysées-Marcel Dassault, 75008 ■ 01 53 76 39 34 ■ Closed Sun ■ €

Modern Italian cuisine is on the menu, along with club sandwiches and home-made burgers, served in a grand former auction house.

4 **Bellota Bellota**
MAP C3 ■ 11 Rue Clément Marot, 75008 ■ 01 47 20 03 13 ■ €

This intimate tapas bar and Spanish deli is a great place for excellent tapas, luxurious carvings of *jamón ibérico* and glasses of Spanish wine.

5 **Taillevent**
MAP C3 ■ 15 Rue Lamennais, 75008 ■ 01 44 95 15 01 ■ Closed Sat, Sun, Aug ■ €€€

One of the city's best dining experiences. The menu changes often, relying on fresh, seasonal ingredients *(see p66)*.

6 **Epicure**
MAP D2 ■ 112 Rue du Faubourg St-Honoré, 75008 ■ 01 53 43 43 40 ■ €€€

In Hotel Le Bristol's elegant dining room or on the garden terrace, diners can choose from chef Eric Frechon's three-Michelin-starred menu.

7 **Gagnaire**
MAP C3 ■ 6 Rue Balzac, 75008 ■ 01 58 36 12 50 ■ Closed Sat, Sun, Aug, 1 week Dec–Jan ■ No disabled access ■ €€€

Chef Pierre Gagnaire is legendary for his artistry in blending flavours.

8 **Bread and Roses**
MAP D3 ■ 25 Rue Boissy d'Anglas, 75008 ■ 01 47 42 40 00 ■ Closed Sun ■ €€

A fabulous tea salon and bakery. Great for breakfast or lunch.

9 **L'Atelier des Chefs**
MAP D2 ■ 10 Rue de Penthièvre, 75008 ■ 01 53 30 05 82 ■ Closed Sun ■ www.atelierdeschefs.fr ■ €

This cooking school offers a range of classes in French, from €17 for a lunchtime session, after which you get to eat the meal you've made.

10 **Le Cinq**
MAP C3 ■ 31 Ave George V, 75008 ■ 01 49 52 70 00 ■ €€€

The George V's *(see p114)* two-Michelin-starred restaurant serves French cuisine with a modern twist.

See map on pp110–11

🔟 Invalides and Eiffel Tower Quarters

Two of Paris's best-known landmarks, the golden-domed Hôtel des Invalides and the Eiffel Tower, are found in these quarters. Large parts of the district were created in the 19th century, when there was still room to construct wide avenues and grassy esplanades. To the east of Les Invalides are numerous stately mansions, now converted into embassies, and the French parliament. Jean Nouvel's Musée du quai Branly is a striking feature beside the Seine.

The top of the Eiffel Tower

AREA MAP OF INVALIDES AND EIFFEL TOWER QUARTERS

1 Hôtel des Invalides
See pp38–9.

2 Eiffel Tower
See pp24–5.

3 Les Egouts
MAP C4 ■ Opposite 93, Quai d'Orsay, 75007 ■ Open May–Sep: 11am–5pm Sat–Wed; Oct–Apr: 11am–4pm Sat–Wed ■ Closed 1 Jan, two weeks mid-Jan, 25 Dec ■ Admission charge

In a city of glamour and grandeur, the sewers *(égouts)* of Paris are an incongruously popular attraction. They date from the Second Empire (1851–70), when Baron Haussmann was transforming the city *(see p43).*

The sewers, which helped to sanitize and ventilate Paris, are considered one of his finest achievements. Engineer Eugène Belgrand provided the designs for the ambitious project. The 2,100-km (1,300-mile) network covers the area from Les Halles to La Villette – if laid end-to-end it would stretch from Paris to Istanbul. An hour-long tour includes a walk through some of the tunnels. The Paris Sewers Museum, which is situated in the sewers beneath the Quai d'Orsay on the Left Bank, tells the story of the city's water and sewers, from their beginnings to the present day through exhibits and an audio-visual show.

4 Musée de l'Armée
MAP C4 ■ Hôtel des Invalides, 75007 ■ Open 10am–6pm Apr-Oct, 10am–5pm Nov-Mar ■ Closed 1 Jan, 1 May, 25 Dec ■ Admission charge

The Army Museum contains one of the largest and most comprehensive collections of arms, armour and displays on military history in the world offering a rich and varied visit. The range of weapons on display include examples from prehistoric times to those used during World War II. Housed in the Hôtel des Invalides, the galleries occupy the old refectories in two wings on either side of the courtyard. The museum's ticket price includes entry to the Musée des Plans-Reliefs, the Historial Charles de Gaulle, the Musée de l'Ordre de la Libération and Napoleon's Tomb *(see pp38–9).*

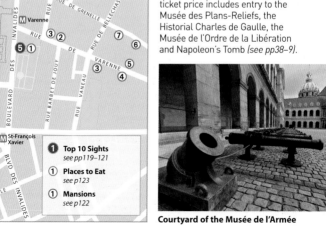

Courtyard of the Musée de l'Armée

(Map legend)

1 **Top 10 Sights**
see pp119–121

1 **Places to Eat**
see p123

1 **Mansions**
see p122

5 Musée Rodin

MAP C4 ■ 79 rue de Varenne, 75007 ■ Open 10am–5:45pm Tue–Sun (until 8:45pm Wed) ■ Closed 1 Jan, 1 May, 25 Dec ■ Admission charge ■ www.musee-rodin.fr

An impressive collection of works by Auguste Rodin (1840–1917) is housed in the splendid 18th-century Hôtel Biron (see p122), where the sculptor and artist spent the last nine years of his life. The museum showcases a broad collection of Rodin's preparatory sketches, watercolours, and bronze and marble masterpieces, including *The Kiss* and *Eve*. Exhibits are displayed chronologically and thematically, showing the creative processes behind the artist's finished sculptures – works that arguably paved the way for modern sculpture. Musée Rodin is also home to the third-largest private garden in Paris, where works such as *The Thinker*, *Monument to Balzac* and *The Gates of Hell* stand amid the lime trees and rose bushes.

6 Musée du Quai Branly

MAP B4 ■ 37 Quai Branly, 75007 ■ Open 11am–7pm Tue–Sun (until 9pm Thu–Sat) ■ Closed 1 May, 25 Dec ■ Admission charge

The purpose of this museum is to showcase the arts of Africa, Asia, Oceania and the Americas. The collection boasts nearly 300,000 artifacts, of which 3,500 are on

display, including a fantastic array of African instruments, Gabonese masks, Aztec statues and 17th-century painted animal hides from North America (once the pride of the French royal family). Designed by Jean Nouvel, the building is an exhibit in itself: glass is ingeniously used to allow the surrounding greenery to act as a natural backdrop to the collection.

7 Rue Cler

MAP C4

The pedestrianized cobblestone road that stretches south of rue de Grenelle to avenue de La Motte-Picquet is the most exclusive street market in Paris. Here greengrocers, fishmongers, butchers and wine merchants sell top-quality produce to the well-heeled residents of the area. Tear yourself away from the mouthwatering displays of cheeses and pastries, however, to feast your eyes on the Art Nouveau buildings at Nos. 33 and 151.

8 Ecole Militaire

MAP C5 ■ 1 Pl Joffre, 75007 ■ Open to the public by special permission only (apply in writing)

At the urging of his mistress Madame Pompadour, Louis XV approved the building of the Royal Military Academy in 1751. Although its purpose was to educate the sons of impoverished officers, a grand edifice was designed by Jacques-Ange Gabriel, architect of the place de la Concorde (see p103) and the Petit Trianon at Versailles, and completed in 1773. The central pavilion with its quadrangular dome

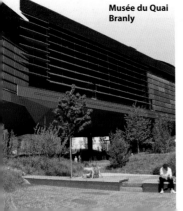

Musée du Quai Branly

and Corinthian pillars is a splendid example of the French Classical style. The massive complex is still in use as a military school today.

Façade of the Ecole Militaire

⑨ UNESCO
MAP C5 ▪ 7 Pl de Fontenoy, 75007 ▪ 01 45 68 10 00
▪ By appointment only

The headquarters of the United Nations Educational, Scientific and Cultural Organization (UNESCO) was built in 1958 by an international team of architects from France, Italy and the United States. The Y-shaped building of concrete and glass may seem unremarkable, but inside, the showcase of 20th-century work by renowned international artists is well worth a visit. There is a huge mural by Picasso, ceramics by Joan Miró, and a 2nd-century mosaic from El Djem in Tunisia. Outside is a giant mobile by Alexander Calder and a peaceful Japanese garden.

⑩ Assemblée Nationale
MAP D4 ▪ 33 Quai d'Orsay, 75007 ▪ Open for tours only (passport required); advance reservation required, see www. assemblee-nationale.fr

Built for the daughter of Louis XIV in 1722, the Palais Bourbon has housed the lower house of the French parliament since 1827. The Council of the Five Hundred met here during the Revolution, and it was the headquarters of the German Occupation during World War II.

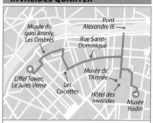

A DAY AROUND THE INVALIDES QUARTER

▶ MORNING

Begin the day with a visit to the **Musée Rodin** *(see p120)*. A magnificent collection of Rodin's works is displayed both indoors, and outside in the attractive garden. Stop for a coffee on the leafy terrace of the garden café.

Stroll through the Esplanade des Invalides, with the **Hôtel des Invalides** *(see pp38–9)* as a grand backdrop. Pause to watch the *pétanque* players who gather in the shade of the trees along the eastern and western sides. Stop in to see **Napoleon's Tomb** and the **Musée de l'Armée** *(see p119)*. Towards the Seine, admire the splendid **Pont Alexandre III** *(see p55)* before heading towards rue Saint-Dominique for lunch at **Les Cocottes** *(see p123)*, top chef Christian Constant's breezy, informal bistro.

AFTERNOON

After lunch, follow the rue de l'Université to the **Musée du Quai Branly** *(see p120)*, where you can enjoy the fascinating collections of tribal art and superb modern architecture. The Café Branly, located in the museum's restful gardens, is the perfect place to stop and enjoy a cup of tea.

Make sure you book ahead, by phone or online, for a late after-noon visit to the **Eiffel Tower** *(see pp24–5)*. The views are spectacular at dusk. Splash out on dinner at the world-famous **Le Jules Verne** on level 2 *(see p66)*, or head back to the Quai Branly museum and its rooftop restaurant, **Les Ombres** *(see p123)*.

See map on p118–19 ←

Mansions

Façade of the elegant Hôtel Biron

1 Hôtel Biron
Built in 1730, from 1904 this elegant mansion was transformed into state-owned artists' studios. Among its residents was Auguste Rodin (1840–1917). After the sculptor's death the house became the Musée Rodin *(see p120)*.

2 Hôtel de Villeroy
MAP D4 ▪ 78–80 Rue de Varenne, 75007 ▪ Closed to the public
Built in 1724 for Comedie-Française actress Charlotte Desmarnes, this is now the Ministry of Agriculture.

3 Hôtel Matignon
MAP D4 ▪ 57 Rue de Varenne, 75007 ▪ Closed to the public
One of the most beautiful mansions in the area is now the official residence of the French prime minister.

4 Hôtel de Boisgelin
MAP D4 ▪ 47 Rue de Varenne, 75007 ▪ Call 01 49 54 03 00 for appointment
Built in 1732 by Jean Sylvain Cartaud, this mansion has housed the Italian Embassy since 1938.

5 Hôtel de Gallifet
MAP D4 ▪ 50 Rue de Varenne, 75007 ▪ Galleries open 10am–1pm, 3–6pm daily
This attractive mansion was built between 1776 and 1792 in Classical style. It is now the Italian Institute.

6 Hôtel d'Estrées
MAP B5 ▪ 79 Rue de Grenelle, 75007 ▪ Closed to the public
Three floors of pilasters feature on the 1713 former Russian embassy. Tsar Nicolas II lived here in 1896. It is now a government building.

7 Hôtel d'Avaray
MAP B5 ▪ 85 Rue de Grenelle, 75007 ▪ Closed to the public
Dating from 1728, this mansion belonged to the Avaray family for nearly 200 years. It became the Dutch Embassy in 1920.

8 Hôtel de Brienne
MAP D4 ▪ 14–16 Rue St Dominique, 75007 ▪ Closed to the public
This mansion houses the Ministry of Defence. Napoleon's mother lived here from 1806 to 1817.

9 Hôtel de Noirmoutiers
MAP B5 ▪ 138–140 Rue de Grenelle, 75007 ▪ Closed to the public
Built in 1724, this was once the army staff headquarters. It now houses ministerial offices.

10 Hôtel de Monaco de Sagan
MAP D4 ▪ 57 Rue St-Dominique, 75007 ▪ Closed to the public
Now the Polish ambassador's house, this 1784 mansion served as the British Embassy until 1825.

Places to Eat

1 Le Jules Verne
MAP B4 ▪ 2nd Level, Eiffel Tower, 75007 ▪ 01 45 55 61 44 ▪ No disabled access ▪ €€€
Book a window table for the view and then sit back and enjoy fine food from kitchen of Alain Ducasse. A reservation is required for dinner.

2 Le Casse-Noix
MAP B5 ▪ 56 Rue de la Fédération, 75015 ▪ 01 45 66 09 01 ▪ Closed Sat & Sun ▪ No disabled access ▪ €€
A charming restaurant serving classic desserts such as *île flottante* (a poached meringue "island" floating on a "sea" of vanilla custard).

3 L'Arpège
MAP D4 ▪ 84 Rue de Varenne, 75007 ▪ 01 47 05 09 06 ▪ Closed Sat, Sun ▪ No disabled access ▪ €€€
Among the best restaurants in the city. Chef Alain Passard produces exquisite food.

4 David Toutain
MAP D4 ▪ 29 Rue Surcouf, 75007 ▪ 01 45 50 11 10 ▪ Closed Sat, Sun ▪ €€
Chef David Toutain delivers eclectic Michelin-starred cuisine that showcases fine seasonal produce and includes vegetarian dishes. The set lunch menu offers good value.

David Toutain interior

5 Café Constant
MAP C4 ▪ 139 Rue St-Dominique, 75007 ▪ 01 47 53 73 34 ▪ No disabled access ▪ €
This classic Parisian establishment serves seasonal, modern French fare to locals and tourists alike.

6 Thoumieux
MAP C4 ▪ 79 Rue St-Dominique, 75007 ▪ 01 47 05 49 75 ▪ €€€
Inventive cuisine by former Crillon chef Jean-François Piège, in a historic brasserie setting.

7 L'Ami Jean
MAP C4 ▪ 27 Rue Malar, 75007 ▪ 01 47 05 86 89 ▪ Closed Sun, Mon ▪ No disabled access ▪ €€€
Inventive dishes such as marinated scallops with ewe's milk cheese.

8 Les Cocottes de Constant
MAP C4 ▪ 135 Rue St-Dominique, 75007 ▪ 01 45 50 10 31 ▪ €
Star chef Christian Constant's French take on a diner, with bar seating and delicious food.

9 Les Ombres
MAP B4 ▪ 27 Quai Branly, 75007 ▪ 01 47 53 68 00 ▪ €€€
Fine food from rising star Sebastien Tasset. Ask for a table with a view of the Eiffel Tower.

10 La Fontaine de Mars
MAP C4 ▪ 129 Rue St-Dominique, 75007 ▪ 01 47 05 46 44 ▪ €€€
The rich, hearty cuisine of southwest France can be found on the menu here, with specialities such as cassoulet and duck confit.

TOP 10 St-Germain, Latin and Luxembourg Quarters

St-Germain-des-Prés is a synonym for Paris's café society, made famous by the writers and intellectuals who held court here in the first half of the 20th century. The Latin Quarter has been the scholastic centre of Paris for more than 700 years, and continues to buzz with student bookshops, cafés and jazz clubs. The area's western border is the bustling Boulevard St-Michel; to the south is the tranquil greenery of the Luxembourg Quarter.

Jardin du Luxembourg

AREA MAP OF ST-GERMAIN, LATIN AND LUXEMBOURG QUARTERS

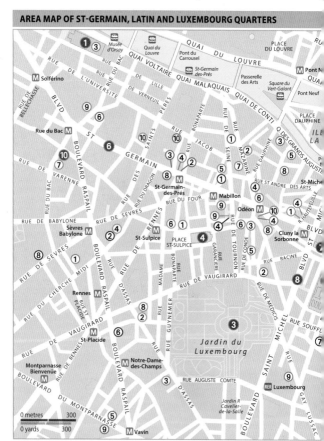

① Musée d'Orsay
See pp16–19.

② The Panthéon
See pp34–5.

③ Jardin du Luxembourg
MAP L6

This 25-ha (60-acre) park is a swathe of green on the very urban Left Bank. The formal gardens are set around the Palais du Luxembourg *(see p47)*, with broad terraces circling the central octagonal pool. A highlight of the garden is the beautiful Medici Fountain *(see p57)*. Statues, erected in the 19th century, include the

Palais du Luxembourg

painter Eugène Delacroix and St Geneviève, patron saint of Paris. There is also a children's playground, open-air café, a bandstand, tennis courts, a puppet theatre and even a bee-keeping school *(see p56)*.

④ St-Sulpice
MAP L5 ▪ **2 Rue Palatine, Pl St-Sulpice, 75006** ▪ **Open 7:30am–7:30pm daily**

Begun in 1646, this vast church took 134 years to build. Its Classical façade features a two-tiered colonnade and two incongruously matched towers. The two holy water fonts by the front door are made from huge shells given to François I by the Venetian Republic. *Jacob Wrestling with the Angel* and other fine murals by Delacroix (1798–1863) are in the chapel to the right of the main door.

⑤ La Sorbonne
MAP M5 ▪ **47 Rue des Ecoles, 75005** ▪ **01 40 46 23 48** ▪ **Group tours only, Mon–Fri and one Sat each month (advance booking)** ▪ **Admission charge**

This famous university *(see p47)* was founded in 1253 as a theology college for poor students. It soon became the country's main centre for religious studies. Philosophers Thomas Aquinas (c.1226–74) and Roger Bacon (1214–92) taught here; Italian poet Dante (1265–1321), founder of the Jesuits St Ignatius Loyola (1491–1556), and church reformer John Calvin (1509–64) are among its list of alumni. Its tradition for conservatism led to its closure during the Revolution (it was reopened by Napoleon in 1806) and also the student riots of 1968.

6 Boulevard St-Germain
MAP J3

This famous Left Bank boulevard runs for more than 3 km (2 miles), anchored by the bridges of the Seine at either end. At its heart is the church of St-Germain-des-Prés, established in 542, although the present church dates from the 11th century. Beyond the famous literary cafés, Flore and Les Deux Magots *(see p131)*, the boulevard runs west past art galleries, bookshops and designer boutiques to the Pont de la Concorde. To the east, it cuts across the Latin Quarter, running through the pleasant street market in the place Maubert, to join the Pont de Sully, which connects to the Ile St-Louis *(see p80)*.

7 Musée National du Moyen Age
MAP N5 ■ 6 Pl Paul Painlevé, 75005
■ Open 9:15am–5:45pm Wed–Mon
■ Closed 1 Jan, 1 May, 25 Dec
■ Admission charge ■ www.musee-moyenage.fr

This impressive mansion was built by the abbots of Cluny at the end of the 15th century and now houses a magnificent collection of art, from the Gallo-Roman period to the 15th century. It adjoins the ruins of 2nd-century Roman baths *(thermes)* with their huge vaulted *frigidarium* (cold bath). Nearby are the 21 carved stone heads of the kings of Judea from Notre-Dame, decapitated during the Revolution. The highlight is the exquisite *Lady and the Unicorn* tapestry series, representing the five senses *(see p50)*.

8 Boulevard St-Michel
MAP M4

The main drag of the Latin Quarter was created in the late 1860s as part of Baron Haussmann's citywide

Trees line the fashionable Boulevard St-Germain

makeover (see p43), and named after a chapel that once stood near its northern end. It is now lined with a lively mix of cafés, clothes shops and cheap restaurants. Branching off to the east are rues de la Harpe and de la Huchette, which date back to medieval times. The latter forms an enclave of the city's Greek community, with many *souvlaki* stands and Greek restaurants. Place St-Michel was a pivotal spot during the Nazi occupation and again in the student riots of 1968. Its huge bronze fountain depicts St Michael killing a dragon.

Statue of St Michael

⑨ Quai de la Tournelle
MAP P5

From this riverbank, just before the Pont de l'Archevêché, there are lovely views across to Notre-Dame. The main attraction of this and the adjacent Quai de Montebello, however, are the dark-green stalls of the *bouquinistes* (see p128). The Pont de la Tournelle also offers splendid views up and down the Seine.

⑩ Musée Maillol
MAP J4 ■ 59–61 Rue de Grenelle, 75007 ■ Currently closed for renovations ■ www.museemaillol.com

Dina Vierny, who modelled for the artist Aristide Maillol (1861–1944) from the ages of 15 to 25, went on to set up this foundation dedicated largely to his works. Located in an 18th-century mansion, it features sculpture, paintings, drawings, engravings and terracotta works. The museum puts on two temporary exhibitions per year, and there are also works by masters of French Naïve art, including Rousseau, as well as drawings by Degas, Matisse and Picasso (see p53).

A DAY ON THE LEFT BANK

▶ **MORNING**

This area is as much about atmosphere as sightseeing, so take time to soak up some of that Left Bank feeling. Begin on the **Quai de la Tournelle**, strolling by the booksellers here and on the adjacent **Quai de Montebello**, which runs parallel to rue de la Bûcherie, home to **Shakespeare and Company** (see p128).

From here head south down any street away from the river to the busy **Boulevard St-Germain**. Turn right for two famous cafés, the **Flore** and **Les Deux Magots**, and stop for a break at either one (see p131), joining the locals talking the morning away.

Cut your way south to the Rue de Grenelle and the **Musée Maillol**, a truly delightful, lesser-known museum. Then enjoy lunch at **l'Épi Dupin** (see p133), a popular bistro that attracts a mix of locals and tourists.

AFTERNOON

The later you reach the **Musée d'Orsay** (see pp16–19) the less crowded it will be, but you'll want to spend at least an hour or two browsing the collections. The most popular works on display are those of the Impressionists, on the upper level.

When you've finished exploring the museum, you can rest and enjoy tea and cake in the stylish **Café Campana** or, if it's dinner time, visit the museum's *belle époque* dining room overlooking the Seine and indulge in their set menu (Thu only).

See map on pp124–5 ⬅

Booksellers

Shakespeare and Company

1 Shakespeare and Company
MAP N5 ■ 37 Rue de la Bûcherie, 75005

Bibliophiles spend hours in the rambling rooms and narrow passageways of Paris's renowned English-language bookshop. There are regular author events and readings in English and French.

2 Bouquinistes
MAP N5

The green stalls of the booksellers (bouquinistes) on the quays of the Left Bank are a Parisian landmark. Pore over the posters, old postcards, magazines, hardbacks, paperbacks, comics and sheet music.

3 Musée d'Orsay Bookshop

As well as its wonderful collections, the museum has a remarkably large and busy art bookshop (see pp16–19).

Abbey Bookshop

4 La Hune
MAP K4 ■ 170 Blvd St-Germain, 75006

This renowned literary hang-out has good collections on art, photography and literature.

5 Gibert Jeune
MAP F5 ■ 5 Place St-Michel, 27 Quai St-Michel, 75006

A couple of bookshops that sell everything from travel guides and French literature to cookery books and children's stories.

6 Album
MAP L4 ■ 8 Rue Dante, 75005

This shop specializes in comic books (big business in France) from Tintin to erotica, as well as related merchandise.

7 Librairie Présence Africaine
MAP P6 ■ 25 Bis, Rue des Ecoles, 75005 ■ Closed Aug

A specialist on books about Africa, as the name suggests. It's an excellent information point, too, if you want to find out where to eat African food or hear African music.

8 San Francisco Book Co.
MAP M5 ■ 17 Rue Monsieur le Prince, 75006

This hodge-podge of all genres carries exclusively used English books at reasonable prices, as well as collectibles and a carefully chosen selection of new titles and classics. If you have books to sell, there is usually a buyer on duty.

9 Librairie Maeght
MAP N5 ■ 42 Rue du Bac, 75007

Books on art are the focus here, next to the Maeght art gallery, as well as posters, postcards and other items.

10 Abbey Bookshop
MAP N5 ■ 29 Rue de la Parcheminerie, 75005

This quirky, Canadian-owned shop stocks books in French and English and serves coffee with maple syrup.

Specialist Food Shops

1 Patrick Roger
MAP F5 ▪ 108 Blvd St-Germain, 75006

One of the new generation of *chocolatiers*, Patrick Roger already has legions of fans thanks to his lifelike sculptures and ganache-filled chocolates.

2 Christian Constant
MAP E5 ▪ 37 Rue d'Assas, 75006 ▪ 01 53 63 15 15

Renowned chef Christian Constant's chocolate shop offers ganache, truffles and filled chocolates in a wide range of flavours.

3 Jean-Paul Hévin
MAP E6 ▪ 3 Rue Vavin, 75006 ▪ Closed Sun, Mon, Aug

Another distinguished *chocolatier*. Elegant, minimalist presentation and superb flavour combinations.

4 Poilâne
MAP E5 ▪ 8 Rue du Cherche-Midi, 75006 ▪ Closed Sun

Founded in the 1930s, this tiny bakery produces rustic, naturally leavened loaves in a wood-fired oven (see p132).

5 La Dernière Goutte
MAP E5 ▪ 6 Rue Bourbon Le Château, 75006

The owners of this English-speaking wine shop, which specializes in bottles from small producers, also run the nearby wine bar Fish.

6 Pierre Hermé Paris
MAP L5 ▪ 72 Rue Bonaparte, 75006

This bakery sells some of the city's very finest cakes and pastries, including innovative flavoured *macarons*.

7 Ryst Dupeyron
MAP N5 ▪ 79 Rue du Bac, 75007 ▪ Closed Sun, Mon am

Atmospheric wine shop specializing in fine Bordeaux, rare spirits and vintage Champagne.

8 Sadaharu Aoki
MAP E5 ▪ 35 Rue de Vaugirard, 75006 ▪ Closed Mon

Aoki cleverly incorporates Japanese flavours such as yuzu, green tea and black sesame into intoxicating classic French pastries that taste as good as they look.

9 Gérard Mulot
MAP L4 ▪ 76 Rue de Seine, 75006 ▪ Closed Wed

Here you'll find some of the finest pastries in Paris, along with some truly miraculous *macarons*.

10 Debauve & Gallais
MAP K4 ▪ 30 Rue des Sts-Pères, 75007 ▪ Closed Sun

This exquisite shop dates from 1800 when chocolate was sold for medicinal purposes.

Historic interior of Debauve & Gallais chocolatier

See map on pp124–5 ←

Late-Night Bars

1 Café de la Mairie
MAP K5 ▪ 8 Pl St-Sulpice, 75006

This is an old-fashioned Parisian café, which offers great views of St-Sulpice church from its busy pavement terrace. It is open until 2am daily except Sunday.

2 Prescription Cocktail Club
MAP L4 ▪ 23 Rue Mazarine, 75006

The expertly mixed drinks are the main attraction at this chic and hip cocktail bar.

3 Le Hibou
MAP M4 ▪ 16 Carrefour de l'Odéon, 75006

Night owls flock to this stylish restaurant and bar serving cocktails till 2am. On a summer night, stake out a spot on the large terrace.

4 Castor Club
MAP M4 ▪ 14 Rue Hautefeuille, 75006 ▪ Closed Sun, Mon

Clandestine cocktail bar with a great menu and a downstairs section.

5 Le 10 Bar
MAP L5 ▪ 10 Rue de l'Odéon, 75006

This incredibly lively sangria bar, with an old jukebox, has been a neighbourhood institution since 1955. Happy hour is 6–8pm.

Interior of Le 10 Bar

Lounge area in Pub Saint-Germain

6 Pub Saint-Germain
MAP L4 ▪ 17 Rue l'Ancienne Comédie, 75006

Sip drinks until dawn at this pub à la français. It has tables and lounge areas on three floors.

7 Mezzanine
MAP L3 ▪ Alcazar, 62 Rue Mazarine, 75006

The lounge bar of the legendary Alcazar is the place to be seen. Drinks are not expensive given the buzz and the wonderful location.

8 Le Bob Cool
MAP M4 ▪ 15 Rue des Grands Augustins, 75006 ▪ Closed Sun

Close to St-Michel, this shabby-chic bar plays host to thirsty local nighthawks as well as trendier partygoers on late-night cocktails.

9 Coolin
MAP L4 ▪ 15 Rue Clément, 75006

An Irish bar that appeals to drinkers, talkers and listeners of all ages, who like their draught Guinness with a blarney chaser.

10 L'Avant Comptoir
MAP M4 ▪ 3 Carrefour de l'Odéon, 75006

It's standing room only at this convivial wine bar next door to the hugely popular Le Comptoir du Relais restaurant (see p133). Tuck in to gorgeous charcuterie, interesting hors d'oeuvres and fantastic wines by the glass.

Literary Haunts

1 La Palette
MAP L4 ■ 43 Rue de Seine, 75006 ■ Open 8am–2am daily

This café has been patronized by the likes of Henry Miller, Apollinaire and Jacques Prévert.

2 Les Deux Magots
MAP K4 ■ 6 Pl St-Germain-des-Prés, 75006 ■ Open 7:30am–1am daily

This was home to the literary and artistic élite of Paris. It was a haunt of Surrealists such as François Mauriac and Existentialists Sartre and de Beauvoir *(see p68)*.

3 Café de Flore
MAP K4 ■ 172 Blvd St-Germain, 75006 ■ Open 7am–2am daily

Guillaume Apollinaire founded his literary magazine, *Les Soirées de Paris*, here in 1913 *(see p68)*.

4 Le Procope
MAP L4 ■ 13 Rue de l'Ancienne Comédie, 75006 ■ Open 11:45am–midnight Sun–Wed, 11:45am–1am Thu–Sat

The oldest café in Paris, this was a meeting place for writers such as Voltaire, Balzac and Zola.

5 Le Sélect
MAP E6 ■ 99 Blvd du Montparnasse, 75006 ■ Open 7am–2am daily (to 3am Fri & Sat)

F. Scott Fitzgerald and Truman Capote are among many American writers who have drunk in this café.

6 Hotel Pont Royal
MAP J3 ■ 5–7 Rue de Montalembert, 75007 ■ Open 11am–midnight daily

Henry Miller drank here at the time of writing his *Tropic of Capricorn* and *Tropic of Cancer*.

7 Shakespeare and Company
This renowned bookshop was once described by novelist Henry Miller as a "wonderland of books" *(see p128)*.

Beautiful Brasserie Lipp

8 Brasserie Lipp
MAP L4 ■ 151 Blvd St-Germain, 75006 ■ Open 9am–1am daily

Ernest Hemingway pays homage to this café in *A Moveable Feast*, and André Gide was also a customer. It sponsors an annual literary prize.

9 La Coupole
MAP E6 ■ 102 Blvd du Montparnasse, 75014 ■ Open 8:30am–midnight (to 11pm Sun & Mon)

This former coal depot became a lavish Art Deco brasserie frequented by Françoise Sagan.

10 Le Petit St-Benoît
MAP K3 ■ 4 Rue St-Benoît, 75006 ■ Open noon–2:30pm, 6:30–10:30pm Tue–Sat

Albert Camus, Simone de Beauvoir and James Joyce once took their daily coffee here.

See map on pp124–5

Picnic Providers

1 Rue de Buci Market
MAP L4

Head for the stalls and shops of this chic daily market to find the very best regional produce, wine and patisserie *(see p71)*.

2 Poilâne
MAP J5 ▪ 8 Rue du Cherche-Midi, 75006

The best bread in France, made from the recipe of the late king of bread-makers, Lionel Poilâne *(see p129)*.

3 Maubert Market
MAP N5 ▪ Pl Maubert, 75006

A small market specializing in organic produce every Tuesday, Thursday and Saturday morning. A good place to pick up olives, cheese, tomatoes and fruit.

4 Gérard Mulot
MAP L4 ▪ 76 Rue de Seine, 75006

Tarts, sandwiches and good breads from this up-market patisserie and deli make for a chic picnic.

5 Naturalia
MAP N6 ▪ 36 Rue Monge, 75005 ▪ Closed Sun

For a fully organic picnic, look no further: excellent breads, wines, cheeses, hams, fruits, desserts and much more.

6 Marché Raspail
MAP J4 ▪ Blvd Raspail, 75006

This food market is held in the morning on Tuesday, Friday and Sunday (when it is all organic). Superb produce but pricey.

7 Bon
MAP N5 ▪ 159 Rue St-Jacques, 75005 ▪ Closed Mon

Wonderful patisserie and chocolatier, with a good line in small fruit tarts, and chocolates in the shape of the Eiffel Tower.

8 La Grande Epicerie de Paris
MAP D5 ▪ Le Bon Marché, 38 Rue de Sèvres, 75007

Hunt for treasures such as Breton seaweed butter and *coucou de Rennes* at the food hall in Le Bon Marché *(see p71)*.

9 Le Pirée
MAP N5 ▪ 47 Blvd St-Germain, 75005

Delicious, freshly prepared Greek and Armenian specialities, such as stuffed vegetables and honey-soaked cakes, are sold here.

10 Kayser
MAP P6 ▪ 14 Rue Monge, 75005

If you don't want to make up your own picnic then try a ready-made sandwich from this bakery. Mouth-watering combinations include goat's cheese with pear.

Interior of Kayser

Places to Eat

PRICE CATEGORIES

For a three-course meal for one with half a bottle of wine (or equivalent meal), taxes and extra charges

€ under €30   €€ €30–€50   €€€ over €50

1 L'Épi Dupin
MAP J5 ■ 11 Rue Dupin, 75006 ■ 01 42 22 64 56 ■ Closed Sat, Sun, Mon L, Aug ■ €€

Dishes such as scallop risotto or mussels and sweet potato are sublime – reserve a table in advance.

2 La Bastide Odéon
MAP L5 ■ 7 Rue Corneille, 75006 ■ 01 43 26 03 65 ■ No disabled access ■ €€

A taste of Provence in an elegant setting. Dishes include bouillabaisse, seared tuna and fried squid.

3 Les Bouquinistes
MAP M4 ■ 53 Quai des Grands Augustins, 75006 ■ 01 43 25 45 94 ■ No disabled access ■ €€€

Creative cooking is served at this bistro, owned by Guy Savoy, on the banks of the Seine.

4 Le Comptoir du Relais
MAP L5 ■ 9 Carrefour de l'Odéon, 75006 ■ 01 44 27 07 97 ■ €

Yves Camdeborde's much-praised restaurant serves excellent bistro lunches and prix-fixe dinners.

5 Lapérouse
MAP M4 ■ 51 Quai des Grands Augustins, 75006 ■ 01 43 26 68 04 ■ Closed Sat L, Sun, Aug ■ €€€

Classic French cuisine is served in a setting that has remained unchanged since 1766.

6 La Crèmerie
MAP L5 ■ 9 Rue des Quatre Vents, 75006 ■ 01 43 54 99 30 ■ Closed Sun ■ €

Beyond the charming façade of this intimate wine bar and informal bistro, you'll find delectable small plates of

La Tour d'Argent

charcuterie, cheese and duck rillettes to share. The gorgeously creamy burrata is a must-try.

7 La Tour d'Argent
MAP P5 ■ 15 Quai de la Tournelle, 75005 ■ 01 43 54 23 31 ■ Closed Sun, Mon, Aug ■ €€€

This historic restaurant with fine views of Notre-Dame serves duckling as its speciality.

8 Le Pré Verre
MAP F5 ■ 8 Rue Thénard, 75005 ■ 01 43 54 59 47 ■ Closed Sun, Mon, Aug, 25 Dec–1 Jan ■ €

Dine on classic French cooking with Asian flourishes.

9 Les Papilles
MAP F6 ■ 30 Rue Gay Lussac, 75005 ■ 01 43 25 20 79 ■ Closed Sun, Mon, Aug, 25 Dec–1 Jan ■ No disabled access ■ €€

Choose your wine straight off the shelves to accompany the great-value Market or Bistro menus.

10 Au Moulin à Vent
MAP P6 ■ 20 Rue des Fossés St-Bernard, 75005 ■ 01 43 54 99 37 ■ Closed Sat L, Sun, Mon, Aug ■ €€€

One of the best bistros in Paris. Have the frogs' legs sauteed in garlic.

See map on p124–5

TOP 10 Jardin des Plantes Quarter

This is traditionally one of the most peaceful areas of Paris. The medicinal herb gardens that give the quarter its name were established here in 1626. Near the gardens is the Arènes de Lutèce, a well-preserved Roman amphitheatre. Rue Mouffetard, winding down the hill from the bustling place de la Contrescarpe, dates from medieval times and has one of the best markets in the city. The area is also home to a sizable Muslim community, focused on the Paris Mosque and the Institut du Monde Arabe cultural centre.

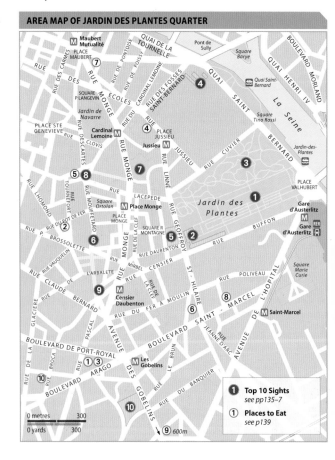

AREA MAP OF JARDIN DES PLANTES QUARTER

❶ Top 10 Sights
see pp135–7

① Places to Eat
see p139

0 metres 300
0 yards 300

1 Jardin des Plantes

MAP G6 ■ 57 Rue Cuvier, 75005
■ 01 40 79 30 00 ■ Open 8am–5:30pm
daily, 7:30am–8pm summer

The 17th-century royal medicinal
herb garden was planted by Jean
Hérouard and Guy de la Brosse,
physicians to Louis XIII. Opened to
the public in 1640, it flourished under
the curatorship of Comte de Buffon.
It contains some 6,500 species, and
10,000 plants. There is also a Cedar
of Lebanon that was planted in 1734,
a hillside maze, and Alpine and rose
gardens (see p138).

2 Muséum National d'Histoire Naturelle

MAP G6 ■ 57 Rue Cuvier, 75005
■ Pavilions: open 10am–5pm Wed–
Mon; Evolution Gallery: open
10am–6pm Wed–Mon ■ Closed 1 May
■ Admission charge ■ www.mnhn.fr

Pavilions in the Jardin des Plantes
house varied exhibits on natural
history. The Grande Galerie de
l'Evolution (see p60) is a magnificent
collection of stuffed African mammals,
a massive whale skeleton and an
endangered species exhibit (see p50).

Flowers in the Jardin des Plantes

3 Ménagerie

MAP G6 ■ Jardin des Plantes,
75005 ■ Open 9am–5pm daily
■ Admission charge

The country's oldest public zoo was
founded during the Revolution to

**Grande Galerie de l'Evolution,
Muséum National d'Histoire Naturelle**

house the surviving animals from the
royal menagerie at Versailles. Other
animals were donated from circuses
around the world. However, during
the Siege of Paris in 1870–71 (see
p43), most of the unfortunate creatures were eaten by hungry citizens.
A favourite with children (see p60),
the zoo has since been restocked.

4 Institut du Monde Arabe

MAP G5 ■ 1 Rue des Fossés
St-Bernard, Pl Mohammed V, 75005
■ 01 40 51 38 38 ■ Open 10am–6pm
Tue–Thu (until 9:30pm Fri, 7pm Sat &
Sun) ■ Admission charge ■ www.
imarabe.org

This institute was founded in 1980 to
promote cultural relations between
France and the Arab world. The
stunning building (1987) designed by
architect Jean Nouvel (see p120)
features a southern wall of 240
ornate photo-sensitive metal screens
that open and close like camera
apertures to regulate light entering
the building. The design is based on
the traditional latticed wooden
screens of Islamic architecture.
Inside is a museum featuring Islamic
artworks, from 9th-century ceramics
to contemporary art, as well as a tea
salon and restaurant.

5 Mosquée de Paris

MAP G6 ▪ 2 Bis Pl du Puits de l'Ermité, 75005 ▪ Tours: 9am–noon, 2–6pm Sat–Thu; closed Islamic hols ▪ Admission charge

Built in 1922–6, the mosque complex is the spiritual centre for Parisian Muslims (see p49). The beautiful Hispano-Moorish decoration, particularly the grand patio, was inspired by the Alhambra in Spain. The minaret soars nearly 33 m (100 ft). The complex has an Islamic school, tearoom and Turkish baths, open to men and women on separate days.

Tearoom in the Mosquée de Paris

6 Rue Mouffetard

MAP F6

Although Rue Mouffetard is most famous today for its lively street market held every Tuesday to Sunday (see p71), it has an equally colourful past. In Roman times this was the main road from Paris to Rome. Some say its name comes from the French word *mouffette* (skunk), as a reference to the odorous River Bièvre (now covered over) where waste was dumped by tanners and weavers from the nearby Gobelins tapestry factory. Though no longer poor nor bohemian, the neighbourhood still

FRENCH NORTH AFRICA

France has long had close connections with North Africa, though not always harmonious. Its annexation of Algeria in 1834 led to the long and bloody Algerian War of Liberation (1954–62). Relations with Tunisia, which it governed from 1883 to 1956, and Morocco, also granted independence in 1956, were better. Many North Africans now live in Paris.

has lots of character, with its 17th-century mansard roofs, old-fashioned painted shop signs and affordable restaurants. In the market you can buy everything from Auvergne sausage to horsemeat and perfectly ripened cheeses.

7 Arènes de Lutèce

MAP G6 ▪ 47 Rue Monge, 75005 ▪ Open 9am–8:30pm daily (summer); 8am–5:30pm daily (winter)

The remains of the 2nd-century Roman amphitheatre from the settlement of Lutetia (see p42) lay buried for centuries and were only discovered in 1869 during construction of Rue Monge. The novelist Victor Hugo, concerned with the preservation of his city's historic buildings, including Notre-Dame (see p23), led the campaign for its restoration. The original arena would have had 35 tiers and could seat 15,000 spectators for theatrical performances and gladiator fights.

8 Place de la Contrescarpe

MAP F5

This bustling square has a village community feel, with busy cafés and restaurants and groups of students from the nearby Lycée Henri-IV hanging out here after dark. In medieval times, it lay outside the city walls, a remnant of which still stands on Rue Clovis. Notice the memorial plaque above the butcher's at No. 1, which marks the site of the old Pine Cone Club, a café where François Rabelais and other writers gathered in the 16th century.

Façade of St-Médard church

⑨ St-Médard

MAP G6 ■ 141 Rue Mouffetard, 75005 ■ Open 8am–12:30pm, 2:30–7:30pm Tue–Sat; 8:30am–12:30pm, 4–8:30pm Sun

The church at the bottom of Rue Mouffetard dates back to the 9th century, when it was a parish church dedicated to St Médard, counsellor to the Merovingian kings. The present church, completed in 1655, is a mixture of Flamboyant Gothic and Renaissance styles. Among the fine paintings inside is the 17th-century *St Joseph Walking with the Christ Child* by Francisco de Zurbarán. The churchyard was the scene of hysterical fits in the 18th century, when a cult of *convulsionnaires* sought miracle cures at the grave of a Jansenist deacon.

⑩ Manufacture des Gobelins

42 Ave des Gobelins, 75013■ Metro Gobelins ■ Guided visits: Tue, Wed, Thu 1pm (3pm during holidays), open for temporary exhibitions only 11am–6pm Tue–Sun ■ Tickets must be bought in advance at branches of FNAC

This internationally renowned tapestry factory was originally a dyeing workshop, founded by the Gobelin brothers in the mid-15th century. In 1662, Louis XIV's minister Colbert set up a royal factory here and gathered the greatest craftsmen of the day to make furnishings for the palace at Versailles *(see p155)*. You can see the traditional weaving process on a guided tour.

A DAY IN THE GARDENS

▶ **MORNING**

Start the day by browsing the stalls at the fabulous market on **Rue Mouffetard**, which gets going by about 8am. Working upwards from the bottom of the street and the church of **St-Médard**, you'll find plenty here to make up a delicious breakfast, whether from the many market stalls or from the grocers and cafés that dot the street. Don't forget to take your eyes off the tempting produce every now and then to see the splendid old buildings on this medieval street.

Follow Rue Mouffetard up to the cheery **Place de la Contrescarpe**, then head to the **Muséum National d'Histoire Naturelle** *(see p135)* and the excellent **Grande Galérie de l'Evolution** *(see p60)*. Stroll through the **Jardin des Plantes** *(see p135)* and take a break on one of the many benches to admire the plantings. Exit through the gate on **Rue Cuvier**, near **Rue Linné**, and make a detour to the **Arènes de Lutèce** on your way to **Le Buisson Ardent** *(see p139)* for a simple, authentic bistro lunch.

AFTERNOON

Spend part of the afternoon at **the Institut du Monde Arabe** *(see p135)*, exploring its beautiful Islamic artworks, before walking down to admire the Moorish architecture of the **Mosquée de Paris**. Finish the day with a mint tea and a selection of maamoul and baklava at the **Café de la Mosquée** *(Pl du Puits de l'Ermité • 01 43 31 18 14)*.

See map on p134 ←

Jardin des Plantes Sights

1 Dinosaur Tree
One of the trees in the Botanical Gardens is a *Ginkgo biloba*, which was planted in 1795, but the species is known to have existed in exactly the same form in the days of the dinosaurs, 125 million years ago.

2 Cedar of Lebanon
This magnificent tree was planted in 1734, and came from London's Botanic Gardens in Kew, although a story grew up that its seed was brought here all the way from Syria in the hat of a scientist.

Cedar of Lebanon

3 Rose Garden
Having only been planted in 1990 and so relatively modern compared to the other gardens, the beautiful *roseraie* has some 170 species of roses and 180 rose bushes on display. Spectacular when in full bloom in spring and summer.

4 Rock Gardens
One of the stars of the Botanical Gardens, with more than 3,000 plants from the world's diverse Alpine regions. There are samples from Corsica to the Caucasus, Morocco and the Himalayas.

5 Sophora Japonica
Sent to Paris under the label "unknown seeds from China" by a Jesuit naturalist living in the Orient, this tree, often called a Pagoda Tree, was planted in 1747, first flowered in 1777, and still flowers today.

6 Iris Garden
An unusual feature is this designated garden which brings together more than 400 different varieties of iris.

7 Dodo Manège
The strange and exotic animals on this magical merry-go-round *(see p61)* include a dodo, a triceratops, a horned turtle and even a sivatherium, which was like a giraffe with antlers.

8 Nile Crocodile
The crocodile in the Reptile House now has a better home than he once did. This creature was found in 1998, when he was six months old, in the bathtub of a Paris hotel room, left behind as an unwanted pet.

9 Young Animal House
One of the zoo's most popular features for children is this house where young creatures, which for one reason or another cannot be looked after by their natural parents, are raised. Once they have reached adulthood they are returned to their natural habitat.

10 Greenhouses
Otherwise known as *Les Grandes Serres*, these 19th-century greenhouses were at one time the largest in the world. Today, they house a rainforest environment, a prickly Mexican cactus garden and a tropical winter garden which is kept at a constant 22°C (74°F) and 80 per cent humidity.

19th-century greenhouse

Places to Eat

La Truffière's vaulted interior

① Le Petit Pascal
33 Rue Pascal, 75013 ■ Metro Gobelins ■ 01 45 35 33 87 ■ Closed Sat, Sun, Aug ■ €

This family-run, provincial-style bistro, popular with locals at dinner, has a menu of regional dishes that changes daily.

② Chez Léna et Mimile
32 Rue Tournefort, 75005 ■ Metro Place Monge ■ 01 47 07 72 47 ■ €€

Those in the know avoid the touristy restaurants around Rue Mouffetard to savour a meal at this ambitious bistro with a peaceful terrace.

③ Au Petit Marguery
MAP F6 ■ 9 Blvd de Port-Royal, 75013 ■ 01 43 31 58 59 ■ €€€

One for meat lovers, with plenty of steak, veal and game on the menu. Boisterous atmosphere.

④ Le Buisson Ardent
MAP G6 ■ 25 Rue Jussieu, 75005 ■ 01 43 54 93 02 ■ Closed Sun D (brunch only Sun) ■ €€

This creative bistro is a romantic night-time destination serving classic French dishes with a twist. Set menus offer good value.

PRICE CATEGORIES

For a three-course meal for one with half a bottle of wine (or equivalent meal), taxes and extra charges

€ under €30 €€ €30–€50 €€€ over €50

⑤ La Truffière
MAP F6 ■ 4 Rue Blainville, 75005 ■ 01 46 33 29 82 ■ Closed Sun, Mon ■ €€€

A 17th-century building, a wood fire and welcoming staff all make for a great little bistro. Naturally, the menu features truffles.

⑥ L'Agrume
MAP G6 ■ 15 Rue des Fossés St-Marcel, 75005 ■ 01 43 31 86 48 ■ No disabled access ■ Closed Sun–Tue ■ €€€

This restaurant is popular for its affordable five-course fixed-price menu of creative modern dishes.

⑦ Patisserie Ciel
MAP N5 ■ 3 Rue Monge, 75005 ■ 01 43 29 40 78 ■ €

This airy Japanese tea house is dedicated to angel cake in a range of imaginative flavours – until nightfall, when it serves Japanese whisky and small savoury plates.

⑧ Au Coco de Mer
MAP G6 ■ 34 Blvd St-Marcel, 75005 ■ 06 20 26 77 67 ■ Closed Sun, Mon L, Aug ■ €€

Spicy Seychelles cuisine, plus a "beach hut" terrace with soft sand. Vegetarians should book ahead.

⑨ L'Avant-Goût
26 Rue Bobillot, 75013 ■ Metro Place d'Italie ■ 01 53 80 24 00 ■ Closed Sun, Mon ■ €€

Small and noisy with tables crammed together. Try the *pot au feu* or apple flan, if available, though the menu changes daily.

⑩ L'Ourcine
92 Rue Broca, 75013 ■ Metro Gobelins ■ 01 47 07 13 65 ■ Closed Sun, Mon ■ €

Locals and visitors like this cozy Basque and Béarnais bistro for its no-fuss, reliably good cooking and affordable southwestern wines. Set menus offer good-value options.

See map on p134

Top10 Chaillot Quarter

Chaillot was a separate village until the 19th century, when it was swallowed up by the growing city and bestowed with wide avenues and grand mansions, many of which now house embassies. The quarter's centrepiece is the glorious Palais de Chaillot, its white-stone wings embracing the Trocadéro Gardens and its terrace facing the Eiffel Tower, across the Seine. Behind the palace is place du Trocadéro, laid out in 1858 and ringed with smart cafés.

Fish sculpture, Cinéaqua

AREA MAP OF CHAILLOT QUARTER

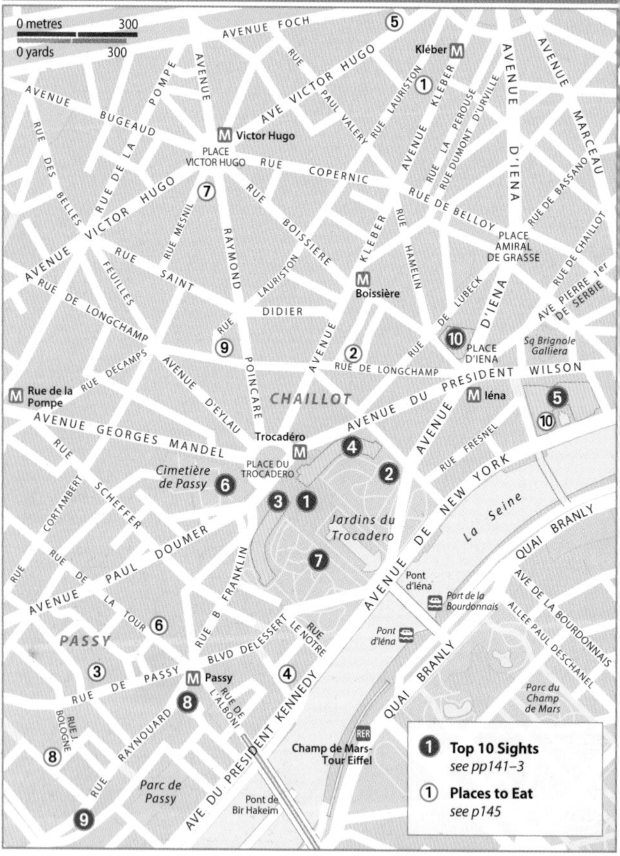

1 **Top 10 Sights**
see pp141–3

1 **Places to Eat**
see p145

View from Palais de Chaillot

① Palais de Chaillot
MAP B4 ■ 17 Pl du Trocadéro, 75016

The fall of his empire scuppered Napoleon's plans for an opulent palace for his son on Chaillot hill, but the site was later used for the Trocadéro palace, built for the Universal Exhibition of 1878. It was replaced by the present Neo-Classical building with its huge colonnaded wings for the prewar exhibition of 1937. The two pavilions house three museums, including the Musée de la Marine. The broad terrace is the domain of souvenir sellers and skateboarders by day, while at night it is crowded with tourists admiring the splendid view of the Eiffel Tower across the Seine. Two bronzes, *Apollo* by Henri Bouchard and *Hercules* by Pommier, stand at the front of the terrace. Beneath the terrace is the 1,200-seat Théâtre National de Chaillot.

② Cinéaqua
MAP B4 ■ 5 Ave Albert de Mun, 75016 ■ Open 10am–7pm daily ■ Closed 14 Jul ■ Admission charge ■ www.cineaqua.com

Originally constructed in 1878 for the Universal Exhibition, this fascinating aquarium is home to over 10,000 species, including seahorses, stonefish and some spectacular sharks and rays. Built into a former quarry, the site has been designed to blend in with the Chaillot hillside. There is also a futuristic cinema complex showing nature films, and a Japanese restaurant.

③ Musée de la Marine
MAP B4 ■ Palais de Chaillot, 17 Pl du Trocadéro, 75016 ■ Open 11am–6pm Wed–Mon (to 7pm Sat & Sun) ■ Closed 1 Jan, 1 May, 25 Dec ■ Admission charge ■ www.musee-marine.fr

Three hundred years of French naval history is the focus of this museum, whether in war, trade and commerce, or industries such as fishing. The displays range from naval art to science to maritime adventure and popular legends and traditions. Among the highlights is an outstanding collection of model ships, from the feluccas of ancient Egypt to medieval galleys and nuclear submarines. You can also watch craftsmen at work on the models. Napoleon's royal barge is another highlight.

④ Cité de l'Architecture et du Patrimoine
MAP B4 ■ Palais de Chaillot, 75116 ■ Open 11am–7pm Wed–Mon (until 9pm Thu) ■ Closed 1 May, 14 Jul, 25 Dec ■ 01 58 51 52 00 ■ Admission charge ■ www.citechaillot.fr

Occupying the east wing of the Palais Chaillot, this museum is a veritable ode to French architectural heritage,

Cité de l'Architecture

GENERAL FOCH

General Ferdinand Foch (1851–1929), whose statue stands in the centre of place du Trocadéro, was commander-in-chief of the Allied armies by the end of World War I. His masterful command ultimately led to victory over Germany in 1918, whereupon he was made a Marshal of France and elected to the French Academy. He is interred at the Hôtel des Invalides (see pp38–9).

---

showcasing its development through the ages as well as contemporary architecture. The Galerie des Moulages (Medieval to Renaissance) contains moulded portions of churches and great French cathedrals including Chartres. The Galerie Moderne et Contemporain includes a reconstruction of an apartment designed by Le Corbusier, and architectural designs from 1990 onwards. The gallery in the Pavillon de Tête has a stunning collection of murals copied from medieval frescoes.

⑤ Musée d'Art Moderne de la Ville de Paris

MAP B4 ▪ 11 Ave du Président Wilson, 75116 ▪ Open 10am–6pm Tue–Sun (until 10pm Thu during temporary exhibitions) ▪ Closed public hols ▪ 01 53 67 40 00 ▪ Admission charge for temporary exhibitions ▪ www.mam.paris.fr

This modern art museum is housed in the east wing of the Palais de Tokyo, built for the 1937 World's Fair. Its permanent collection includes such masters as Chagall, Picasso, Modigliani and Léger; further highlights include Raoul Dufy's enormous mural *The Spirit of Electricity* (1937) and Picabia's *Lovers (After the Rain)* (1925). The museum also showcases the work of up-and-coming artists in the west wing.

⑥ Cimetière de Passy

MAP A4 ▪ Pl du Trocadéro (entrance rue du Commandant Schloessing), 75016

This small cemetery covers only 1 ha (2.5 acres), yet many famous people have been laid to rest here with the Eiffel Tower as their eternal view (see p144). It is worth a visit just to admire the striking sculptures on the tombs.

⑦ Jardins du Trocadéro

MAP B4

Designed in 1937, the tiered Trocadéro Gardens descend gently down Chaillot hill from the palace to the Seine and the Pont d'Iéna. The centrepiece of this 10-ha (25-acre) park is the long rectangular pool lined with stone and bronze statues, including *Woman* by Georges Braque (1882–1963). Its illuminated fountains are spectacular at night. With flowering trees, walkways and bridges over small streams, the gardens are a romantic place for a stroll (see p57).

⑧ Musée du Vin

MAP A4 ▪ 5 Square Charles Dickens, Rue des Eaux, 75016 ▪ Open 10am–6pm Tue–Sun ▪ Admission charge ▪ www.museeduvinparis.com

The vaulted 14th-century cellars where the monks of Passy once made wine are an atmospheric setting for this wine museum. Waxwork figures recreate the history

Aerial view, Jardins du Trocadéro

Exhibits in the Musée du Vin

of the wine-making process, and there are displays of wine paraphernalia. The museum also has tasting sessions, wine for sale and an excellent restaurant.

⑨ Maison de Balzac

MAP A4 ■ 47 Rue Raynouard, 75016 ■ Open 10am–6pm Tue–Sun ■ Closed public hols ■ Admission charge for temporary exhibitions ■ www.balzac.paris.fr

The writer Honoré de Balzac (see p44) rented an apartment here from 1840 to 1844, assuming a false name to avoid his many creditors. He worked on several of his famous novels here, including *La cousine Bette* and *La comédie humaine*. The house is now a museum displaying first editions and manuscripts, personal mementoes and letters, and paintings and drawings of his friends and family. It also houses temporary exhibitions.

⑩ Musée National des Arts Asiatiques–Guimet

MAP B3 ■ 6 Pl d'Iéna, 75116 ■ Open 10am–6pm Wed–Mon ■ Closed 1 Jan, 1 May, 25 Dec ■ Admission charge ■ www.guimet.fr

One of the world's foremost museums of Asiatic and Oriental art, founded in 1889. The Khmer Buddhist temple sculptures from Angkor Wat are the highlight of a fine collection of Cambodian art. Guimet's collection tracing Chinese and Japanese religion from the 4th to 19th centuries is also on display, as are artifacts from India, Indonesia and Vietnam.

A DAY IN CHAILLOT

▶ MORNING

It would be hard to imagine a better start to a day in Paris than going to the **Palais de Chaillot** (see p141) and seeing its perfect view of the **Eiffel Tower** (see pp24–5) across the Seine. Then tour the fascinating collections of the **Cité de l'Architecture** (see pp141–2) and, if marine history is your thing, the **Musée de la Marine** (see p141), both here.

Outside the palace, have lunch at the **Café du Trocadéro** (8 Pl du Trocadéro • 01 44 05 37 00) and watch the comings and goings in the square. Or, for something a little fancier, call ahead and make reservations at the excellent **Le Jamin** (see p145).

AFTERNOON

Revived, walk up to the place d'Iéna, to the refurbished and much improved **Musée National des Arts Asiatiques–Guimet** for its spectacular collection of Eastern artifacts and artworks. On the first floor, spend some time with the remarkable Riboud collection of textiles from India, Japan, China and Indonesia, which includes a number of rare Indian textiles not usually on display elsewhere because of their fragility.

By now you will surely be in need of a rest, so return to the Place du Trocadéro for tea and éclairs at **Café Carette** at No. 4 (01 47 27 98 85). End the day in the peaceful **Cimetière de Passy** before an unforgettable dinner overlooking the lights of the city at the stylish **Le Jules Verne** (see p123).

See map on p140 ⬅

Graves in Cimetière de Passy

1 Edouard Manet

Born in Paris in 1832, Manet became the most notorious artist in the city when works such as *Olympia* and *Le Déjeuner sur l'Herbe (see p16)* were first exhibited. He died in Paris in 1883.

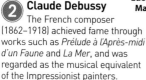

Edouard Manet

2 Claude Debussy

The French composer (1862–1918) achieved fame through works such as *Prélude à l'Après-midi d'un Faune* and *La Mer*, and was regarded as the musical equivalent of the Impressionist painters.

3 Berthe Morisot

The French Impressionist artist was born in Paris in 1841, posed for Edouard Manet and later married his lawyer brother Eugène. She never achieved the fame of the male Impressionists and died in Paris in 1895.

4 Fernandel

The lugubrious French film actor known as Fernandel was born Fernand Contandin in Marseille in 1903.He made more than 100 films in a career that lasted from 1930 until his death in Paris in 1971.

5 Marie Bashkirtseff

This Russian artist became more renowned as a diarist after her death from tuberculosis in 1884. Despite living for only 24 years she produced 84 volumes of diaries and their posthumous publication created a sensation due to their intimate nature.

6 Henri Farman

The French aviator was born in Paris in 1874 and died here in 1958. He was the first man to make a circular 1-km (0.5-mile) flight, and the first to fly cross-country in Europe. His gravestone shows him at the controls of a primitive plane.

7 Comte Emanuel de las Cases

Born in 1766, this historian and friend of Napoleon shared the emperor's exile on the island of St Helena and recorded his memoirs. The Comte himself died in Paris in 1842.

8 Gabriel Fauré

The French composer, probably best known today for his *Requiem*, was a great influence on the music of his time. He died in Paris in 1924, at the age of 79.

9 Octave Mirbeau

The satirical French novelist and playwright was also an art critic and an outspoken journalist. Born in 1848, he died in Cheverchemont in 1917 and his body was brought to Passy for burial.

10 Antoine Cierplikowski

The grave of this fairly obscure artist of the 1920s attracts attention because of its immensely powerful sculpture of a man and woman joined together and seeming to soar from the grave to the heavens.

Grave of Antoine Cierplikowski

Places to Eat

PRICE CATEGORIES
For a three-course meal for one with half
a bottle of wine (or equivalent meal),
taxes and extra charges
....
€ under €30 ■ €€ €30–€50 ■ €€€ over €50

1 Akrame
MAP B2 ■ 19 Rue Lauriston,
75016 ■ 01 40 67 11 16 ■ Closed Sat,
Sun ■ €€€

Chef Akrame Benallal has been
awarded a Michelin star for his
brilliant modern cooking at this
buzzy, relaxed restaurant. Dinner-
time tasting menus are a splurge;
set lunches offer better value.

2 Le Jamin
MAP A3 ■ 32 Rue de
Longchamp, 75116 ■ 01 45 53 00 07
■ Closed Sat L, Sun, Aug ■ No
disabled access ■ €€€

Former Guy Savoy disciple Alain Pras
presides over this elegant, formal
restaurant, offering an inventive
approach to French classics, and
good vegetarian options.

3 Le Bistrot du Chineur
MAP A4 ■ 5 Impasse des
Carrières, 75016 ■ 01 42 88 17 73
■ Closed D, Sat, Sun, Mon ■ €

This is a minuscule, friendly bistro
in an antiques shop, serving good
value, thoughtfully prepared food.
Advance reservation essential, due to
the tiny number of tables available.

4 L'Astrance
MAP B4 ■ 4 Rue Beethoven,
75116 ■ 01 40 50 84 40 ■ Closed Sat–
Mon ■ No disabled access ■ €€€

Pascal Barbot serves fusion food at
its best. Book at least a month in
advance to secure a table.

5 Maison Prunier
MAP B3 ■ 16 Ave Victor Hugo,
75016 ■ 01 44 17 35 85 ■ Closed Sat
L, Sun ■ No disabled access ■ €€€

Fish dishes reign at this restaurant,
with its dazzling Art Deco interior.

6 Comme des Poissons
MAP A4 ■ 24 Rue de la Tour,
75016 ■ 01 45 20 70 37 ■ Closed Mon,
Sun L ■ €

This tiny Japanese sushi restaurant
serves good food at reasonable
prices. Book ahead.

7 Le Petit Rétro
MAP B3 ■ 5 Rue Mesnil, 75016
■ 01 44 05 06 05 ■ Closed Sun ■ No
disabled access ■ €€

Cozy atmosphere and affordable
prices at this 1900s bistro. The
Blanquette de Veau is delicious.

8 Le Bistrot des Vignes
MAP B4 ■ 1 Rue Jean Bologne,
75016 ■ 01 45 27 76 64 ■ No disabled
access ■ €€

Unpretentious little bistro of the type
everyone hopes to find in Paris.

9 La Table Lauriston
MAP A3 ■ 129 Rue Lauriston,
75116 ■ 01 47 27 00 07 ■ Closed Sun,
Sat L, Aug, 1 week over Christmas
■ €€€

Chef Serge Barbey's La Table
Lauriston is a hit with local gourmets
who tuck into his gargantuan steak
and rum-doused *baba* in the jewel-
toned dining room.

Monsieur Bleu terrace

10 Monsieur Bleu
MAP B4 ■ 20 Ave de New York,
75116 ■ 01 47 20 90 47 ■ €€€

A glamorous modern brasserie
within the Palais de Tokyo, near the
Musée d'Art Moderne *(see p142)*.
Nibbles from the bar menu are
perfect for enjoying on the terrace
facing the Eiffel Tower.

See map on p140

TOP 10 Montmartre and Pigalle

In the 19th and early 20th centuries, painters and poets put the "art" in Montmartre, and it will forever be associated with their bohemian lifestyle. Throngs of tourists climb the hill for the view from Sacré-Coeur, but you can still discover village-like charms in the winding back streets. Pigalle, once home to dance halls and cabarets, is now better known for its adult shows and sex shops.

Church of St-Pierre de Montmartre

AREA MAP OF MONTMARTRE AND PIGALLE

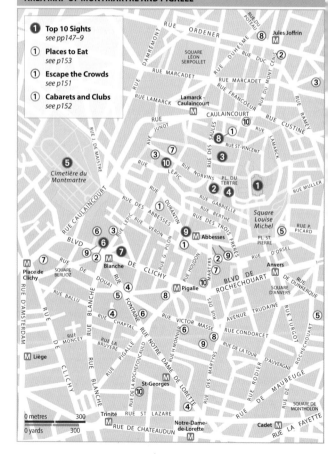

- **1** Top 10 Sights
  see pp147–9
- **1** Places to Eat
  see p153
- **1** Escape the Crowds
  see p151
- **1** Cabarets and Clubs
  see p152

1 Sacré-Coeur

See pp26–7.

2 Espace Montmartre Salvador Dalí

MAP F1 ■ 11 Rue Poulbot, 75018 ■ Open 10am–6pm daily (Jul–Aug to 8pm) ■ Admission charge ■ www. daliparis.com

The Dalí works here may not be the artist's most famous or best, but this museum is still a must for any fan of the Spanish Surrealist *(see p150)*. More than 300 of his drawings and sculptures are on display amid high-tech lighting and sound effects, including Dalí's voice, which creates a "surreal" atmosphere. There are also bronzes of his memorable "fluid" clocks.

3 Musée de Montmartre

12 Rue Cortot, 75018 ■ Open 10am–6pm daily (until 7pm Jul & Aug) ■ Admission charge ■ www. museedemontmartre.fr

The museum is set in Montmartre's finest town house, known as Le Manoir de Rose de Rosimond after the 17th-century actor who once owned it. From 1875 it provided living quarters and studios for numerous artists. Using drawings, photographs and all sorts of memorabilia, the museum presents the history of the Montmartre area, from its 12th-century convent days to the

Portrait artist in the Place du Terte

present, with an emphasis on the bohemian lifestyle of the *belle époque*. There is even a recreated 19th-century bistro, as well as lovely gardens where Renoir painted.

4 Place du Tertre

MAP F1

At 130 m (430 ft), Montmartre's old village square, whose name means "hillock", is the highest point in the city. Any picturesque charm it might once have had is now sadly hidden under the tourist-trap veneer of overpriced restaurants and portrait artists hawking their services, although the fairy lights at night are still atmospheric. No. 21 houses the Old Montmartre information office, with details about the area. Nearby is the church of St-Pierre de Montmartre, all that remains of the Benedictine abbey which stood here from 1133 until the Revolution.

5 Cimetière de Montmartre

MAP E1 ■ 20 Ave Rachel, 75018

The main graveyard for the district lies beneath a busy road in an old gypsum quarry, though it's more restful than first appears when you actually get below street level. The illustrious tombs, many with ornately sculpted monuments, packed tightly into this intimate space, reflect the artistic bent of the residents, who include composers Berlioz and Offenbach, writers Stendhal and Dumas, Russian dancer Nijinsky and the film director François Truffaut.

Cimetière de Montmartre

Cancan dancers on stage at the Moulin Rouge

⑥ Moulin Rouge

MAP E1 ▪ 82 Blvd de Clichy, 75018 ▪ Shows daily at 9pm & 11pm (dinner at 7pm) ▪ www.moulinrouge.fr

The Moulin Rouge ("red windmill") is the most famous of the *belle époque* dance halls that once scandalized respectable citizens and attracted Montmartre's artists and other bohemian characters. Henri de Toulouse-Lautrec immortalized the era with his sketches and posters of dancers such as Jane Avril, some of which now grace the Musée d'Orsay *(see p17)*. Cabaret is still performed here *(see p64)*.

⑦ Musée de l'Erotisme

MAP E1 ▪ 72 Blvd de Clichy, 75018 ▪ Open 10am–2am daily ▪ Admission charge ▪ www.musee-erotisme.com

Exhibiting more than 2,000 items from all around the world, this museum presents all forms of erotic art from painting, sculpture, photographs and drawings to objects whose sole purpose seems to be titillation. It is all tastefully presented, however, which reflects the sincere interest of the three collectors who founded the museum in 1997 in order to explore the cultural aspects of eroticism. The displays range from the spiritual objects of primitive cultures to whimsical artworks.

⑧ Au Lapin Agile

MAP F1 ▪ 22 Rue des Saules, 75018 ▪ Open 9pm–1am Tue–Sun ▪ www.au-lapin-agile.com

This *belle époque* restaurant and cabaret was a popular hang-out for Picasso and Renoir, and poets Apollinaire and Paul Verlaine. It took its name from a humorous painting by André Gill of a rabbit *(lapin)* leaping out of a cooking pot, called the *Lapin à Gill*. In time it became known by its current name ("nimble rabbit") *(see p152)*.

Lapin à Gill by André Gill

⑨ Place des Abbesses
MAP E1

This pretty square lies at the base of the Butte Montmartre, between Pigalle and the place du Tertre. Visit it via the metro station of the same name to appreciate one of the few original Art Nouveau stations left in the city. Designed by the architect Hector Guimard in 1900, it features ornate green wrought-iron arches, amber lanterns and a ship shield, the symbol of Paris, on the roof. Along with Porte Dauphine, it is the only station entrance to retain its original glass roof. A mural painted by local artists winds around the spiral staircase at the entrance. But don't walk to the platform, take the elevator – it's the deepest station in Paris, with 285 steps.

THE MONTMARTRE VINEYARDS

It's hard to imagine it today, but Montmartre was once a French wine region said to match the quality of Bordeaux and Burgundy. There were 20,000 ha (50,000 acres) of Parisian vineyards in the mid-18th century, but today just 1,000 bottles of wine are made annually from the remaining 2,000 vines in Montmartre (below), and are sold in aid of charity.

⑩ Moulin de la Galette
MAP E1 ■ 83 Rue Lepic, 75018

Montmartre once had more than 30 windmills, used for pressing grapes and grinding wheat; this is one of only two still standing. During the siege of Paris in 1814 its owner, Pierre-Charles Debray, was crucified on its sails by Russian soldiers. It became a dance hall in the 19th century and inspired paintings by Renoir and Van Gogh (see p150). It is now a restaurant. Rue Lepic is worth a visit for its shops and cafés.

A DAY IN MONTMARTRE

▶ **MORNING**

As with all the city's attractions, the sooner you get to **Sacré-Coeur** (see pp26–7) the more you will have it to yourself – it opens at 8am. Later in the morning, enjoy the bustle of Montmartre and watch tourists having their portraits painted by the area's street artists in the **Place du Tertre** (see p147). There are plenty of places to choose for a coffee, but the one most of the artists frequent is the **Clairon des Chasseurs** (3 Pl du Tertre • 01 42 62 40 08).

For art of a more surreal kind, visit the **Espace Montmartre Salvador Dalí** (see p147). Head down rue des Saules to continue the artistic theme with lunch at La Maison Rose (2 Rue de l'Abreuvoir • 01 42 57 66 75). Utrillo once painted this pretty pink restaurant.

AFTERNOON

The **Musée de Montmartre** (see p147) is close by, as are the Montmartre Vineyards, and also the little **Cimetière St-Vincent** where you will find Maurice Utrillo's grave.

Walk back up to Rue Lepic to see the **Moulin de la Galette** before heading towards the boulevard de Clichy. Here you will find the sleazier side of Pigalle, although the **Musée de l'Erotisme** offers a more tasteful interpretation.

To the east is a great bar for an apéritif, **La Fourmi** (74 Rue des Martyrs • 01 42 64 70 35). Then finish off the day in style with a show at the world-famous **Moulin Rouge** cabaret.

See map on p146 ←

Artists who Lived in Montmartr

Pablo Picasso

5 Edouard Manet

Manet (1832–83) frequented Montmartre's artist haunts and scandalized the art world with his paintings of nudes, including the famous *Olympia (see p16)*.

6 Maurice Utrillo

Utrillo (1883–1955) often painted the Auberge de la Bonne-Franquette, giving an atmospheric depiction of old Montmartre. His mother was the artist Suzanne Valadon and they both lived at 12 Rue Cortot, now the Musée de Montmartre *(see p147)*.

7 Henri de Toulouse-Lautrec

More than any other artist, Toulouse-Lautrec (1864–1901) is associated with Montmartre for his sketches and posters of dancers at the Moulin Rouge and other dance halls. For most people, they epitomize the era to this day *(see p17)*.

1 Pablo Picasso

Picasso (1881–1973) painted *Les Demoiselles d'Avignon* in 1907 while living at the Bateau-Lavoir. It is regarded as the painting that inspired the Cubism movement, which he launched with fellow residents Georges Braque and Juan Gris.

2 Salvador Dalí

The Catalan painter (1904–89) came to Paris in 1929 and held his first Surrealist exhibition that year. He kept a studio in Montmartre, and his work is now celebrated in the Espace Montmartre Salvador Dalí *(see p147)*.

3 Vincent van Gogh

The Dutch genius (1853–90) lived for a time on the third floor of 54 Rue Lepic. Many of his early paintings were inspired by the Moulin de la Galette windmill *(see p149)*.

8 Raoul Dufy

The painter Dufy (1877–1953) lived at Villa Guelma on the Boulevard de Clichy from 1911 to 1953, when he was at the height of his career.

9 Amedeo Modigliani

The Italian painter and sculptor (1884–1920) arrived in Paris in 1906, when he was 22, and was greatly influenced by Toulouse-Lautrec and the other bohemian artists on the Montmartre scene.

Toulouse-Lautrec

4 Pierre-Auguste Renoir

Renoir (1841–1919) is another artist who found inspiration in the Moulin de la Galette, when he lived at 12 Rue Cortot. For a time he laid tables at Au Lapin Agile *(see p148)*.

10 Edgar Degas

Edgar Degas was born in Paris in 1834 and lived in the city for the whole of his life, most of the time in Montmartre, painting many of its street scenes and characters. He died here in 1917 and is buried in Montmartre cemetery *(see p147)*.

Places to Escape the Crowds

1 St-Jean l'Evangéliste de Montmartre

MAP E1 ▪ 21 Rue des Abbesses, 75018 ▪ Open daily

This 1904 church is a clash of styles, from Moorish to Art Nouveau.

2 Montmartre City Hall

1 Pl Jules Joffrin, 75018 ▪ Metro Jules Joffrin

On display in this building are two Utrillo paintings.

3 Hameau des Artistes

MAP E1 ▪ 11 Ave Junot, 75018

This little hamlet of artists' studios is private, but no one will mind if you take a quiet look round.

4 Musée de la Vie Romantique

MAP E1 ▪ 16 Rue Chaptal, 75009 ▪ Open 10am–6pm Tue–Sun ▪ Admission charge for temporary exhibitions

George Sand was a frequent visitor to this house, which is now devoted to the writer.

5 Halle Saint Pierre

MAP F1 ▪ 2 Rue Ronsard, 75018 ▪ 01 42 58 72 89 ▪ Open 11am–6pm Mon–Fri (until 7pm Sat) noon–6pm Sun ▪ Closed public hols ▪ Admission charge

A fascinating cultural centre that exhibits naive folk art and Art Brut.

6 Cité Véron

MAP E1 ▪ 92 Blvd de Clichy, 75018

This cul-de-sac is home to the Académie des Arts Chorégraphiques, a prestigious dance school.

7 Square Suzanne Buisson

MAP E1

Named after a World War II Resistance fighter, this square is a romantic spot.

8 Rue de Poteau Market

Metro Jules Joffrin

Great food market that is a long way from the tourist crowds.

9 Crypte du Martyrium

MAP E1 ▪ 11 Rue Yvonne Le Tac, 75018 ▪ 01 42 23 48 94 ▪ Open 3–6pm Fri

A simple, peaceful 19th-century chapel, this is said to be on the spot where St Denis, the patron saint of Paris, was beheaded by the Romans in AD 250.

10 Musée Gustave Moreau

MAP E2 ▪ 14 Rue de La Rochefoucauld, 75009 ▪ Open 10am–12:45pm, 2–5:15pm Wed–Mon (all day Fri–Sun) ▪ Admission charge ▪ www.musee-moreau.fr

The former home of Symbolist artist Moreau displays a large collection of his imaginative works.

Musée Gustave Moreau

See map on p146 ←

Cabarets and Clubs

Old photograph of Au Lapin Agile

1 Au Lapin Agile
Poets and artists not only drank in this cabaret club, some – such as Renoir and Verlaine – also laid tables. Picasso even paid his bill with one of his Harlequin paintings *(see p148)*.

2 Moulin Rouge
MAP E1 ■ 82 Blvd de Clichy, 75018

As old as the Eiffel Tower (1889) and as much a part of the Parisian image, today's troupe of 60 Doriss Girls are the modern versions of Jane Avril and La Goulue *(see p148)*.

3 Autour de Midi et Minuit
MAP E1 ■ 11 Rue Lepic, 75018 ■ Closed Sun, Mon, end Feb, Aug

Tuck into delicious bistro food before heading into the small vaulted cellar for a jazz concert.

4 Le Carmen
MAP E1 ■ 34 Rue Duperré, 75009 ■ 01 45 26 50 00

This trendy hang-out offers excellent cocktails and hosts themed nights featuring live music.

5 La Nouvelle Eve
MAP E1 ■ 25 Rue Pierre Fontaine, 75009

One of the lesser-known cabaret venues. The intimate venue produces professional shows that feature colourful displays of the celebrated French cancan.

6 Le Bus Palladium
MAP E1 ■ 6 Rue Pierre Fontaine, 75009 ■ 01 45 26 80 35 ■ Closed Sun

This 1960s club, which was graced by The Beatles, now hosts concerts with an alternative/rock vibe.

7 Cabaret Michou
MAP E1 ■ 80 Rue des Martyrs, 75018

With outrageous drag artists and a legendary compère whose behaviour can never be predicted, this place is close to the original spirit of Montmartre cabaret.

Cabaret Michou

8 Folies Pigalle
MAP E1 ■ 11 Pl Pigalle, 75018

This former strip club is now a leading dance venue and popular among the gay community.

9 La Machine du Moulin Rouge
MAP E1 ■ 90 Blvd de Clichy, 75018

This venue next to the Moulin Rouge hosts both club nights and concerts.

10 Le Divan du Monde
MAP E1 ■ 75 Rue des Martyrs, 75018

World music is played here, both live and DJs, with regular dance events and concerts too.

Places to Eat

PRICE CATEGORIES
For a three-course meal for one with half a bottle of wine (or equivalent meal), taxes and extra charges

€ under €30 €€ €30–€50 €€€ over €50

1 Café Burq
MAP E1 ▪ 6 Rue Burq, 75018 ▪ 01 42 52 81 27 ▪ Closed L, Sun, 1 week Christmas ▪ No disabled access ▪ €

A genuine Montmartre bistro with a trendy clientele. Roasted Camembert with honey is a speciality.

2 Le Miroir
MAP E1 ▪ 94 Rue des Martyrs, 75018 ▪ 01 46 06 50 73 ▪ No disabled access ▪ €€

Chef Sébastien Guénard creates fine French fare using classical techniques and seasonal ingredients.

3 Table d'Eugène
18 Rue Eugène Sue, 75018 ▪ 01 42 55 61 64 ▪ Closed Sun, Mon, Aug ▪ €

This chic restaurant serves fantastic gastronomic tasting menus at very reasonable prices.

4 Restaurant Jean
MAP E1 ▪ 8 Rue St-Lazare, 75009 ▪ 01 48 78 62 73 ▪ Closed Sat, Sun ▪ €€€

This restaurant boasts creative, beautifully presented, contemporary cuisine and a Michelin star.

5 Le Pétrelle
MAP F1 ▪ 34 Rue Pétrelle, 75009 ▪ 01 42 82 11 02 ▪ Closed Sun, Mon, 1st week May, Aug ▪ €€

A restaurant with offbeat, eccentric decor, an intimate atmosphere and a menu using only local produce.

6 Buvette
MAP E1 ▪ 28 Rue Henry Monnier, 75009 ▪ 01 44 63 41 71 ▪ €

Under a gorgeous tin ceiling, this comfortable New York-style bistro serves cocktails, classic French dishes and a mouthwatering chocolate mousse. Linger over a hearty brunch on the weekend.

7 Charlot "Roi des Coquillages"
MAP E1 ▪ 81 Blvd de Clichy, 75009 ▪ 01 53 20 48 00 ▪ No disabled access ▪ €€

A sumptuous Art Deco brasserie, specializing in seafood.

8 Le Cul de Poule
MAP F2 ▪ 53 Rue des Martyrs, 75009 ▪ 01 53 16 13 07 ▪ Closed Sun L, a few weeks Dec–Jan ▪ €

This bistro offers modern French dishes and a good selection of wines.

9 Hotel Amour
MAP F2 ▪ 8 Rue de Navarin, 75009 ▪ 01 48 78 31 80 ▪ €

The cozy restaurant in this hip hotel serves Anglo-inspired food.

10 Chamarré de Montmartre
MAP E1 ▪ 52 Rue Lamarck, 75018 ▪ 01 42 55 05 42 ▪ No disabled access ▪ €€€

Creative Mauritanian-French fusion food is served on a terrace at this fine-dining restaurant.

Buvette, with its beautiful tin ceiling

See map on p146

🔟 Greater Paris

Central Paris has more than enough on offer to keep any visitor occupied, but if time permits you should make at least one foray out of the centre, whether it be to the sumptuous Palace of Versailles, former home of the "Sun King" Louis XIV, or to the Magic Kingdom of Disneyland® Paris. The excellent metro system makes for easy day trips to the area's two main parks, the Bois de Boulogne and the Bois de Vincennes, for a wide range of outdoor activities,

from boating to horse riding or in-line skating, or just strolling amid pleasant greenery. In contrast to these bucolic pleasures is the cutting-edge modern architecture of La Défense. Visually stunning, it comprises Paris's high-rise business district, with added attractions in its exhibition centres. Two large cemeteries outside the centre are worth a visit for their ornate tombs.

The Grande Arche de la Défense

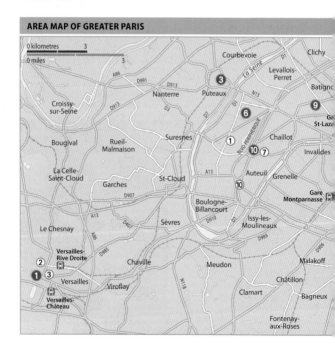

AREA MAP OF GREATER PARIS

1 Versailles

Versailles, 78000 ■ RER line C to Versailles-Rive Gauche ■ Château open Apr–Oct: 9am–6:30pm Tue–Sun; Nov–Mar: 9am–5:30pm Tue–Sun; gardens open 8am–8:30pm daily (to 6pm winter) ■ Closed public hols ■ Admission charge ■ www.chateauversailles.fr

The top day trip from Paris has to be Versailles. This stunning chateau, begun by Louis XIV in 1664, is over-whelming in its opulence and scale. Plan what you want to see and arrive early, as even a full day may not be long enough. Much of the palace is only accessible by guided tour *(see p158)*. Buy a Versailles Passport online to avoid the queues.

Fountain at Versailles

2 Disneyland® Paris

Marne-la-Vallée ■ RER line A to Marne-la-Vallée Chessy/Disneyland ■ See website for opening times and prices ■ www.disneylandparis.com

Despite grumblings that the Paris branch of Disneyland® may have lost some of its lustre since opening in 1992, the theme park still draws more people than the Louvre and the Eiffel Tower combined. In the shadow of the extravagant Chateau de la Belle au Bois Dormant (Sleeping Beauty Castle), visitors – whether young or young-at-heart – will enjoy the high-tech workings and imagination behind such attractions as the multisensory, 3D Ratatouille ride and of course Pirates of the Caribbean. At the adjacent Walt Disney Studios® Park, dedicated to Disney's movies and television shows, visitors can experience the thrill of special-effects rides and professional stunt shows.

3 La Défense

Metro Esplanade de la Défense or RER line A to Grande-Arche-de-la-Défense

French vision and flair coupled with Parisian style are clearly shown by this modern urban development. This business and government centre was purposely built to the west of the city to allow the centre to remain unmarred by skyscrapers. More than just offices, however, the area is also an attraction in its own right, with stunning sights such as the Grande Arche, a cube-like structure with a centre large enough to contain Notre-Dame, and surrounded by artworks, a fountain, cafés and restaurants.

4 Bois de Vincennes

Vincennes, 94300 ▪ Metro Château de Vincennes/RER Vincennes ▪ Park: open dawn–dusk daily; château: Sep–Apr: 10am–5pm; May–Aug: 10am–6pm ▪ Closed public hols ▪ www.chateau-vincennes.fr

Southeast of the city lies the Bois de Vincennes, which has several lakes with boating facilities, beautiful formal gardens, a Buddhist centre, a zoo and an amusement park. The Château de Vincennes was a royal residence before Versailles and has the tallest keep in Europe. The more energetic can walk here all the way from the Bastille along the lovely Promenade Plantée (see p58), formerly a railway viaduct.

5 Parc de la Villette

30 Ave Corentin-Cariou, 75019 ▪ Metro Porte de Pantin ▪ 01 40 03 75 75 ▪ Opening times vary depending on the attraction ▪ Admission charge for certain attractions ▪ www.villette. com

More than just a park, this landscape was created in 1993 to a futuristic design. It provides the usual park features of paths and gardens, but modern sculptures, zany park benches and several major high-tech attractions offer a different edge. These include the interactive science museum, the Cité des Sciences et de l'Industrie, a 60-seater mobile hydraulic cinema, an Omnimax cinema in a geodesic dome. There are also play areas for children and a music institute (see p60).

Parc de la Villette's Géode

6 Bois de Boulogne

MAP A2

This enormous park is Parisians' favourite green retreat, especially on summer weekends when its 865 ha (2,135 acres) can become crowded. There is plenty to do here, apart from simply walking and picnicking, such as cycling, horse riding, boating or visiting the various attractions – including parks within the park, two race courses and the striking Frank Gehry-designed Fondation Louis Vuitton contemporary arts centre (see p159). The park is open 24 hours a day, but is best avoided after dark.

7 Montparnasse

Metro Gare Montparnasse ▪ Tour du Montparnasse: open 9:30am–11:30pm daily (winter until 10:30pm, 11pm Fri & Sat); admission charge ▪ Cemetery: open 8:30am–5:30pm daily ▪ www. tourmontparnasse56.com

The area of Montparnasse is always recognisable due to the 209-m (685-ft) Tour du Montparnasse, which offers spectacular views. Five minutes' walk away is the area's main draw, the Montparnasse Cemetery, where the great writers Maupassant, Sartre, de Beauvoir, Baudelaire and Samuel Beckett are buried (see p160). For breathtaking views of Paris by night, visit the rooftop restaurant Le Ciel de Paris.

8 Père Lachaise Cemetery

16 Rue du Repos ▪ Metro Père-Lachaise ▪ 01 55 25 82 10 ▪ Open 8am–5:30pm Mon–Fri, 8:30am–5:30pm Sat, 9am–5:30pm Sun (Mar–Nov: to 6pm)

This is the most visited cemetery in the world, largely due to rock fans who come from around the world to see the grave of the legendary singer Jim Morrison of The Doors. There are about one million other graves here, and some 70,000 different tombs, including those of Chopin, Oscar Wilde, Balzac, Edith Piaf, Colette, Molière and Delacroix (see p160). There are maps posted around the cemetery to help you find the most detailed graves, and a more detailed plan can be bought at kiosks in the grounds

Père Lachaise Cemetery

⑨ Parc Monceau
Blvd de Courcelles, 75008
■ Metro Monceau

This civilized little park is no further from the city centre than Montmartre, yet it goes unnoticed by many visitors. It was created in 1778 by the Duc de Chartres and is still frequented by well-heeled residents. The park grounds are full of statues (see p56).

⑩ Musée Marmottan-Claude Monet
2 Rue Louis-Boilly, 75016 ■ Metro Muette ■ Open 10am–6pm Tue–Sun (9pm Thu) ■ Admission charge ■ www.marmottan.fr

Paul Marmottan was an art historian and his 19th-century mansion now houses the world's largest collection of works by Claude Monet, including his *Impression Soleil Levant*, which gave the Impressionist movement its name. The collection was donated by the artist's son in 1966, and includes Monet's own collection of works by Renoir and Gauguin.

THE TREATY OF VERSAILLES

France, Great Britain, the USA, Italy and Germany negotiated this agreement after World War I at Versailles, which required Germany to demilitarize parts of its territory, reduce the size of its army, abolish conscription, cease trading in military equipment and to pay compensation. The Treaty was signed on 28 June 1919.

A DAY IN THE BOIS DE VINCENNES

▶ MORNING

To escape the bustle and crowds of the city, put on your walking shoes and head to the **Bois de Vincennes**. Take metro line 1 to **Château de Vincennes**, stopping off at **Maison Cailleaud** (104 Cours de Vincennes • Metro Porte de Vincennes) on the way to stock up on the excellent sandwiches and tarts for a picnic later.

From the Château de Vincennes metro station, follow the sign-posts to the medieval castle that was at the heart of the French monarchy until 1682, when Louis XIV decided to settle in Versailles. Look out for the ornate gate and stained-glass windows of the Gothic Sainte-Chapelle.

For a sit-down lunch, try **La Rigadelle** (23 Rue de Montreuil • 01 43 28 04 23), just outside the fortress, which specializes in fish and seafood dishes.

AFTERNOON

Walk off lunch amid the flowers and botanical plants in the **Parc Floral** within the Bois, then head for the charmingly kitsch mini-golf course featuring models of Parisian monuments. Afterwards, if you're still feeling energetic, stroll to **Lac Daumesnil**, where you can rent a boat to row around the lake's two islands.

Time to rejoin urban life? Head to the Porte Dorée metro station via **Avenue du Général Laperrine** and take the metro to the jolly hubbub of the Aligre quarter. From Ledru-Rollin metro station, walk to the lively **Baron Rouge** (see p101) for a well-earned aperitif.

See map on pp154–5

Versailles Sights

1 The Hall of Mirrors
The spectacular 70-m (233-ft) long Galerie des Glaces has been magnificently restored. It was in this room that the Treaty of Versailles was signed in 1919, formally ending World War I.

2 Chapelle Royale
The Royal Chapel is regarded as one of the finest Baroque buildings in the country. Finished in 1710, its elegant, white marble Corinthian columns and numerous murals make for an awe-inspiring place of prayer.

3 Salon de Venus
In this elaborate room, which is decorated predominantly in marble, a statue of Louis XIV, the creator of Versailles, stands centre stage, exuding regal splendour beneath the fine painted ceiling.

4 Queen's Bedroom
Nineteen royal infants were born in this opulent room, which has been meticulously restored to exactly how it appeared when it was last used by Marie-Antoinette in 1789.

5 Marble Courtyard
Approaching the front of the palace across the vast open forecourt, visitors finally reach the splendour of the black-and-white marble courtyard, which is the oldest section of the palace. The north and south wings were added later.

Salon d'Apollon

6 Salon d'Apollon
Louis XIV's throne room is, naturally, one of the palace's centrepieces, and features a suitably regal portrait of the great Sun King. Dedicated to the god Apollo, it strikingly reflects the French monarchy's divine self-image.

7 L'Opéra
The opulent opera house was built in 1770 for the marriage of the *Dauphin*, the future Louis XVI, to Marie-Antoinette. The floors were designed so that they could be raised to stage level during special festivals.

8 Le Trianon
In the southeast corner of the gardens, Louis XIV and Louis XV had the Grand and Petit Trianon palaces built as "private" retreats. Marie-Antoinette was given Petit Trianon by Louis XVI.

9 Palace Gardens
The palace gardens feature many walkways, landscaped topiary, fountains, pools, statues and the Orangery, where exotic plants were kept in the winter. The magnificent Fountain of Neptune is situated to the north of the North Wing.

10 Stables of the King
The magnificent stables have been restored and they now house the famous Bartabas Academy of Equestrian Arts.

Black-and-white marble courtyard

Bois de Boulogne Features

1 **Parc de Bagatelle**
Differing garden styles feature in this park, including English and Japanese, though for most visitors the major attraction is the huge rose garden, best seen in June.

2 **Pré Catelan**
This park-within-a-park is at the very centre of the Bois. Its lawns and wooded areas include a magnificent 200-year-old beech tree and the idyllic eponymous restaurant (see p161).

3 **Jardin d'Acclimatation**
The main children's area of the Bois incorporates a small amusement park, a zoo with a farm and a pets' corner, and a Herb Museum aimed especially at children (see p61).

4 **La Grande Cascade**
This artificial waterfall was a major undertaking when the park was built, requiring concrete to be shipped down the Seine.

5 **Lakes**
Two long, thin lakes adjoin each other. The larger of the two, confusingly called Lac Inférieur (the other is Lac Supérieur) has boats for hire and a motor boat to take you to the islands.

6 **Fondation Louis Vuitton**
A thrilling example of modern architecture, this glass Frank Gehry-designed building hosts art events and exhibitions (see p53).

7 **Château de Longchamp**
While he redesigned central Paris (see p43), Baron Haussmann landscaped the Bois de Boulogne. This chateau was given to him as a thank-you by Napoleon III.

8 **Shakespeare Garden**
Inside Pré Catelan is a little garden planted with all the trees, flowers and herbs mentioned in the plays of Shakespeare. There is a lovely open-air theatre.

9 **Jardin des Serres d'Auteuil**
This 19th-century garden has a series of greenhouses where ornamental hothouse plants are grown. In the centre is a palm house with tropical plants.

10 **Horse-Racing**
The Bois is home to two race courses. To the west is the Hippodrome de Longchamp, where flat racing takes place, including the Prix de l'Arc de Triomphe (see p75); in the east, the Hippodrome d'Auteuil holds steeplechases.

Lac Inférieur

Notable Graves

1 Jim Morrison, Père Lachaise Cemetery

The American lead singer of The Doors rock band spent the last few months of his life in Paris and died here in 1971. Fans still hold vigils at his grave, which is covered with scrawled messages from those who come from all over the world.

2 Oscar Wilde, Père Lachaise Cemetery

The Dublin-born author died in 1900, after allegedly uttering: "My wallpaper and I are fighting a duel to the death. One or the other of us has to go." His tomb is unmissable, with a huge monument by Jacob Epstein.

3 Frédéric Chopin, Père Lachaise Cemetery

The Polish composer was born in 1810 and died in Paris at the age of 39. The statue on his tomb represents "the genius of music sunk in grief".

4 Edith Piaf, Père Lachaise Cemetery

The iconic French *chanteuse*, known as the "little sparrow", was born in poverty in the Belleville district of Paris in 1915, less than 1,500 m (5,000 ft) from where she was buried in 1963 in a simple black tomb.

5 Marcel Proust, Père Lachaise Cemetery

The ultimate chronicler of Paris, Proust was born in the city in 1871. He is buried in the family tomb *(see p44)*.

6 Samuel Beckett, Montparnasse Cemetery

The Irish-born Nobel Prize-winning writer settled in Paris in 1937, having previously studied here. He died in 1989 and his gravestone is a simple slab, reflecting the writer's enigmatic nature *(see p45)*.

7 Jean-Paul Sartre and Simone de Beauvoir, Montparnasse Cemetery

Joined together in death as in life, even though they never actually lived together, their joint grave is a remarkably simple affair. Both of these philosophers were born, lived and died in Paris.

8 Guy de Maupassant, Montparnasse Cemetery

The great French novelist and short-story writer died in Paris in 1893, and his grave, with its luxuriant growth of shrubs, stands out because of the open book carving *(see p44)*.

9 Charles Baudelaire, Montparnasse Cemetery

The poet who shocked the world with his frank and decadent collection of poems *Les Fleurs du Mal*, published in 1857, was born in Paris in 1821 and died here in 1867.

10 Charles Pigeon Family, Montparnasse Cemetery

This charming and touching grave shows Charles Pigeon and his wife in bed, reading by the light of the gas lamp he invented.

Edith Piaf's gravestone

Places to Eat

PRICE CATEGORIES

For a three-course meal for one with half a bottle of wine (or equivalent meal), taxes and other charges
....

€ under €30   €€ €30–€50   €€€ over €50

1 Le Pré Catelan
Route de Suresnes, Bois de Boulogne, 75016 ▪ Metro Porte Maillot ▪ 01 44 14 41 14 ▪ Closed Sun, Mon, 2 weeks Feb, 3 weeks Aug, 1 week Nov ▪ €€€

Tucked away in the Bois de Boulogne *(see p156)* is this high-class dining pavilion. Romantic setting and elegant service.

2 Gordon Ramsay au Trianon
1 Blvd de la Reine, Versailles ▪ RER line C to Versailles ▪ 01 30 84 50 18 ▪ Closed L Sun–Thu ▪ €€€

Celebrity chef Gordon Ramsay's protégé Simone Zanoni is the chef at this two-Michelin-starred restaurant.

3 Le Resto du Roi
1 Ave de St-Cloud, Versailles ▪ 01 39 50 42 26 ▪ Closed Wed, D Mon, Tue & Sun ▪ €

Close to the château *(see p155)*, this informal bistro serves inventive dishes. Specialities include salmon smoked with birch branches.

4 Roseval
1 Rue d'Eupatoria, 75020 ▪ Metro Ménilmontant ▪ 09 53 56 24 14 ▪ Closed Sat, Sun ▪ €€

Imaginative menus of modern French cooking draw foodies to this restaurant.

5 La Closerie des Lilas
MAP E6 ▪ 171 Blvd du Montparnasse, 75006 ▪ 01 40 51 34 50 ▪ €€€

With its piano bar and terrace, this is a Montparnasse institution. The brasserie is cheaper than the main restaurant. The steak tartare is recommended.

6 Chatomat
6 Rue Victor Letalle, 75020 ▪ Metro Ménilmontant ▪ 01 47 97 25 77 ▪ Closed L, Mon, Sun ▪ €

Locals love the concise but creative modern menu on offer here.

7 La Gare
19 Chaussée de la Muette, 75016 ▪ Metro La Muette ▪ 01 42 15 15 31 ▪ €€

Any visit to the Bois de Boulogne, should include a stop at La Gare. This stylish brasserie in a former railway station has a terrace.

Interior of La Gare

8 Le Baratin
3 Rue Jouye-Rouve, 75020 ▪ Metro Pyrénées ▪ 01 43 49 39 70 ▪ Closed Sun, Mon ▪ No disabled access ▪ No vegetarian options ▪ €

A local favourite in Belleville, this bistro serves modern French cuisine with excellent wines. The fixed-price lunch is particularly popular.

9 Le Chapeau Melon
92 Rue Rébeval, 75019 ▪ Metro Pyrénées ▪ 01 42 02 68 60 ▪ Closed Mon, Tue, 2 weeks Aug ▪ €

This wine shop turns into a charming bistro by night, offering a fixed-price menu and, of course, an excellent selection of wines.

10 Relais d'Auteuil
31 Blvd Murat, 75016 ▪ Metro Michel Ange Molitor ▪ 01 46 51 09 54 ▪ Closed L Sat, Sun, Mon, Aug ▪ €€€

At the southern end of the Bois de Boulogne is this gourmet restaurant. Try the sea bass in a pepper crust.

See map on pp154–5

Streetsmart

**Art Nouveau entrance to
St-Michel metro station**

Getting To and Around Paris

Arriving by Air

Roissy-Charles-de-Gaulle Airport is the arrival point for most international flights, 23 km (14 miles) northeast of central Paris. Its main terminals are some distance apart, so check which one you need when returning. A 24-hour English-language information service is available.

CDG is connected to central Paris by Air France and **Roissy** bus services, and (the easiest option) the **RER** train line B3. This links with Gare du Nord, Les Halles and St-Michel. A taxi to the city centre takes between 30 minutes and 1 hour, depending on the traffic, and costs about €55.

Orly is 14 km (8.5 miles) south of the city centre and is used by French domestic services and some international airlines. It has two terminals: **Orly-Sud** is mainly for international flights; **Orly-Ouest** is for domestic flights. English-language information is available 6am–11:30pm.

Air France coaches run to and from Etoile, Invalides and Montparnasse metro and mainline stations. The high-speed **Orlyval** shuttle train serves both of Orly's terminals from Antony on RER line B4. Note that metro signs to Orly on RER C refer to Orly town (not Orly airport). Taxis take about 30 minutes and cost about €35.

Beauvais Tillé Airport is some 70 km (43 miles) north of Paris and is used by some low-cost airlines.

There is a connecting bus link with Porte Maillot metro station. You should allow at least an hour for the journey.

Arriving by Train

Eurostar trains arrive at the Gare du Nord, slightly north of the city centre. There is a tourist office by the Grandes Lignes exit. The station is served by three metro lines and three RER lines. The metro station is reached from the concourse and is clearly signposted. There is also a taxi rank outside.

Arriving by Coach

The main bus operator, **Eurolines**, has services from the UK, Ireland, Germany and several other European countries. Coaches arrive at Gare Routière Internationale, east of the city centre but linked to the metro by the Galliéni station on Line 3.

Arriving by Car

All French autoroutes, from whichever direction, eventually align with Paris's busy Boulevard Périphérique (Inner Ring Road). Access to central Paris is via different exits (*portes*), so drivers should always check their final destination before setting off and know which exit they will need.

To park on the street you will need the nerves and manoeuvring ability of a local. Meters take the prepaid *carte* only, which is available to buy from tobacconists (*tabac*).

Otherwise use one of the many underground car parks in the city, which are clean and safe.

Travelling by Metro

The Paris metro system is cheap and efficient. The network is comprehensive and the service is very frequent. It operates roughly 5:30am–12:30am (until 1:30–2am Fri, Sat and the evening before public holidays); exact times for each line are given at stations.

Travelling by RER

The RER train system (5am–12:30am; to 1:30am Fri, Sat and the evening before public holidays) has only five lines, but the network goes further into the suburbs. Metro tickets are only valid on RER trains in Zone 1. If you are travelling further, such as to Versailles or one of the airports, you must buy a separate RER ticket.

Travelling by Bus

Buses run approximately 6:30am–8:30pm, with some services continuing until 12:30am and others operating through the night (**Noctilien** buses). A *Grand Plan de Paris* available from metro stations shows all bus routes. Metro tickets are valid in Zones 1 and 2, but you cannot switch between bus and metro on the same ticket. You can also buy a ticket from the driver for a little more than from a machine. Bus stops show the line route.

Taxis

Taxis may not always stop if you hail them on the street. The best way to find one is to head for one of the 470 taxi ranks (look for the taxi icon on a blue background), or ask your hotel or restaurant to call for one. Some taxi companies also accept bookings by phone or internet, though they cost a bit more, as you also pay for the time that it takes for them to get to you. Many drivers will not take more than three people, to avoid front-seat passengers. In general, fares are not expensive but there may be a charge for extra luggage.

On Foot

Central Paris is fairly compact, and even a walk from the Arc de Triomphe to the Bastille should only take about an hour. Be sure to look up to see the beautiful old buildings – and down to avoid the evidence of Parisian dogs. A particularly pleasant walk is the Promenade Plantée, a leafy former railway viaduct that puts you high above the city streets (see p58).

Cycling

Paris is an excellent city for cyclists. You can hire bikes via **Allovelo** or **Parisvelosympa**, or try the self-service scheme **Vélib'**. These bike stands are found every 300 metres (330 yards) and payment for the scheme can be made online or by credit card at the access terminals, which operate in eight languages.

Riverboat

The **Batobus** runs year round and its eight stops link all the major sights on the river. Boats run every 20–25 minutes, from 10am to 9:30pm (until 7pm in winter). One-day, two-day and five-day passes are available (you can't buy single tickets).

Buying Tickets and Travel Cards

Tickets, valid for metro, bus and RER Zone 1, can be bought in batches of 10 (un carnet), which offer considerable savings on the price of a single ticket. Each ticket is valid for one journey in central Paris, no matter how many changes are made. They must be stamped when you enter the metro or bus and retained until you leave. Spot checks are frequent and you will be fined if you are not in possession of a valid ticket; on the RER you need your ticket to exit the machines. If staying for a few days, consider buying a Navigo Découverte (photo ID needed), or a Paris Visite card, available for up to five days and which offers savings at some attractions too.

Arrondissements

The city is divided into 20 arrondissements (districts), radiating out in a clockwise spiral from the centre. The first is abbreviated to 1er (Premier) and they follow on as 2e, 3e (Deuxième, Troisième) etc. The post code for the first district is 75001, the second is 75002, and so on.

Practical Information

Passports and Visas

No visa is required for citizens of EU countries, the USA, Canada, Australia or New Zealand if you are staying for fewer than three months, although your passport will need to be valid for at least three months beyond the end of your stay. Citizens of other countries should consult their French embassy or consulate for information before travelling.

Customs

For EU citizens there are no limits on goods that can be taken into or out of France, provided they are for your personal use. Outside the EU, you may import the following allowances duty-free: 200 cigarettes or equivalent in tobacco; 1 litre of spirits (more than 22% alcohol); 2 litres if less than 22%, 4 litres of wine and 16 litres of beer; €430 (if you're travelling by air) worth of other items.

Health and Travel Insurance

French medical treatment is excellent but it can be expensive. Visitors from EU countries should carry with them a European Health Insurance card (EHIC) to avoid emergency fees. All other nationalities should take out private insurance. Report all crimes or lost property, and keep a copy of the statement you make to the police so that you can claim back on insurance.

Pharmacies

A green cross (usually in flashing neon) indicates a pharmacy (chemist). They are usually open 9am–7pm Monday to Saturday. At other times, the address of the duty pharmacy will usually be displayed, or ask at the local *gendarmerie*. Pharmacies will advise on minor health problems and can give details of the nearest doctor.

Hospitals

Paris hospitals are listed in the phone directory, or check the website of the **Assistance Publique**. The most centrally located hospital is the **Hôtel Dieu**. If you need an ambulance, dial the **SAMU** number. Fire stations also have ambulances and are qualified to give first aid.

Dentists

These are listed in the Paris *Pages Jaunes (Yellow Pages)* under *Dentistes*. In the case of a dire emergency, a service called **SOS Dentistes** will provide a prompt house call, but be prepared to pay a substantial amount for this visit. A large dental practice can be found at the **Centre Médical Europe**.

Personal Security

Petty theft is as common in Paris as in any major city. Pickpockets frequent tourist spots such as the Eiffel Tower and the Arc de Triomphe, as well as wandering the metro system and RER. Some are amateur gangs and easy to spot, but others are more subtle, so guard your belongings at all times. To report a theft, go to the *commissariat de police*. These are listed in the phone book, or call the **Préfecture Centrale** for details (open 24 hours a day). All crimes should be reported, if only for insurance purposes.

Mugging is less of a problem in Paris than in other big cities, but it can happen. Try not to walk alone late at night and avoid unlit streets. Try to avoid long changes between metro lines too: better a longer journey than an unfortunate experience. The main stations you should avoid at night are Les Halles and Gare du Nord.

Women travellers are unlikely to experience any particular problems. Parisian men are generally courteous towards women. A firm rebuttal usually halts unwanted attention. If not, try to seek the help of another man.

Take care when crossing Paris's roads. French drivers are not known for respecting pedestrians, though a red light will usually – though not always – make them stop. Pedestrians do not have automatic priority on a crossing, unless the lights are also in their favour. At pedestrian crossings, motorists often have the right to turn right, so always look before you start to cross.

Lost Property

If you lose any of your belongings you could try **Objets Trouvés** (the city's lost-and-found office).

Currency

France's currency is the euro (€). Euro banknotes come in seven denominations: 5, 10, 20, 50, 100, 200 and 500. There are also eight coins: €1 and €2, and 50, 20, 10, 5, 2 and 1 cents (also referred to as centimes). Both notes and coins are valid and interchangeable all over the euro zone.

Credit and Debit Cards

These are widely accepted throughout Paris and you should have no difficulty paying for things with plastic. The only exception is American Express because of the heavy commission it incurs.

Cash Dispensers (ATMs)

There are cash dispensers all over Paris, and each one indicates which cards it accepts. Many of them give instructions in a range of languages. If you know your PIN, obtaining cash in this way is very easy, though most banks levy a charge on foreign withdrawals. Note that the metro/RER and SNCF ticket vending machines do not always work with North American credit cards, as they are designed for a chip-and-PIN system rather than with magnetic-strip cards.

Changing Money

Bureaux de Change exist throughout Paris, especially near tourist hotspots. Many banks also have either a *bureau de change* or foreign desk. "No commission" signs can be misleading, as they may well mean an unfavourable rate.

Driving Licences

All European and US driving licences are valid in France. UK visitors need both parts of their licence. Visitors from other countries should check with their local motoring organizations.

Time Difference

France is in the Central European Time Zone (GMT+1): 1 hour ahead of the UK, 6 hours ahead of North American EST and 9 hours ahead of PST.

Electrical Appliances

Electricity runs on 220V out of double, round-pin wall sockets. You will need adaptors, and possibly a transformer (for some US electrical appliances).

DIRECTORY

EMBASSIES AND CONSULATES

Australia
MAP B4 ■ 4 Rue Jean-Rey, 75015
01 40 59 33 00
france.embassy.gov.au

Canada
MAP C3 ■ 35 Ave Montaigne, 75008
01 44 43 29 00
canadainternational.gc.ca/france

New Zealand
MAP D4 ■ 103 Rue de Grenelle, 75007
01 45 01 43 43
nzembassy.com/france

UK
MAP D3 ■ 35 Rue du Faubourg St-Honoré, 75008
01 44 51 31 00
ukinfrance.fco.gov.uk

US
MAP D3 ■ Ave Gabriel, 75001
01 43 12 22 22
france.usembassy.gov

EMERGENCY NUMBERS

All Emergencies
112

Ambulance (SAMU)
15

Fire Department
18

Police
17

HEALTH AND SAFETY

Assistance Publique
aphp.fr

Centre Médical Europe
MAP E2 ■ 44 Rue d'Amsterdam, 75009
01 42 81 93 33

Hôtel Dieu
MAP N4 ■ Place du Parvis Notre Dame, 75004
01 42 34 82 34

Objets Trouvés
36 Rue des Morillons, 75007
08 21 00 25 25

Prefecture Centrale
01 53 71 53 71

SOS Dentistes
MAP F6 ■ 87 Blvd Port Royal, 75013
01 43 37 51 00

Communications

Paris phone numbers begin with 01 or 09 and have eight subsequent digits, usually written in four sets of two digits. If calling Paris from overseas, use the IDD code for your country (00 or 001 in most cases), then France's country code (33), then the local number minus the initial zero. Mobile phone numbers begin with 06 and 07. Check the roaming rates with your operator before your trip. Pay-as-you-go SIM cards can be bought for unlocked phones and topped up at tobacconists.

Most public telephones require a *télécarte* (phonecard), which can be bought from post offices, metro stations and tobacconists.

Most hotels and many cafés provide free Wi-Fi access. You can also connect for free to the Paris Wi-Fi network from more than 260 parks and libraries.

The main post offices in the heart of Paris are at 52 rue de Louvre (open 24 hours) and 71 ave des Champs-Elysées. They do not exchange currency or travellers' cheques but will exchange international postal cheques, giros and money orders. For simple letters and postcards, you can buy stamps at a *tabac* (tobacconist) rather than try to find a post office. Not all of them advertise the service, but if they sell postcards it is worth asking. Some hotels and newsagents also sell postage stamps.

A wide choice of the major foreign newspapers is available on the day of publication throughout Paris. The closer you are to the Champs-Elysées, the more you will see. The popular *International New York Times* is published in Paris.

Most hotels subscribe to multilingual cable and satellite channels, which vary the diet of French-language entertainment.

Opening Hours

Department stores and chain boutiques are usually open 9:30am–7pm Monday to Saturday. Late-night shopping is on Thursdays until 9pm. Independent shops often don't open up until 10 or 11am, and may be closed during the holidays, on Mondays and/or between noon and 2pm, but some open on Sundays in main tourist areas. Many food shops are open on a Sunday morning.

Museums are generally open 9/10am to 5/6pm and some have a late opening one evening a week. Most museums close either on a Monday or Tuesday. Banks are usually open Monday to Friday 9am–4pm, with some closing for lunch.

Businesses, banks, most shops and many restaurants are closed on New Year's Day, Easter Monday, 1 May (Labour Day), 8 May (VE Day), Ascension Day (40 days after Easter), Whitsun (7th Sunday after Easter), Whit Monday (the day after Whitsun), 14 July (Bastille Day), 15 August (Assumption), 1 November (All Saints' Day), 11 November (Armistice Day) and 25 December (Christmas Day).

Weather

Paris has a temperate and pleasant climate. Summers can be hot, with temperatures sometimes reaching 35–40°C (95–105°F). Both spring and autumn are mild, with a fair amount of rain, but there are also many bright days. Winter is cold, though the light then can be beautiful.

Tourist Information

The main tourist office is located close to the Pyramides metro station. It is well stocked with brochures, and has hotel and tour reservation services. There are also Welcome Points at Gares du Nord, de Lyon and de l'Est, and by Anvers metro station.

The **Espace du Tourisme d'Ile de France** tourist facility serves both Paris and the wider Ile de France region, and is the best source of advice and information on visiting places outside the city. It has offices in airports and train stations, plus a useful website.

Aside from the Paris tourist office, another useful official site is the **Paris City Hall**, with lots of information and links in French and English. There are also countless English-language blogs and websites on Paris. **Bonjour Paris** is a weekly email newsletter with articles and current information on cultural activities, as well as restaurant openings and closings in the city.

Other blogs include **Spotted by Locals**, with lots of tips from local residents; Alexander Lobrano's **Hungry for Paris**, a restaurant guide by a respected food critic and long-time Paris resident; and Davis Lebovitz's **My Paris**, with restaurant and other reviews plus recipes from a former Chez Panisse chef and food writer based in Paris.

For information about what's on, there are two indispensable weekly listings magazines, the **Officiel des Spectacles** and **Pariscope**, which has a small English section; both are available from newsagents and kiosks. Also handy are the free weekly **A Nous Paris**, which is available in metro stations, and the Sortir insert in the weekly magazine **Télérama**.

Paris Voice is a monthly magazine published by the American Church and aimed at US residents in Paris. Available from English-language bookshops, it is a good source of information and also has a website.

Disabled Travellers

The Paris tourist office site has a great deal of information on facilities for the disabled, including useful addresses.

Another good source of information, but in French only, is the **Association des Paralysés de France (APF)**, which publishes a guide to disabled access at Paris's museums, theatres and cinemas.

All buses are wheelchair accessible. Line 14 is the only metro line that is fully accessible. Around 20 RER stations are accessible and most require a member of station staff to operate lifts. The website **infomobi** details exactly which stations are wheelchair accessible.

It is a legal requirement for taxi drivers to help people with disabilities in and out of their vehicle, and to carry guide dogs as passengers. This does not mean that all taxis are able to carry wheelchairs, so check when booking. **Taxi G7** has a special service for clients in wheelchairs.

Many older hotels are unsuitable for people with mobility problems as they are without elevators – check before booking. Newer hotels and modern chain hotels are usually wheelchair accessible, but always check.

Tourism for All, in the UK, has a useful list of specialist tour operators; in the US, **Sage Traveling** offers a range of packages and assistance.

DIRECTORY

FRENCH TOURIST OFFICES
The French Tourist Office (Atout France) has branches in many world capitals and other international cities.

Australia and New Zealand
W au.rendezvous enfrance.com

Britain
W uk.rendezvous enfrance.com

Canada
W ca.rendezvous enfrance.com

USA
W us.rendezvous enfrance.com

Espace du Tourisme d'Île de France
W visitparisregion.com

Office de Tourisme de Paris
MAP K1 ■ 25 Rue des Pyramides, 75001
Open 10am–7pm daily (9am–7pm May–Oct)
W parisinfo.com

WEBSITES

Bonjour Paris
W bonjourparis.com

Hungry for Paris
W alexanderlobrano. com

My Paris
W davidlebovitz.com/ paris

Officiel des Specacles
W offi.fr

Paris City Hall
W paris.fr

Paris Voice
W parisvoice.com

Pariscope
W spectacles.premiere.fr

Spotted by Locals
W spottedbylocals.com

DISABLED ACCESS

APF
W apf.asso.fr

infomobi
W infomobi.com

Sage Traveling
C 1 888 645 7920
W sagetraveling.com

Taxi G7
C 01 47 39 00 91
W taxisg7.fr

Tourism for All
C 0845 124 9971; outside UK +44 1539 726 111
W tourismforall.org.uk

Shopping

As the world capital of fashion, Paris is simply unbeatable for clothes shopping and is home to all the top names. Don't forget, too, to look out for independent designers and labels often found nowhere else, such as **Antoine et Lili** *(see p96)*. For vintage clothes try **Vintage Désir** *(32 rue des Rosiers, 75004)* and **Didier Ludot** in the **Palais Royal's arcades** *(see p104)*.

Parisians are fiercely loyal to their local food shops: each *quartier* has its own boulangerie, patisserie, fromagerie and charcuterie, each one selling top-quality produce. One of the best areas for exquisite delis is **Place de la Madeleine** *(see p70)*, where you'll find **Maille**, **Hédiard**, **Fauchon** and **Ladurée**; and don't miss **La Grande Epicerie** at Le Bon Marché, with its fabulous array of fresh and packed foods. Check out the street markets, too *(see pp70–71)*.

Worth a visit for their wonderful *belle époque* interiors alone are the city's department stores, **Galeries Lafayette**, **Au Printemps** and **Le Bon Marché** *(see pp70–71)*. There are also a number of good concept stores, handy for a one-stop shop: try **L'Eclaireur** *(26 Champs-Elysées)*, which sells clothes and hosts art exhibitions and events, or **Merci** *(see p96)*.

The vast flea market at **Saint-Ouen** *(see p71)* is excellent for bric-a-brac, while **Marché Malassis** *(142 rue des Rosiers, 93400)* stocks a range of 20th-century treasures.

Dining

Paris is almost synonymous with good food and eating well; it is, after all, the city that invented the restaurant, and Michelin-starred gastronomic restaurants abound. Recently, however, there has been a movement against the pricey, somewhat stuffy haute cuisine establishments, and young, innovative chefs are opening up more informal dining rooms and experimenting with uncommon flavours and ingredients. Wine bars, too, have undergone something of a revolution and many now pay as much attention to the food as the wine, going beyond the usual meat and cheese platters to offer well-sourced, inventive dishes. It's still possible, of course, to find old-fashioned bistros serving well-cooked, traditional French classics such as *confit de canard*, *poulet rôti* and *steak-frites*. Traditional dishes are also served in *brasseries*, many of which, with their beautiful Art Nouveau decor, have become hallowed institutions and haven't changed a bit in decades. Cafés usually serve food, too, and are often open on weekends when many restaurants are closed.

It's worth booking ahead if there's a particular restaurant you have in mind; often the day before will be enough, though for the most popular places you'll need to book some weeks in advance. Many restaurants close at the weekend, in August and at other holiday periods.

Parisians are casual but chic, so it's worth taking a few smart outfits for dining out. Only the most expensive restaurants require men to wear a jacket and tie.

Trips and Tours

A wide range of tours is available, from traditional boat rides along the Seine to leisurely wine-tasting cruises. Or you could tap into the expertise of a local and be guided to the best food and fashion shops.

The long-established river boats, the **Bateaux-Mouches**, run regular day and evening dinner cruises. Other boat trip operators include **Paris Canal** (see p58), **Bateaux Parisiens**, **Vedettes de Paris** and **Vedettes du Pont-Neuf**.

City tours are available on a wide range of themes and in several languages. **Secrets of Paris**, **Paris Walks** and **Context Travel** are three leading English-language companies. For many **DiscoverWalks** tours you pay what you think is fair at the end of the tour. Several companies offer guided cycling tours with multilingual guides, including **Paris à Vélo** and **Fat Tire Bike Tours**. For the less energetic, there are **City Segway Tours**.

Numerous bus tours are available – ask at the main **Office de Tourisme** on rue des Pyramides *(see p169)*. Tours usually last up to two hours but many companies allow you to hop on and off.

Promenades Gourmandes runs tours of food markets and other foodie haunts, while **Edible**

Paris offers self-guided itineraries. **O-Chateau** runs wine-tasting cruises on the Seine.

There are also well-informed guides to direct you to the very best shops. With **Chic Shopping Paris** you take your choice from a range of themes.

Accommodation

The Left Bank is a good area to stay if you fancy a bohemian atmosphere with cafés and plenty of student life. The Marais has many museums, shops and restaurants, while the Opéra and Louvre quarters are central. To save money, stay just outside the centre and use the excellent, cheap metro.

There are numerous sumptuous hotels in Paris with stratospheric prices to match; prices over €400 are not uncommon, though off-season and online deals can bring the rates down. A modest 2-star hotel will be around €80–€130 per room; for something a bit classier you'll pay more like €130–€250. Boutique hotels are increasingly common and can be good value. The cheapest rooms (costing around €55) will often have only a sink in the room with the bathroom on the landing.

When choosing a hotel, it's a good idea to ask about the size of the rooms: some can be very cramped. It is also worth checking whether the rooms face busy, noisy roads. Rooms at the back, on the other hand, can sometimes be rather dark. Ask if there is an elevator to all floors, as in some older buildings this may not be the case.

It's worth booking as far in advance as you can, as the best hotels get booked up quickly, especially in spring and autumn.

If you're staying for more than a few days and/or you're a family or group of friends, renting an apartment can often be better value than a hotel. There's a wide choice, ranging from studio garrets to luxury apartments. It's also worth considering B&Bs, often cheaper and less impersonal than a hotel; most accommodate couples, but some can host families and some offer extras such as French conversation or guided tours. Hostels, aimed mostly at younger visitors, are another budget option; they tend to be slightly on the outskirts, but are well connected by metro.

DIRECTORY

BOAT TRIPS

Bateaux-Mouches
📞 01 42 25 96 10
🌐 bateaux-mouches.fr

Bateaux Parisiens
🌐 bateauxparisiens.com

Vedettes de Paris
📞 01 44 18 19 50
🌐 vedettesdeparis.com

Vedettes du Pont-Neuf
📞 01 46 33 98 38
🌐 vedettesdupontneuf.fr

GUIDED TOURS

Chic Shopping Paris
📞 09 77 19 77 85
🌐 chicshoppingparis.com

City Segway Tours
📞 01 56 58 10 54
🌐 citysegwaytours.com

Context Travel
🌐 www.contexttravel.com

DiscoverWalks
🌐 discoverwalks.com/paris-walking-tours

Edible Paris
🌐 edible-paris.com

Fat Tire Bike Tours
📞 01 56 58 10 54
🌐 fattirebiketours.com

O-Chateau
📞 01 44 73 97 80
🌐 o-chateau.com

Paris à Vélo
📞 01 48 87 60 01
🌐 parisvelosympa.com

Paris Walks
📞 01 48 09 21 40
🌐 paris-walks.com

Promenades Gourmandes
📞 01 48 04 56 84
🌐 promenadesgourmandes.com

Secrets of Paris
🌐 secretsofparis.com

WHERE TO STAY

Accomodation booking sites
🌐 airbnb.com
🌐 booking.com
🌐 hostelbookers.com
🌐 housetrip.com
🌐 parisinfo.com
🌐 perfectlyparis.com

B&BS

Alcove & Agapes
🌐 bed-and-breakfast-in-paris.com

Good Morning Paris
🌐 goodmorningparis.fr

HOSTELS

FUAJ
📞 01 44 89 87 27
🌐 fuaj.org

St Christophers Inn
🌐 st-christophers.co.uk

Places to Stay

PRICE CATEGORIES
For a standard double room per night (with breakfast if included), taxes and extra charges.

€ under €150   €€ €150–€350   €€€ over €350

Boutique Hotels

Hôtel Baume
MAP M5 ▪ 7 Rue Casimir Delavigne, 75006 ▪ 01 53 10 28 50 ▪ www.baume-hotel-paris.com/en/ ▪ €€
Minutes from the Jardin de Luxembourg, this modern hotel has recently been refurbished with a glamorous Art Deco-inspired interior. On the upper floors, spacious suites with a large terrace overlook the Neo-Classical Théâtre de l'Odéon.

Hôtel Bel Ami
MAP K4 ▪ 7/11 Rue St-Benoît, 75006 ▪ 01 42 61 53 53 ▪ www.hotel belami-paris.com ▪ €€
Occupying a former 19th-century printing works, this bright, stylish hotel is on a small side street in the heart of lively St-Germain-des-Prés. A good choice for design-conscious families, it has connecting rooms, as well as larger rooms that include a sofabed.

Hôtel de NELL
MAP F2 ▪ 9 Rue du Conservatoire, 75009 ▪ 01 44 83 83 60 ▪ www. www.hoteldenell.com ▪ €€€
The sleek, minimalist rooms in this contemporary hotel are ideal for a chic Parisian stay. . Twenty minutes on foot from the Louvre, the hotel is on a quiet street away from the crowds. For a more serene experience, ask for a room facing the interior courtyard.

Hôtel du Temps
MAP F2 ▪ 11 Rue de Montholon, 75009 ▪ 01 47 70 37 16 ▪ www.hotel-du-temps.fr ▪ €€
Vintage furniture and textiles give this creatively decorated small hotel, near the Gare du Nord, a home-away-from-home feel. Some rooms can be snug, but the imaginative touches fill the space with charm and style.

Hôtel Vernet
MAP C3 ▪ 25 Rue Vernet, 75008 ▪ 01 44 31 98 00 ▪ www.hotelvernet-paris.fr ▪ €€
Steps away from the Champs-Elysées, this recently renovated hotel combines cutting-edge contemporary design with the elegant framework of the post-Haussmannian building that it occupies. To have breakfast underneath the ornate, Gustave-Eiffel-designed glass dome is a stunning way to start the day.

La Maison Favart
MAP E3 ▪ 5 Rue de Marivaux, 75002 ▪ 01 42 97 59 83 ▪ www.lamaisonfavart.com ▪ €€
There is a sense of theatre at this graceful, small hotel dedicated to the colourful lives of Charles-Simon and Justine Favart, the 'It' couple of the 18th-century Opéra-Comique. Well-appointed, cheerfully decorated rooms have a courtesy tray; guests also have access to the small pool downstairs.

Hôtel Amour
MAP F1 ▪ 8 Rue Navarin, 75009 ▪ 01 48 78 31 80 ▪ www.hotelamourparis.fr ▪ €€€
Situated just below the hill of Montmartre, this extremely trendy vintage hotel and bistro has medium-sized rooms decorated with cutting-edge photography and pop art (bare bottoms and more much are in evidence). As it is on a quiet residential street, guests can experience Parisian bohemia without the usual crowds.

W Paris - Opéra Hotel
MAP E2 ▪ 4 Rue Meyerbeer, 75009 ▪ 01 77 48 94 94 ▪ www.wparis opera.com ▪ €€€
Ideally located next to the Opéra National de Paris Garnier, the W brings its trendy, modern flair to Paris with 91 ultra-chic rooms and suites. Nab one with a view of the opera house.

Luxury Hotels

Hôtel Molitor
13 Rue Nungesser et Coli, 75016 ▪ Metro Michel-Ange – Molitor ▪ 01 56 07 08 50 ▪ www.mgallery.com ▪ €€
Stunningly refurbished in 2014, this immaculate hotel breathes new life into the historic Art Deco

Piscine Molitor, where the beautiful people of 1930s Paris made waves. Minutes from the elegant botanical gardens in the Bois de Boulogne, it is within easy walking distance of the metro to central Paris.

Four Seasons George V
MAP C3 ■ 31 Ave George V, 75008 ■ 01 49 52 70 00 ■ www.fourseasons.com/paris ■ €€€
One of the most luxurious and fashionable hotels in Paris, the George V combines period features with modern amenities. Bedrooms are spacious, beautifully decorated and have marble bathrooms. The two-Michelin-starred restaurant, Le Cinq (see p117), is unquestionably one of the finest places to dine in the whole of Paris.

Hotel Plaza Athénée
MAP C3 ■ 25 Ave Montaigne, 75008 ■ 01 53 67 66 65 ■ www.plaza-athenee-paris.com ■ €€€
Surrounded by designer shops (see p116) is this venerable but thoroughly modernized hotel, famed for its old-world air of luxury and its immaculate service. Alain Ducasse has a dazzling restaurant in the hotel.

Hôtel Raphaël
MAP B3 ■ 17 Ave Kleber, 75016 ■ 01 53 64 32 00 ■ www. raphael-hotel. com ■ €€€
This is one of the city's finest hotels. The rooms have antique decor but they have been fully modernized in terms of the facilities they offer. Rooms on higher floors

have stunning Parisian city skyline views. The fitness room comes complete with hammam and sauna.

Mandarin Oriental
MAP E3 ■ 251 Rue St-Honoré, 75001 ■ 01 70 98 78 88 ■ www. mandarinoriental.com/paris ■ €€€
Centrally located on one of Paris's most fashionable streets, the interiors of this hotel are both Art Deco and Oriental. The rooms and suites are luxurious and spacious, and the service is impeccable.

Meurice
MAP E3 ■ 228 Rue de Rivoli, 75001 ■ 01 44 58 10 10 ■ www.lemeurice. com ■ €€€
The sumptuous antique decor of the Meurice may not be original, but you would never know it. The once-fading glory of this hotel has been completely restored, and it now offers spacious guest rooms and state-of-the-art facilities, as well as interiors by designer Philippe Starck. And the location could not be better.

The Peninsula Paris
MAP B3 ■ 19 Ave Kléber, 75016 ■ 01 58 12 28 88 ■ paris.peninsula.com ■ €€€
Occupying a sumptuously restored 1908 building, this grand hotel feels modern and has some great contemporary art-works on display in its vast public areas. Among the six drinking and dining outlets in the hotel, the Oiseau Blanc restaurant stands out for its spectacular views.

Prince de Galles
MAP C3 ■ 33 Ave George V, 75008 ■ 01 53 23 77 77 ■ www.prince degallesparis.com ■ €€€
Steps from the luxury and haute couture boutiques, this gloriously restored Art Deco hotel features handsome rooms, some with a balcony or terrace, and the Michelin-starred restaurant, La Scène. Guests can use the on-site spa and gym.

Le Royal Monceau
MAP C2 ■ 37 Ave Hoche, 75008 ■ 01 42 99 88 00 ■ www.raffles.com/paris ■ €€€
This Paris branch of the Raffles hotel chain features interiors by Philippe Starck and two superb restaurants.

Shangri-La Paris
MAP A3 ■ 10 Ave d'Iéna, 75116 ■ 01 53 67 19 98 ■ www.shangri-la.com ■ €€€
Housed in the former home of Napoleon's grand-nephew, this fabulous hotel is located in the elegant 16th arrondissement. Most of the rooms have views of the Eiffel Tower.

The Westin Paris
MAP E3 ■ 3 Rue de Castiglione, 75001 ■ 01 44 77 11 11 ■ www.westin.com ■ €€€
The Westin is world away from the usual anonymity of chain hotels, being set in a 19th-century building designed by Charles Garnier and overlooking the Tuileries gardens. The original atmosphere has been retained, but the rooms offer everything you would expect from a hotel of this class.

Romantic Hotels

Five Hotel

3 Rue Flatters, 75005
■ Metro Les Gobelins
■ 01 43 31 74 21 ■ www.
thefivehotel.com ■ €
Fibre-optic lighting
creates a glittering
atmosphere in many
of this boutique hotel's
24 rooms. The rooms
come in nine different
colours, ranging from
sleek black to cheerful
plum-and-pink, and five
"olfactory ambiences" by
Esteban. The Five has
already established a
reputation as the perfect
lovers' hideaway hotel.

Hôtel Caron de Beaumarchais

MAP R2 ■ 12 Rue Vieille
du Temple, 75004 ■ 01 42
72 34 12 ■ www.caron
debeaumarchais.com
■ No disabled access ■ €
Wooden beams,
candlelight, a log fire,
authentic decor and
sparkling crystal
chandeliers evoke the
essence of 18th-century
romance. Rooms are
beautiful and guests
are truly pampered.

Hôtel d'Aubusson

MAP M4 ■ 33 Rue
Dauphine, 75006 ■ 01 43
29 43 43 ■ www.hotel
daubusson.com ■ €€
The rooms in this
17th-century building
are spacious and many
of them have beams.
In winter there is a log fire
in the guests' lounge.

Hôtel Bourg Tibourg

MAP P3 ■ 19 Rue du
Bourg Tibourg, 75004
■ 01 42 78 47 39 ■ www.
bourgtibourg.com ■ €€
The lavishly decorated
rooms in this intimate

boutique hotel are
furnished with antiques
and luxurious fabrics.
Public spaces are hung
with tapestries, and
there's a peaceful library
lounge. Most rooms are
small – and the lift is
possibly the tiniest in the
city – but the location, in
the heart of the Marais,
makes up for it.

Le Relais Christine

MAP M4 ■ 3 Rue
Christine, 75006 ■ 01 40
51 60 80 ■ www.relais-
christine.com ■ No
disabled access ■ €€
This historic mansion
with a spa offers a quiet
side-street escape from
the St-Germain bustle.
Opt for a terraced room
overlooking the secluded
garden and take breakfast
in the vaulted dining room
which was once the
refectory of an abbey.

Hôtel Bellechasse

MAP J2 ■ 8 Rue de
Bellechasse, 75007
■ 01 45 50 22 31 ■ www.
lebellechasse.com ■ No
disabled access ■ €€€
The fabulously opulent
rooms at this hotel were
designed by Christian
Lacroix. Special packages,
such as Pour Une Nuit,
include a 3pm checkout,
Champagne and other
indulgent treats. The
hotel is located just a
few minutes' walk from
the Musée d'Orsay.

Hôtel Costes

MAP E3 ■ 239 Rue
St-Honoré, 75001 ■ 01 42
44 50 00 ■ www.hotel
costes.com ■ €€€
Book a first-floor room
overlooking the courtyard
for a romantic place to
stay. Low lighting and
dark furniture add to

the seductive mood,
as does the Oriental-style
swimming pool and
trendy restaurant.

L'Hôtel

MAP E4 ■ 13 Rue des
Beaux-Arts, 75006
■ 01 44 41 99 00 ■ www.
l-hotel.com ■ €€€
This hotel has come up
in the world since Oscar
Wilde expired here, having
uttered the famous words,
"My wallpaper and I
are fighting a duel to the
death. One or the other of
us has to go." Fashionable
as it has become, with
stylish decor by Jacques
Garcia and a Michelin-
starred restaurant, the
hotel still retains its
quirky charm.

Hôtel Particulier Montmartre

MAP E1 ■ 23 Ave Junot,
Pavillon D, 75018 ■ 01 53
41 81 40 ■ www.hotel-
particulier-montmartre.
com ■ No disabled access
■ €€€
This hotel is a romantic
hideaway right in the
heart of Montmartre,
housed in a former
private residence. The five
suites are individually
decorated by artists in
quirky and decadent style.

Hotels in Great Locations

Hôtel Brighton

MAP K1 ■ 218 Rue de
Rivoli, 75001 ■ 01 47 03
61 61 ■ www.paris-hotel-
brighton.com ■ €€
Enjoy the Rue de Rivoli,
within walking distance
of numerous attractions,
without paying the usual
prices associated with this
location. The venerable
Hôtel Brighton has been
completely refurbished –

ask for a room with a view over the Tuileries gardens opposite or, even better, of the Eiffel Tower.

Hôtel des Deux-Iles
MAP Q5 ▪ 59 Rue St-Louis-en-l'Ile, 75004 ▪ 01 43 26 13 35 ▪ www. hoteldesdeuxiles.com ▪ No disabled access ▪ €€
To stay on one of the Seine islands is a treat, and to do it in this hotel is a double treat. The bedrooms may be small, due to the building's 17th-century origins, but the cheerful decor, the intimacy (only 17 rooms) and the hidden patio with its flowers and fountain more than compensate.

Hôtel du Jeu de Paume
MAP Q5 ▪ 54 Rue St-Louis-en-l'Ile, 75004 ▪ 01 43 26 14 18 ▪ www. jeudepaumehotel.com ▪ €€
Tucked away on the Ile St-Louis is this beautiful old building with ancient beamed ceilings. Some rooms overlook a peaceful courtyard, and all are quite small, however the welcoming atmosphere makes up for that.

Hôtel d'Orsay
MAP J2 ▪ 93 Rue de Lille, 75007 ▪ 01 47 05 85 54 ▪ www.paris-hotel-orsay. com ▪ €€
Art-lovers will enjoy this hotel, in an 18th-century building near to the magnificent Musée d'Orsay. The hotel's bright and modern decor is strikingly offset with choice items of elegant antique furniture here and there. Several more expensive suites are also available. A buffet

breakfast is served in a light and airy room under a glass roof.

Hôtel de la Place du Louvre
MAP M2 ▪ 21 Rue des Prêtres-St-Germain-l'Auxerrois, 75001 ▪ 01 42 33 78 68 ▪ www.paris-hotel-place-du-louvre. com ▪ No disabled access ▪ €€
The 20 rooms in this neat little hotel may be small, but many of them offer a superb view onto the colonnade of the Louvre museum. The decor is bright and fresh, and cleverly mixes classic and modern influences.

Hôtel Le Bristol Paris
MAP D3 ▪ 112 Rue du Faubourg St-Honoré, 75008 ▪ 01 53 43 43 00 ▪ www.lebristolparis.com ▪ €€€
Prices reflect the level of luxury and the location, on the Faubourg St-Honoré. Rooms are spacious, and fitted out with antique furniture. They offer indulgently large marble bathrooms, as well as all the latest modern facilities. There are also two restaurants.

Hôtel Edouard VII
MAP E3 ▪ 39 Ave de l'Opéra, 75002 ▪ 01 42 61 56 90 ▪ www.edouard 7hotel.com ▪ €€€
An elegant boutique hotel with eclectic design features and oodles of charm. Most rooms have the bonus of breath-taking balcony views over the spectacular Opéra National de Paris Garnier. The bar serves tailor-made cocktails and the restaurant offers inventive seasonal cuisine.

Hôtel Les Dames du Panthéon
MAP N6 ▪ 19 Pl du Panthéon, 75005 ▪ 01 43 54 32 95 ▪ www. hotellesdamesdu pantheon.com ▪ €€€
A small, charming hotel set in an 18th-century building right by the Panthéon.

Pavillon de la Reine
MAP R3 ▪ 28 Pl des Vosges, 75003 ▪ 01 40 29 19 19 ▪ www.pavillon-de-la-reine.com ▪ €€€
This may well be the best hotel in the Marais, right on the Place des Vosges. Lovely rooms, a spa and a quiet courtyard.

Starhotels Castille
MAP E3 ▪ 33 Rue Cambon, 75001 ▪ 01 44 58 44 58 ▪ www.castille. com ▪ €€€
This elegant hotel is located near Place Vendôme. The bedrooms are decorated in either a contemporary style or classic 1930s French, depending on which wing you stay in. The hotel also boasts an Italian restaurant, l'Assaggio.

Rooms with a View

Hôtel du Quai Voltaire
MAP K2 ▪ 19 Quai Voltaire, 75007 ▪ 01 42 61 50 91 ▪ www.quaivoltaire. fr ▪ No air conditioning ▪ No disabled access ▪ €
Impressionist artist Camille Pissarro (1830–1903) painted the view of the Seine and Notre-Dame visible from most of the guest rooms here. Rooms are small, but the warm welcome and the location more than make up for that.

Artus Hôtel
MAP L4 ▪ 34 Rue de Buci, 75006 ▪ 01 43 29 07 20 ▪ www.artushotel.com ▪ No disabled access ▪ €€

You'll be able to indulge yourself in the food shops of the Rue de Buci, then pamper yourself even more back in this hotel – especially if you have booked the suite with a Jacuzzi, from which there are views of the rooftops of the Latin Quarter.

Bourgogne & Montana
MAP D4 ▪ 3 Rue de Bourgogne, 75007 ▪ 01 45 51 20 22 ▪ www.bourgogne-montana.com ▪ No disabled access ▪ €€

A stylish hotel, with the Musée d'Orsay and the Invalides close by. Rooms feature Empire-style furnishings and Kenzo-designed wallpaper. Some top-floor rooms have views across the Seine.

Hôtel des Grands Hommes
MAP N6 ▪ 17 Pl du Panthéon, 75005 ▪ 01 46 34 19 60 ▪ www.hoteldesgrandshommes.com ▪ No disabled access ▪ €€

Great upper floor views of the Panthéon from this intimate 30-room hotel in an 18th-century house. Rooms are a good size.

Le Notre-Dame St-Michel
MAP N4 ▪ 1 Quai St-Michel, 75005 ▪ 01 43 54 20 43 ▪ www.hotelnotredameparis.com ▪ No disabled access ▪ €€

This hotel is in a great location right by the Seine with magnificent views of Notre-Dame. The bright

decor by Christian Lacroix here makes up for the small size of the rooms.

Radisson Blu Le Metropolitan
MAP A3 ▪ 10 Pl de Mexico, 75016 ▪ 01 56 90 40 04 ▪ www.radissonblu.com ▪ €€

Five upper suites offer striking views of the Eiffel Tower; the best has a giant bull's-eye window. Lower-floor rooms have good, but less spectacular, balcony views.

Les Rives de Notre-Dame
MAP N4 ▪ 15 Quai St-Michel, 75005 ▪ 01 43 54 81 16 ▪ www.rivesdenotredame.com ▪ No disabled access ▪ €€

The views of Notre-Dame from this 10-room Latin Quarter hotel are arguably the best in Paris. The spacious and airy rooms feature charming wooden ceiling beams.

Hôtel Régina
MAP K1 ▪ 2 Pl des Pyramides, 75001 ▪ 01 42 60 31 10 ▪ www.regina-hotel.com ▪ €€

Across the Rue de Rivoli from the Louvre, with views of the museum and the Tuileries, this is a splendid old hotel. The rooms are elegantly decorated and there's a terrace for al fresco dining. The bar is reminiscent of Victorian England, with its oak panelling and plush sofas.

Hotel Square
MAP A5 ▪ 3 Rue de Boulainvilliers, 75016 ▪ 01 44 14 91 90 ▪ www.hotelsquare.com ▪ €€€

The Square is an ultra-chic boutique hotel with

22 rooms and views over Paris. The dramatic architecture includes a four-storey exhibition wall featuring modern art. Classic and inventive cuisine is served at hip Zebra Square restaurant, and there's also a spa.

Terrass Hôtel
MAP E1 ▪ 12–14 Rue Joseph de Maistre, 75018 ▪ 01 46 06 72 85 ▪ www.terrass-hotel.com ▪ €€€

Located in Montmartre, the Terrass has fabulous views over the city from its rooftop terrace. Most rooms in this early 19th-century building have air conditioning. There is a bar, restaurant and other facilities.

Family-Friendly Hotels

Hôtel des Arts
MAP F2 ▪ 7 Cité Bergère, 6 Rue du Faubourg Montmartre, 75009 ▪ 01 42 46 73 30 ▪ www.hoteldesarts.fr ▪ No disabled access ▪ €

This hotel is an excellent choice for families on a budget, with triple rooms and cots available. It's tucked away in one of Paris's pretty *passages* in arty Montmartre.

Hôtel Elysées Flaubert
MAP C1 ▪ 19 Rue Rennequin, 75017 ▪ 01 46 22 44 35 ▪ www.parishotelflaubert.com ▪ €

This hotel, slightly out of the centre but not far from the metro, offers terrific value. The new owners have given it a smart makeover, and the lush garden is a delight. A continental buffet breakfast is free if you book directly through their website.

Ibis Paris Bastille Faubourg Saint Antoine

MAP H5 ▪ 13 Rue Trousseau, 75011 ▪ 01 48 05 55 55 ▪ www.ibis.com ▪ €
A popular budget option, this hotel in the Ibis chain is a five-minute walk from the bustling Marché d'Aligre. Triple rooms and smartly designed duplex rooms are perfect for families.

Hôtel Baltimore

MAP B3 ▪ 88 Bis, Ave Kléber, 75016 ▪ 01 44 34 54 54 ▪ www.accorhotels. com ▪ €€
Part of the Accor hotel chain and located in between the Trocadéro and the Arc de Triomphe, the Baltimore caters well for families, with good facilities and a friendly attitude. Rooms and suites are elegant.

Hôtel St-Jacques

MAP N5 ▪ 35 Rue des Ecoles, 75005 ▪ 01 44 07 45 45 ▪ www.paris-hotel-stjacques.com ▪ €€
Numerous Left Bank attractions are within walking distance of this comfortable hotel with triple-bed rooms and cots available. The Toulouse-Lautrec Bar is excellent.

Pullman Paris Montparnasse

MAP D6 ▪ 19 Rue du Commandant René Mouchotte, 75014 ▪ 01 44 36 44 36 ▪ www. pullmanhotels.com ▪ €€
Facilities here include family rooms with two double beds. Breakfast

and accommodation is free for two under-13s when sharing a room with their parents. The hotel also lays on children's entertainment during Sunday brunch.

Relais du Louvre

MAP M2 ▪ 19 Rue des Prêtres-St-Germain-l'Auxerrois, 75001 ▪ 01 40 41 96 42 ▪ www.relais dulouvre.com ▪ No disabled access ▪ €€
Right by the Louvre, this great family hotel offers a self-catering apartment for five, plus several family suites and communicating rooms, as well as a host of extras for children.

Relais St-Germain

MAP L4 ▪ 9 Carrefour de l'Odéon, 75006 ▪ 01 44 27 07 97 ▪ www.hotel-paris-relais-saint-germain.com ▪ No disabled access ▪ €€
A delightful 17th-century town-house hotel in the heart of the Left Bank. The Louvre, Musée d'Orsay and Notre-Dame cathedral are all within walking distance. The Jardin du Luxembourg is also nearby, for when the children simply want to let off steam and play in the gardens.

Résidence NELL

MAP E2 ▪ 60 Rue Richer, 75009 ▪ 01 53 24 98 98 ▪ www.residencenell.com ▪ €€
The 17 chic, understated apartments and suites in this handsomely renovated building each have a kitchenette so families can stock up at the grocery stores and bakeries nearby. Large families should ask for adjoining suites.

Medium-Priced Hotels

Le Citizen

MAP H2 ▪ 96 Quai de Jenmapes, 75010 ▪ 01 83 62 55 50 ▪ www.lecitizen hotel.com ▪ €€
This modern eco-hotel boasts views over the chic Canal St-Martin. There are 12 rooms and suites and each one comes with a complimentary minibar and iPad for use during your stay. There's a wide choice of restaurants nearby, too.

Hôtel de l'Abbaye Saint–Germain

MAP K5 ▪ 10 Rue Cassette, 75006 ▪ 01 45 44 38 11 ▪ www. hotelabbayeparis.com ▪ No disabled access ▪ €€
This delightful hotel, in a 16th-century former convent, is set around a leafy cobbled courtyard in a quiet location near St-Sulpice. It is perfect for exploring much of the Left Bank, and is a haven to return to afterwards. The 44 rooms are all different, the best being the top-floor suites with their rooftop views.

Hôtel d'Angleterre

MAP N5 ▪ 44 Rue Jacob, 75006 ▪ 01 42 60 34 72 ▪ www.hotel-dangleterre. com ▪ No air conditioning ▪ No disabled access ▪ €€
Hemingway once stayed in this long-established hotel. Most of the rooms have high ceilings, and some are furnished with antiques. Standard rooms can be on the small side, but more spacious superior rooms can be reserved at an extra cost.

For a key to hotel price categories see p172

Hôtel de Banville
166 Blvd Berthier, 75017 ▪ Metro Porte de Clichy ▪ 01 42 67 70 16 ▪ www. hotelbanville.fr ▪ €€
This wonderful 1928 mansion may be away from the centre but it oozes class and is filled with antiques. On Thursdays, there is live music in the hall. Several bedrooms have balconies.

Hôtel Le Clos Médicis
MAP M5 ▪ 56 Rue Monsieur-le-Prince, 75006 ▪ 01 43 29 10 80 ▪ www.closmedicis.com ▪ 1 room suitable for disabled guests ▪ €€
This was built in 1773 for the Médici family; historic features now seamlessly combine with modern design. Rooms are small, but compensations are the garden, bar, and the location, in a quiet street off boulevard St-Michel.

Hôtel Notre-Dame Paris Maître Albert
MAP N5 ▪ 19 Rue Maître Albert, 75005 ▪ 01 43 26 79 00 ▪ www.hotel-notre dame-charmeparis.com ▪ No disabled access ▪ €€
Situated in a quiet street opposite Notre-Dame, close to the Latin Quarter and the Marais, this hotel combines sleek modern design and high-tech facilities with the odd beam or stone wall.

Hôtel Saint-Paul
MAP M5 ▪ 43 Rue Monsieur-le-Prince, 75006 ▪ 01 43 26 98 64 ▪ www.hotelsaint paulparis.fr ▪ €€
This 17th-century building features antique furniture, beamed ceilings and even some four-poster beds. Several rooms have great views over Paris and the Sorbonne. Breakfast is served in a cellar with a vaulted ceiling.

Hôtel le Senat
MAP M5 ▪ 10 Rue de Vaugirard, 75006 ▪ 01 43 54 54 54 ▪ www.hotel senat.com ▪ €€
In an excellent central location, just a few steps away from the Jardin de Luxembourg, this small modern hotel is smartly decorated in cheery colours. Some rooms can accommodate families, and the two duplex terrace suites on the top floors have fantastic panoramic views.

Hôtel des Trois Poussins
MAP E1 ▪ 5 Rue Clauzel, 75009 ▪ 01 53 32 81 81 ▪ www.les3poussins.com ▪ €€
This hotel is in the Pigalle area but well away from the sleazier side of the district. Some rooms are small, but the higher up they are, the better the view of the city becomes. The decor is modern with warm colours and each room has a quirky artwork on the wall.

La Régence Etoile Hôtel
MAP B2 ▪ 24 Ave Carnot, 75017 ▪ 01 58 05 42 42 ▪ www.laregenceetoile. com ▪ No disabled access ▪ €€
Very reasonably priced considering its standard of luxury and its location (just a short walk from the Arc de Triomphe), the Régence Etoile features handsome public spaces and plush modern bedrooms with plasma TVs, mini-bars and safes.

Budget Hotels

Le Caulaincourt Square Hôtel
MAP E1 ▪ 2 Square Caulaincourt, 75018 ▪ 01 46 06 46 06 ▪ www. caulaincourt.com ▪ No air conditioning ▪ No disabled access ▪ €
Part budget hotel, part hostel, with a friendly atmosphere and easy access to the sights of Montmartre.

Ermitage Hôtel
MAP E1 ▪ 24 Rue Lamarck, 75018 ▪ 01 42 64 79 22 ▪ www. ermitagesacrecoeur.fr ▪ No credit cards ▪ No air conditioning ▪ No disabled access ▪ €
A wonderful family-run hotel in Montmartre. Some rooms have views over the city, others overlook a garden, and the furniture is antique or retro.

Grand Hôtel Lévêque
MAP C4 ▪ 29 Rue Cler, 75007 ▪ 01 47 05 49 15 ▪ www.hotel-leveque. com ▪ No disabled access ▪ €
The only thing grand about this hotel is its name, but it remains a favourite for budget accommodation. Almost all rooms have fans, phone, TV and a hairdryer, and a free Continental breakfast is served daily.

Hôtel Arvor Saint-Georges
MAP E2 ▪ 8 Rue Laferrière, 75009 ▪ 01 48 78 60 92 ▪ hotelarvor. com/en/ ▪ No air conditioning ▪ No disabled access ▪ €
A budget boutique hotel at the foot of Montmartre, with comfortable rooms,

many boasting views across Paris. Two-room suites, one in the attic and one opening onto a small patio, are good for families.

Hôtel Chopin

MAP F2 ▪ 46 Passage Jouffroy, 75009 ▪ 01 47 70 58 10 ▪ www.hotelchopin. fr ▪ No air conditioning ▪ No disabled access ▪ €

The rooms have heaps of charm – and some picture-perfect rooftop views – at this characterful, historic hotel which dates from 1846.

Hôtel du Cygne

MAP N1 ▪ 3–5 Rue du Cygne, 75001 ▪ 01 42 60 14 16 ▪ www.hoteldu cygne.fr ▪ Not all en-suite ▪ No air conditioning ▪ No disabled access ▪ €

This lovely hotel is housed in a restored 17th-century building, just five minutes' walk away from Forum Les Halles. Free Wi-Fi is available in all the rooms, and breakfast is included.

Hôtel Familia

MAP P6 ▪ 11 Rue des Ecoles, 75005 ▪ 01 43 54 55 27 ▪ www.familia hotel.com ▪ €

This popular budget option in the heart of the Latin Quarter is a friendly hotel within walking distance of many landmarks. The best rooms have a charming wrought-iron balcony.

Hôtel des Grandes Ecoles

MAP P6 ▪ 75 Rue du Cardinal Lemoine, 75005 ▪ 01 43 26 79 23 ▪ www. hotel-grandes-ecoles.com ▪ No air conditioning ▪ €

A secret hideaway in a lovely part of Paris, the three buildings that make

up this 51-room hotel are set around a garden. The rooms are attractively decorated and the location is perfect for exploring the Latin Quarter.

Hôtel Jeanne d'Arc

3 Rue de Jarente, 75004 ▪ Metro St-Paul ▪ 01 48 87 62 11 ▪ www.hotel jeannedarc.com ▪ No air conditioning ▪ €

You could easily spend a whole weekend in Paris without wandering far from this well-equipped hotel, surrounded as it is by the many Marais district attractions.

Hôtel Joyce

MAP E2 ▪ 29 Rue la Bruyère, 75009 ▪ 01 55 07 00 01 ▪ www.astotel. com ▪ €

This wittily decorated modern hotel has a fresh, informal feel and well-equipped rooms with organic toiletries. Room rates include a good-value buffet breakfast.

Hôtel de Nesle

MAP L4 ▪ 7 Rue de Nesle, 75006 ▪ 01 43 54 62 41 ▪ www.hoteldenesleparis. com ▪ No disabled access ▪ €

Centrally located, this atmospheric hotel, complete with a large courtyard garden, is colourfully decorated with murals and vintage wallpaper. Not all rooms are en-suite. Phone reservations only.

Hôtel de Nice

MAP Q3 ▪ 42 bis Rue de Rivoli, 75004 ▪ 01 42 78 55 29 ▪ www.hoteldenice. com ▪ No disabled access ▪ €

A ten-minute walk to Notre-Dame cathedral,

and even less to the shops and cafés of the Marais, this quirky small hotel has a romantic, 19th-century charm.

Hôtel Regyn's Montmartre

MAP E1 ▪ 18 Pl des Abbesses, 75018 ▪ 01 42 54 45 21 ▪ www.paris-hotels-montmartre.com ▪ No air conditioning ▪ No disabled access ▪ €

Colourful Toile de Jouy wallpaper livens up the smallish rooms in this budget hotel, well-placed in the heart of Montmartre and just minutes away on foot from Sacré-Coeur. The amenities are basic, but the stunning views of the Eiffel Tower from the upper floors are priceless.

Hôtel Saint-André-des-Arts

MAP M4 ▪ 66 Rue St-André-des-Arts, 75006 ▪ 01 43 26 96 16 ▪ www. hotel-saintandredesarts. fr ▪ No air conditioning ▪ No disabled access ▪ €

This modest hotel has ancient exposed beams and stone walls, plus an enviable Left Bank location at bargain prices. The rooms are tiny, but for a cheap bolt-hole and truly Parisian feel, it can't be beaten.

Mama Shelter

109 Rue de Bagnolet, 75020 ▪ Metro Gambetta ▪ 01 43 48 48 48 ▪ www. mamashelter.com ▪ €

Created by world-famous designer Philippe Starck, this trendy hotel close to Père Lachaise cemetery offers ultra-stylish yet affordable rooms. The lively restaurant is very popular, and there's a great rooftop sundeck.

For a key to hotel price categories see p172

General Index

Acknowledgments

Author
Donna Dailey and Mike Gerrard are award-winning journalists, specializing in travel, food and wine and have written more than 30 guidebooks between them. Mike Gerrard's *Time for Food* guide to Paris for Thomas Cook won the Benjamin Franklin Award for the best new guidebook in 2001. Their work has appeared in international publications such as the *Times*, *Washington Post* and *Global Adventure*.

Additional contributors
Ruth Reisenberger, M Astella Saw

Publishing Director Georgina Dee

Publisher Vivien Antwi

Design Director Phil Ormerod

Editorial Michelle Crane, Rachel Fox, Fay Franklin, Fíodhna Ní Ghríofa, Freddie Marriage, Sally Schafer, Christine Stroyan

Design Tessa Bindloss, Marisa Renzullo

Picture Research Phoebe Lowndes, Susie Peachey, Ellen Root, Oran Tarjan

Cartography Mohammad Hassan, Suresh Kumar, Casper Morris, Simonetta Giori

DTP Jason Little, George Nimmo

Production Nancy-Jane Maun

Factchecker Bryan Pirolli

Proofreader Kate Berens

Indexer Patricia Baker

Illustrator Chris Orr & Associates

Commissioned Photography Max Alexander, Neil Lukas, Eric Meacher, Rough Guides/ Lydia Evans, Rough Guides/James McConnachie, Jules Selmes, Valerio Vincenzo, Peter Wilson.

First edition created by Book Creation Services Ltd, London

Picture Credits
The publisher would like to thank the following for their kind permission to reproduce their photographs:
(**Key:** a-above; b-below/bottom; c-centre; f-far; l-left; r-right; t-top)

4Corners: SIME/Stefano Brozzi 4b.

Abbey Bookshop: Picasa 128cb.

Alamy Images: Bildarchiv Monheim GmbH 21tl;Godong 20bc; Glenn Harper 79tr; Hemis 94tr; 135bl, hemis.fr / Pascal Ducept 87bl; hemis.fr/Bertrand Gardel 59cla;hemis.fr/ Gilles Rigoulet 137tl; hemis.fr /Sylvain Sonnet 59br; Heritage Image Partnership Ltd 144br; Peter Horree 33tl; John Kellerman 38br, 112tl; Lautaro 127cla; Eddie Linssen/ADAGP, Paris and DACS, London 2015 84tr; macdonald_churches 22tr; Claude Thibault 152cr.

Anatomica: 96tl.

Au Lapin Agile: 148br;Peter Koslowski 152tl.

Au Pied de Cochon: Raoul Dobremel 88t.

AWL Images: Danita Delimont Stock 1; Hemis 2tr, 3tl, 40-1, 76-7.

Barbara Bui: David Picchiottino 116br.

Benoit: C.Sarramon 90br.

Bridgeman Images: Musée de l'Armée, Paris, France 38bl.

Buvette: Nicole Franzen 153br.

Café Castiglione: Eric Fenot 107br.

Clair de Rêve: 82bl.

Clown Bar Paris: Galland 69tr.

Corbis: Bettmann 45tr; 150c; Patrick Escudero 47br; The Gallery Collection 19cl, 45bl, 64cla; The Gallery Collection/Louvre Paris *The Raft of the Medusa* by Théodore Géricault 13tl; The Gallery Collection/Louvre *The Lacemaker* Jan Vermeer Louvre 13cr; The Gallery Collection Musée d'Orsay *Dancers in Blue* Edgar Degas 18bl; Godong /Fred de Noyelle 49cr; Hemis/ Arnaud Chicurel 80t; hemis.fr/Bertrand Gardel 159b; Hulton-Deutsch Collection 114tr, 135tr; Peter Langer 143tl; Leemage 19b; Mosaic Images 126cla; Musée d'Orsay, Paris *The Siesta (after Millet)* by Vincent van Gogh,10cl; Musée D'Orsay *Van Gogh's Bedroom at Arles* by Vincent Van Gogh, 16-7c; Gianni Dagli Orti 10tr, 15bl, 43tr; Bertrand Rieger/Louvre *Captives or Slaves Dying* Michelangelo 12bl; Robert Harding World Imagery/Godong 42tl; David Sailors 120bl; Vittorio Sciosia 141br; Leonard de Selva 44cr; John Springer Collection 23b; Sygma/Jacques Pavlovsky 86cra; Michael Le Poer Trench 44tl; Tim de Waele 74tc.

Dreamstime.com: Alfonsodetomas 78cla; Andersastphoto 10br; Andrey Anisimov 85tr; Aprescindere 57tr; Ardazi 70tl; Baghitsha 48tr; Bargotiphotography 6cl; Christian Bertrand 147tr; Mikhail Blajenov 48bl; Bukki88/SOCIETE D'EXPLOITATION DE LA TOUR EIFFEL/SETE/Copyright Tour Eiffel-illuminations Pierre Bideau 24cl; Cecoffman 56br; Mircea Costina 56t; Dabldy 118cla; Matthew Dixon 54t; Dennis Dolkens 4t, 12cra; Chris Dorney 125tr; Viorel Dudau 33bl, 64b; Alexandre Fagundes De Fagundes 98tl; Flynt 108-9; freephoton 138br; Goghy73 46bl; Nataliya Hora 61tr; Infomods 104-5; Javarman 36clb; Javierjmt 75tr; Pavel Kavalenkau 142br; Ladiras81 146tl; Lornet 110cla; Meunierd 53tl, 86bl; Miketanct 10bl; Moharrim 4cr; Monticello 7tr; Juan Moyano 4cla, 7cr; Nikonaft 3tr, 162-3; Ohmaymay 62-3; Andrey Omelyanchuk 2tl, 8-9; Francisco Javier Gil Oreja 4crb, 11ca, 32clb; Anna Penigina 158bl; Janusz Pieńkowski 73clb; Pixattitude 121cla; ProductionPerig 20-1; Evgeny Prokofyev 119br; Puppie2008 11br,

36br; Olivier Le Queinec 11clb; Sborisov 28-9; Scaliger 58tl; Juergen Schonnop 36-7c; Lee Snider 57tl; Sognolucido 54br; Peter Spirer 72tl; Tinamou 93tr; Vitalyedush 124tr; Adam Wasilewski 4cl; Yulan 155tr.

Epicure: 117tr.

Fotolia: JL 31tl; lornet 30br, 111tr; petunyia 34-5c.

Four Seasons Hotel George V: 114bl.

Fragonard Parfumeur: 97bl.

The Frog & Rosbif: Samuel Hense 91tr.

Getty Images: AFP/Stringer 85br; Alinari Archives 23tl; DEA/G. DAGLI ORTI 17tl; Ralph Gatti 150tl; Hekimian/Rindoff Petroff 105tl; Fernand Ivaldi 32-3c; Keystone-France 22bl; Patrick Kovarik 148t; Leemage 15tl; Francois Xavier Marit 115crb; Print Collector 42cr, 43bl; Yvan Travert 149clb.

Kayser: Thierry Samuel 132b.

L'Atelier de Joel Robuchon: 67tr.

L'Atelier de l'Eclair: 89br.

La Rose de France: 83tr.

La Truffiere: 139tl.

Le Bon Marche: 71bc.

Le Jules Verne: Matt Aletti 25bl.

Le Pub Saint-Germain: Crea PR 130tr.

Ministere Français de la Culture et de la Communication: 74br.

Monsieur Bleu: Adrien Dirand 145crb.

Musée de la Magie et des Automates: Mikelkl 60tl.

Parc de la Villette: Marie-Sophie Leturcq 60br, 156bl.

Paris Tourist Office: Marc Bertrand 72br, 73tr.

Restaurant Chez Paul: 101bl.

Restaurant David Toutain: Thai Toutain 123bl.

Restaurant La Tour d'Argent: 133tr.

Restaurant Septime: François Flohic 66br.

Shakespeare and Company: Tobias Staebler 128tl.

SuperStock: Peter Willi 14tr.

Le Taillevent: Arnaud Meyer 66t.

Jacket

Front and spine – **Getty Images:** Travelpix Ltd ©Tour Eiffel-illuminations Pierre Bideau/ SOCIETE D'EXPLOITATION DE LA TOUR EIFFEL/SETE.

Back – **Dreamstime.com:** Flynt.

Pull-out map cover
Getty Images: Travelpix Ltd ©Tour Eiffel-illuminations Pierre Bideau/SOCIETE D'EXPLOITATION DE LA TOUR EIFFEL/SETE.

All other images are: © Dorling Kindersley. For further information see www.dkimages.com.

Penguin Random House

Printed and bound in China

First published in Great Britain in 2002 by Dorling Kindersley Limited 80 Strand, London WC2R 0RL

Copyright 2002, 2016 © Dorling Kindersley Limited

A Penguin Random House Company

15 16 17 18 10 9 8 7 6 5 4 3 2 1

Reprinted with revisions 2003, 2004, 2005, 2006, 2007, 2008, 2009, 2010, 2011, 2012, 2013, 2014, 2016

A CIP catalogue record is available from the British Library.

ISBN 978 0 2411 9844 5

MIX
Paper from responsible sources
FSC™ C018179

SPECIAL EDITIONS OF DK TRAVEL GUIDES

Phrase Book

In an Emergency

Help!	**Au secours!**	oh sekoor
Stop!	**Arrêtez!**	aret-ay
Call…	**Appelez…**	apuh-lay
…a doctor!	**…un médecin!**	uñ medsañ
…an ambulance!	**…une ambulance!**	oon oñboo-loñs
…the police!	**…la police!**	lah poh-lees
…the fire brigade!	**…les pompiers!**	leh poñ-peeyay

Communication Essentials

Yes/No	**Oui/Non**	wee/noñ
Please	**S'il vous plaît**	seel voo play
Thank you	**Merci**	mer-see
Excuse me	**Excusez-moi**	exkoo-zay mwah
Hello	**Bonjour**	boñzhoor
Goodbye	**Au revoir**	oh ruh-vwar
Good night	**Bonsoir**	boñ-swar
What?	**Quel, quelle?**	kel, kel
When?	**Quand?**	koñ
Why?	**Pourquoi?**	poor-kwah
Where?	**Où?**	oo

Useful Phrases

How are you?	**Comment allez-vous?**	kom-moñ talay voo
Very well, Pleased to meet you.	**Très bien, Enchanté de faire votre connaissance.**	treh byañ oñshoñ-tay duh fehr votr kon-ay-sans
Where is/are…?	**Où est/sont…?**	oo ay/soñ
Which way to..?	**Quelle est la direction pour..?**	kel ay lah deer-ek-syoñ poor
Do you speak English?	**Parlez-vous anglais?**	par-lay voo oñg-lay
I don't understand.	**Je ne comprends pas.**	zhuh nuh kom-proñ pah
I'm sorry.	**Excusez-moi.**	exkoo-zay mwah

Useful Words

big	**grand**	groñ
small	**petit**	puh-tee
hot	**chaud**	show
cold	**froid**	frwah
good	**bon**	boñ
bad	**mauvais**	moh-veh
open	**ouvert**	oo-ver
closed	**fermé**	fer-meh
left	**gauche**	gohsh
right	**droit**	drwah
entrance	**l'entrée**	l'on-tray
exit	**la sortie**	sor-tee
toilet	**les toilettes**	twah-let

Shopping

How much is it?	**Ça fait combien?**	sa fay kom-byañ
What time…	**A quelle heure…**	ah kel urr
…do you open?	**…êtes-vous ouvert?**	et-voo oo-ver
…do you close?	**…êtes-vous fermé?**	et-voo fer-may
Do you have?	**Est-ce que vous avez?**	es-kuh voo zavay

I would like …	**Je voudrais…**	zhuh voo-dray
Do you take credit cards?	**Est-ce que vous acceptez les cartes de crédit?**	es-kuh voo zaksept-ay leh kart duh krehdee
This one.	**Celui-ci.**	suhl-wee-see
That one.	**Celui-là.**	suhl-wee-lah
expensive	**cher**	shehr
cheap	**pas cher, bon marché,**	pah shehr, boñ mar-shay
size, clothes	**la taille**	tye
size, shoes	**la pointure**	pwañ-tur

Types of Shop

antique shop	**le magasin d'antiquités**	maga-zañ d'oñteekee-tay
bakery	**la boulangerie**	booloñ-zhuree
bank	**la banque**	boñk
bookshop	**la librairie**	lee-brehree
cake shop	**la pâtisserie**	patee-sree
cheese shop	**la fromagerie**	fromazh-ree
chemist	**la pharmacie**	farmah-see
department store	**le grand magasin**	groñ maga-zañ
delicatessen	**la charcuterie**	sharkoot-ree
gift shop	**le magasin de cadeaux**	maga-zañ duh kadoh
greengrocer	**le marchand de légumes**	mar-shoñ duh lay-goom
grocery	**l'alimentation**	alee-moñtasyoñ
market	**le marché**	marsh-ay
newsagent	**le magasin de journaux**	maga-zañ duh zhoor-no
post office	**la poste, le bureau de poste, le PTT**	pohst, booroh duh pohst, peh-teh-teh
supermarket	**le supermarché**	soo pehr-marshay
tobacconist	**le tabac**	tabah
travel agent	**l'agence de voyages**	l'azhoñs duh vwayazh

Sightseeing

art gallery	**la galerie d'art**	galer-ree dart
bus station	**la gare routière**	gahr roo-tee-yehr
cathedral	**la cathédrale**	katay-dral
church	**l'église**	l'aygleez
garden	**le jardin**	zhar-dañ
library	**la bibliothèque**	beebleeo-tek
museum	**le musée**	moo-zay
railway station	**la gare (SNCF)**	gahr (es-en-say-ef)
tourist office	**l'office du tourisme**	ohfees doo tooreesm
town hall	**l'hôtel de ville**	l'ohtel duh veel

Staying in a Hotel

Do you have a vacant room?	**Est-ce que vous avez une chambre?**	es-kuh voo zavay oon shambr
I have a reservation.	**J'ai fait une réservation.**	zhay fay oon rayzehrva-syoñ
single room	**la chambre à une personne**	shambr ah oon pehr-son
twin room	**la chambre à deux lits**	shambr ah duh lee
room with a bath, shower	**la chambre avec salle de bains, une douche**	shambr avek sal duh bañ, oon doosh